C. E. Brown

Knight Printing Co

ONE DAY

THIS VOLUME IS DESIGNED TO SHOW HOW
ONE COPY OF THE EVENING BULLETIN
APPEARS WHEN PUBLISHED IN BOOK FORM

THE EVENING BULLETIN
PHILADELPHIA

FOREWORD

"One Day" is the record of events of a single day.

With the exception of this introduction, the running headline at the top of each page and an occasional footnote, this volume presents in book form the contents of one edition of a single day's issue of The Philadelphia Evening Bulletin.

All advertising has been omitted. All else has been reproduced here, not in the size in which it appeared in the newspaper, but in a type and form normally used in books. Photographs and cartoons in most cases have been reduced in size.

The interesting thing is that nothing has been added, nothing eliminated, except the advertising.

In selecting a copy of The Bulletin for this purpose, it was desired to reproduce an issue that was as nearly normal in size and contents as possible. The issue of June 4, 1928—Night Extra Edition—was decided upon. This issue is slightly below the normal size. It contains 102.48 columns of news, editorials, pictures and reading matter of all kinds. The average number for June, 1928 was 112.89 columns. The average for the first six months of 1928 was 108.54.

The following table, giving the average number of columns of reading matter appearing in The Bulletin, will be interesting, particularly to those who have not been conscious of the increased quantity of news matter added year by year:

Year	Average Columns of reading matter published per issue	Year	Average Columns of reading matter published per issue
1895	36.65	1912	69.47
1900	61.50	1913	63.83
1905	56.79	1914	67.06
1908	65.55	1915	73.74
1909	60.92	1916	65.81
1910	66.41	1917	75.50
1911	69.44	1918	71.69

58011

Year	Average Columns of reading matter published per issue		Year	Average Columns of reading matter published per issue
1919	74.69		1924	99.80
1920	65.81		1925	98.12
1921	76.46		1926	104.63
1922	93.09		1927	102.04
1923	99.01			

The circulation of The Evening Bulletin has shown a consistent growth over the years. Its position in its city as the newspaper with the largest circulation (one of the largest in America) has resulted from an increasing demand on the part of the people of this community. At no time has circulation been obtained by the use of premiums, prizes or contests.

The average net paid daily circulation for the past thirty-three years is given in the following table:

Year	Net Paid Daily Average Circulation		Year	Net Paid Daily Average Circulation
1895	6,317		1912	281,285
1896	33,625		1913	291,868
1897	59,281		1914	326,714
1898	113,973		1915	356,531
1899	112,970		1916	402,644
1900	124,855		1917	367,766*
1901	130,084		1918	430,614
1902	130,439		1919	448,126
1903	144,375		1920	488,687
1904	182,904		1921	494,629
1905	211,134		1922	493,240
1906	222,480		1923	505,035
1907	241,400		1924	518,357
1908	240,797		1925	524,662
1909	249,811		1926	537,974
1910	244,063		1927	549,148
1911	253,565		1928	550,159†

*Retail price increased from one to two cents, Jan. 29, 1917.
†First six months.

ONE DAY

ANTIPODES FLIERS 2,388 MILES OUT ON HOP FOR FIJIS

Flying in Circles to Dodge Storm Clouds When 750 Miles from Suva, Goal of Second Leg of California to Australia Flight

'ALL'S WELL,' 'DOING FINE,' SAYS RADIO NEAR EQUATOR

Fly Past Night Storms Leaving Hawaii—Due to End Trip at Midnight Tonight

CAN CUT JOURNEY 300 MILES BY SEEKING SAMOA

(By Associated Press)

Honolulu, Hawaii, June 4.—Sometimes flying in circles to dodge storm clouds, while soaring 8,500 feet over the South Pacific Ocean, the Australia-bound monoplane Southern Cross was endeavoring at 9.50 A. M. Pacific Coast time today (1.50 P. M. Philadelphia daylight time) to reach Suva, Fiji, 750 miles away.

A message heard from the giant plane by the Radio Corporation of America read:

"Five A. M., seven degrees, six minutes south, latitude. Longitude 179 west, 800 miles to Suva. Bad weather."

Thus the Southern Cross, which with four men had taken flight at 7.50 A. M., Pacific Coast time (11.50 A. M. in Philadelphia) yesterday from Kauai Island, near Honolulu, had traversed 2,338 miles of its epochal 3,138 miles journey toward Suva, Fiji Islands.

Of the total journey to Sydney, Australia, begun at Oakland, California, Thursday morning, the Southern Cross had flown 5,462 miles over the Pacific.

Should the weather become menacing, gasoline supply near exhaustion or engines misbehave, the men of the Southern Cross were in a position to shorten today's flight by at least 300 miles, veering southwestward from their course and alighting at Apia or elsewhere in Samoa.

The Southern Cross had radioed at 9.10 A. M. Pacific time (1.10 P. M. in Philadelphia) today:

"Hello, Samoa. How are you getting us."

The message was picked up by the Navy radio station here.

(By Associated Press)

Fanning Island, June 4.—This cable station 1,200 miles south of the Hawaiian Islands, heard this message at 9.30 A. M. Pacific Coast time (1.30 P. M. in Philadelphia) today, from the Southern Cross:

"Having poor flying conditions now. Weather changeable. We have been dodging rain clouds and flying in circles sometimes. It certainly would have been unfortunate were it not for our old friend the Moon."

After a long silence the Southern Cross had radioed at 3.20 A. M. Fanning Island time (10.20 A. M. Philadelphia daylight time) the following message:

"Doing fine. Been expecting sight land, but none yet. It's not so clear as one would like. Altitude 1,000. Speed eighty knots."

The Southern Cross, reporting its position at 1 A. M. Fanning Island time (8 A. M. Philadelphia daylight time), had stated:

"Rain, 1 A. M. Position: Latitude, 3 South; Longitude, 171, West. Now over Phoenix group. All well."

A radio message from the plane at 12.15 A. M., Fanning Island time (7.15 A. M. in Philadelphia), had said the plane had dropped down to 1,000 feet and that "all was well."

Throughout the night this island was treated to a continuous story of the flight.

A series of radio messages put on the air as the plane played tag with a storm told of the fight the huge craft was making with the elements.

Once the radio man in the Southern Cross, James Warner, called the radio station here directing the subjoined message:

"Hello, old man. Nice place. Hope we have permission to trespass upon your domain."

"Going good. Breeze is slight help," said another message.

COURSE OF PACIFIC FLIGHT

Map showing the route of the Southern Cross on its flight from the Hawaiian Islands to the Fiji Islands, the second leg of its proposed trip from Oakland, Calif. to Sydney, Australia.

"Average speed made good 82. Altitude 500. We all well. Good spirit."

The tense situation in the Southern Cross control cabin was

mixed with humor when C. P. T. Ulm, co-pilot, drew a cartoon of Captain Charles Kingsford-Smith, the Australian commander, as the latter heard the starboard motor sputter.

Another message told of flying above the clouds with a clear sky and a bright moon above.

"That's when one enjoys the moon."

"Dodging about to miss a storm," was the text of another broadcast sent from an altitude of 4,600 feet, with the comment "looks pretty stormy here. What a beautiful sight."

As the plane continued there was apprehension about the change of air currents. "It's going to be a bad night. Getting dark. Circling for altitude."

Then the fliers told of enjoying "sandwiches with nice hot coffee, thanks to our host, Mr. and Mrs. Faye, of Kauai."

And so it went through the night, and Fanning Island enjoyed the treat, for the principal industry of this remote settlement is communication, this being the midway relay point of a cable operating between Australia and British Columbia.

(By Associated Press)

Suva, Fiji Islands, June 4.—So confident is the Hon. Henry Marks, Mayor of Suva, of the success of the flight of the Southern Cross, that he announced today that the four men comprising the crew would be his guests while they are here.

Natives awaited the thrill of their lives—the arrival of the Southern Cross here before sundown. The craft will be the first to land here.

Just how the natives will regard the huge plane should it reach Suva was a matter of conjecture. The populace was apprised of the coming of the Southern Cross last week when trees and poles were removed from a clearing in order to permit the plane to land.

Arrival of the plane will be the signal for a celebration among the 1,200 white inhabitants of the island who understand some of the practical difficulties connected with the adventure.

(By Associated Press)

San Francisco, June 4.—The steamship Sonoma, bound from San Francisco to Sydney, reported to the Mackay Radio and Telegram Company at 3.55 A. M. (7.55 A. M. in Philadelphia) today that the Southern Cross had passed overhead at 3 A. M. Pacific Coast time (7 A. M. in Philadelphia), at a position 3,505 miles from San Francisco.

The ship said she sighted the plane in the vicinity of the Phoenix Islands and attempted to radio the airmen on 600 meters wave length. The plane failed to answer.

The plane was flying at 1,400 feet altitude. The ship said the air was rough, but that the weather was fair.

The message was the first report that the plane had been sighted since the fliers started the Hawaii-Suva leg of their flight to Australia.

The first leg from Oakland, Cal., to Honolulu, a distance of 2,400 miles, was made in twenty-seven hours and twenty-eight minutes. The entire distance to Sydney is approximately 7,800 miles.

Radio despatches picked up at San Francisco and Honolulu vividly described the second leg of the flight, and told of the dangers.

First there were ominous dark clouds, a little rain and then a sputtering motor caused the navigators temporarily to slacken speed. This difficulty apparently disappeared as the plane roared its way through the night with a full moon furnishing the only light.

Flying first at a low altitude to save precious fuel, the ship was forced to take altitude, the radio message announced, to avoid the storm in its path.

They were forced to seek a course above the clouds. "There's our friend the moon," one message said, and thereafter through the night the message spoke frequently of the beautiful sight of the full moon beaming down upon the clouds beneath the navigators.

Only two small coral island groups dot the Pacific between the Hawaiians and Suva. Fanning Island, 1,200 miles distant from the Barking Sands take-off, was passed early in the night. The Phoenix group lies 1,866 miles southeast of Kauai.

The monoplane, Southern Cross, weighed seven tons fully loaded with her 1,200 gallons of gasoline, cargo and crew of four men when she started out on her flight to the Antipodes from Oakland, Calif., on May 31.

The craft was assembled from the broken parts of the two monoplanes which were wrecked in 1926 during the attempts of Captain George H. Wilkins to explore the Arctic from Alaska. Only the motors are new.

The personnel are: Australians, Captain Charles Kingsford-Smith, commander and chief pilot; C. T. P. Ulm, co-pilot; Americans, Lieutenant Harry Lyon, navigator, and James Warner, radio man, both former U. S. Navy men.

LOG OF PACIFIC FLIERS

(By Associated Press)

Second leg of California-Australia flight: (Honolulu time is six and a half hours behind Philadelphia daylight time. Pacific time is four hours behind Philadelphia daylight time). Sunday:

5.20 A. M. (11.50 A. M. in Philadelphia): Took off from Barking Sands, Island of Kauai, Hawaii, for Suva in Fiji Islands.

6.12 A. M. (8.42 Pacific Coast time), (12.42 P. M. in Philadelphia): "Receiving radio beacon O. K."

6.50 A. M. (9.20 A. M. Pacific Coast time): "Average speed good, eighty-two miles an hour. Altitude 500 feet. Our generator not delivering current. Will investigate later."

8 A. M. (10.30 A. M. Pacific Coast time): "18.45 North latitude; 159.42 West. Elevation 400 feet. Speed eighty knots. Slightly overcast."

9 A. M. (11.30 A. M. Pacific Coast time): "Speed ninety knots. Wind about ten knots on our tail. Position about 340 miles on course."

10 A. M. (12.30 P. M. Pacific Coast time): "Speed eighty-eight miles. Going to fix trouble now. Position about 430 miles on course."

11 A. M. (1.30 P. M. Pacific Coast time): "Speed eighty-two knots. Altitude 400. Position estimated 600 miles from Kauai, on plotted course."

11.48 A. M. (2.18 P. M. Pacific Coast time): "Rain ahead." Message received two minutes later said "rain squalls."

12 noon (2.30 P. M. Pacific Coast time): "Latitude, by

observation, 12.47 North, by dead reckoning 12.58. Longitude 163.13. Running time seven hours. Distance 630. Average speed ninety. Sea smooth. Partly cloudy. Occasional squalls. Wind approximately fifteen miles east by north. Ship behaving good. Motors doing well."

2 P. M. (4.30 P. M. Pacific Coast time): "Position 10.10 North; 164.55 West." Position estimated about 810 miles out.

3.40 P. M. (6.10 P. M. Pacific Coast time): "One motor sounds bad. Dropped to sixty miles an hour."

3.55 P. M. (6.25 P. M. Pacific Coast time): Message intercepted by Naval Radio San Francisco, indicated position 910 land miles from Kauai.

4.25 P. M. (6.55 P. M. Pacific Coast time): Another message through San Francisco Naval Radio said: "Have been flying low all day to insure gasoline economy. Have encountered many small rainstorms and recently the starboard (right) motor started fluttering. All O. K. now. Altitude 600 feet. Speed 72 knots. Quartering winds helping us. Revolutions more economical than on Hawaiian hop. Regards to all."

5 P. M. (7.30 P. M. Pacific Coast time): Southern Cross reported position slightly more than 1,100 miles from Kauai.

6.24 P. M. (8.54 Pacific Coast time): Naval Radio Station at San Francisco heard: "Black Clouds ahead."

6.30 P. M. (9 P. M. Pacific Coast time): "We are gaining altitude, going up near 2,000 feet now."

7 P. M. (9.30 P. M. Pacific Coast time): San Francisco Naval Radio received another radiogram saying the plane was "dodging about" and climbing to avoid the storm."

7.36 P. M. (10.26 P. M. Pacific time)—Message to San Francisco naval radio said the plane had climbed to 7,800 feet to avoid the storm clouds, but still found clouds overhead and all around. Message added that the fliers were using auxiliary lights. One generator having quit three hours after the start.

8 P. M. (10.30 P. M. Pacific time)—The San Francisco naval radio received a message from the Southern Cross setting her 7 P. M. position at about 1,370 miles from Kauai.

8.45 P. M. (11.15 Pacific time)—San Francisco naval radio

station received a message saying the fliers had climbed above the clouds and were "sailing fine, with a nice full moon."

9.00 P. M. (11.30 P. M. Pacific time)—Reported to San Francisco naval radio through Honolulu naval station: "Latitude 0-30, north longitude 169.59 West." That would place the plane directly over the magnetic equator, with only twenty miles to go before entering the Southern Hemisphere. Estimated position, 1,650 miles from Kauai, 216 miles from Canton Island in the Phoenix group, and 1,488 miles from Suva.

9.30 P. M. (12 P. M. Pacific time)—"All is well, cloudy, but not so bad. Clouds lower and clear over us, with nice moon. That's when one enjoys the moon."

10.50 P. M. (1.20 A. M. Monday, Pacific time)—"Latitude .:41 south; Longitude 171.18 west. All's well." This placed the plane approximately 1,740 miles from Kauai.

11.35 P. M. (1.55 A. M. Monday, Pacific time)—"Everything O. K."

Monday:

12.25 A. M. (2.55 A. M. Pacific time)—"Now flying 1,000 feet altitude. Going good."

12.45 A. M. (3.15 A. M. Pacific time)—Mackay radio received message giving midnight position of Southern Cross at Latitude 2.00 south, Longitude 170.33 west. Speed 78 knots. This would place ship near Phoenix Islands, 1,866 miles from Honolulu.

12.15 A. M. Fanning Island time (3.15 A. M. Pacific time) —Southern Cross radioed the monoplane had dropped down to 1,000 feet altitude. "All well."

3.55 A. M. (Pacific Coast time)—Mackay radio and telegraph company at San Francisco picked up report from steamship Sonoma that Southern Cross had passed overhead at 3 A. M. (Pacific time), plane flying at 1,400 feet in vicinity of Phoenix Islands. Sonoma reported air rough, weather fair.

1 A. M., Fanning time (4 A. M. Pacific time)—"Rain, position, Latitude 3 south, Longitude 171 west. Now over Phoenix group. All well."

3.20 A. M., Fanning Island time (6.20 A. M. Pacific time) —Southern Cross radioed: "Doing fine. Been expecting sight land, but none yet. It's not so clear as one would like. Altitude 1,000; speed 80 knots."

AUSTRALIAN FLIERS LOSE DAY BY INTERNATIONAL DATE LINE

It's Now Tuesday in Fiji Island, Goal of Second Lap

If all goes well with the airplane Southern Cross, winging its way southwestward across the South Pacific on the second leg of its flight from Oakland, Calif., to Australia, it will reach Suva, in the Fiji Islands, some time late today, only to find that it is Tuesday, not Monday.

A radio message received from the plane gave its position at 8 A. M., Philadelphia daylight saving time, as over the group of tiny islands known as the Phoenix Islands, indicating that it had passed the Equator and is flying a direct course, straight as an arrow, according to the map, from Honolulu to Suva.

Between that position and its destination in the Fijis, and some 700 miles from Suva, the plane will cross the International Date Line, and its time will at once advance twenty-four hours. Thus, assuming that the plane approaches the line at 4 P. M. on Monday, the time will at once become 4 P. M. Tuesday.

The International Date Line was established by agreement of the nations of the world to simplify difficulties of time adjustment due to the differences of travel from east to west and west to east. It is an imaginary line extending in a northerly and southerly direction in the Pacific Ocean, and separating the islands of the Pacific in such a way that all those to the east of it carry the same date as the United States and all those to the west of it carry the same date as Japan and Australia. Travelers who cross the line from east to west find their time made one full day later and those crossing it from west to east find themselves one full day earlier.

The question arises, when or at what time did the traveler change from noon of one day to noon of the next? It is to him apparently still Monday noon, and to obtain the correct date he must drop a day.

GIANT PLANE CROSSING U. S.

Seven Passengers Aboard Palatial Craft Leaving New Jersey

(By Associated Press)

Teterboro, N. J., June 4.—Bearing seven passengers, including its new owner J. Talbot, president of the Richfield Oil Company of California, and two pilots, a luxurious trimotored Fokker cabin monoplane is on the way to the Pacific coast.

The plane took off Sunday morning. It was planned to stop at Buffalo, N. Y., Detroit and Chicago.

The monoplane equipment includes a washroom with running water, kitchenette, upholstered seats and racks for light baggage and a writing desk. It has a capacity for twelve passengers.

BALTIMORE LAWYER SLAIN

Disgruntled Client is Supposed Murderer of Clifton S. Brown

(By Associated Press)

Baltimore, June 4.—Clifton S. Brown, member of a Baltimore law firm, was shot dead today as he approached his office, by a man who had waited for him in the corridor of the office building. The slayer, seized by policeman, collapsed at a police station before his name had been obtained.

Five shots struck Brown as he staggered toward the door of his office. A statement by Mrs. Brown expressed belief that a client who had held a grudge for several years over what he thought was an excessive fee did the shooting.

KEAN'S CAMPAIGN COST NEAR LIMIT

Senatorial Nominee Testifies He Gave $50,000—
All but $633.70 Spent

QUIZZED BY 'JIM' REED

Washington, June 4.—Hamilton F. Kean spent exactly $49,366.30 in the campaign which resulted in his winning the Republican nomination for the United States Senate in New

Jersey in the primary of May 15, he declared in the investigation begun today by the Reed Campaign Fund Committee into the reports that money was spent in the New Jersey Senatorial campaign greatly in excess of the limit fixed by law.

This is $633.70 within the limit of $50,000 fixed by both the Federal and New Jersey laws. Kean stuck to that statement during a grilling of over an hour by Senator James A. Reed, Democrat, of Missouri, chairman of the investigating committee and Senators Charles L. McNary, of Oregon, Republican, and William H. King, of Utah, Democrat, who compose the sub-committee appointed to conduct the inquiry into New Jersey campaign expenditures.

John H. Scott, of Montclair, county clerk of Essex county and Kean's State campaign manager, followed Kean on the stand.

There was no conflict between the testimony of Kean and his campaign manager, and the three members of the Senate committee who cross-examined them were unable to shake the statements of either.

Kean laughed heartily at reports that he had given Enoch Johnson, of Atlantic county, a blank check, which was later filled in and cashed for $200,000 to carry on the campaign in Atlantic county and other Southern New Jersey counties for him. He had not given a penny to Enoch Johnson, and neither had his campaign manager, Scott, Kean asserted.

Kean described Enoch Johnson as a man of great influence in Atlantic county.

"Johnson got up a meeting there which was addressed by Johnson, five or six of his aids and myself," Kean continued. "To show how they regard Johnson down there I will tell you that every speaker began his talk by declaring he was devoted to God and Johnson."

Senator Reed thought that over a minute, and then asked if the speakers said "to God and Johnson," or "Johnson and God." Kean said it was as he first said.

Kean, who is also Republican national committeeman for New Jersey, was the first witness called.

Senator Reed asked him directly if he knew of any other money than the $50,000 fund which was spent in his behalf.

2

Kean then discussed an advertisement appearing in a Philadelphia paper for which former Governor Edward C. Stokes, his leading opponent, charged him with violation of the law. He insisted he did not know who put the advertisement in the paper. It might have been put in by some one in the Camden organization, he said.

Senator Reed's first questions were in regard to reports that Kean began his campaign about two years ago and that the money he spent during all that time in furthering his candidacy should be considered in making up the total he has spent, instead of his expenditures since he announced his candidacy on January 5, 1928.

Kean replied that he has been working actively for the Republican cause in New Jersey forty years, and has talked about running for the Senate for ten years, but did practically nothing like campaigning for the nomination until January 5, when he was unanimously urged by the Union county Republican committee to make the race.

As for the many meetings he attended and addressed, Kean said he didn't help pay for them, although he had been asked to.

Asked why he didn't help pay for the meetings, he replied he "couldn't afford to."

Senator Reed said it was "generally understood you are comfortably fixed." Kean chuckled and said he would like to organize a syndicate to cash in on the "rumors." He explained he could not afford to go beyond the $50,000 limit.

The primary winner hesitated when asked to name his business and finally said: "You better call it merchant in securities."

Kean described himself in the campaign as a "chicken with its head off, more or less, moving around all over the State, shaking hands and renewing acquaintances."

Senator Reed read from Kean's original statement that only $39,000 had been spent, but Kean said a supplemental statement has been prepared covering later bills.

"I notice that this $10,000 was spent between May 12 and the primary on May 15," Reed said, "Why was that?"

"I guess it was for use on election day," replied Kean.

"For workers?"

"Yes, of course, there are always workers, and I don't know that they worked for me any more than for the rest of the ticket."

---

100 IN RECORDER'S OFFICE LOSE JOBS

Political Circles Excited on Learning Superfluous Transcribers Were to Go

DUE TO CALM IN REALTY

A flurry of excitement occurred today in political circles when it became known that about 100 transcribers employed by Recorder of Deeds James M. Hazlett will be dropped from the payroll June 15.

Ward leaders were active about City Hall, seeking to persuade Mr. Hazlett to keep their men at work. Mr. Hazlett, who is chairman of the Republican City Committee, informed them that exhaustion of an appropriation forced the elimination of the transcribers who are listed as extra help.

It has been a custom to appeal to City Council for additional funds for the payment of the extra workers, but the lull in real estate the last year has enabled the Recorder's staff to catch up almost with its work.

When the real estate boom was at its height, deliveries of deeds, mortgages and other papers at the Recorder of Deeds gradually lagged twelve months behind.

This was reduced to nine months by employment of extra clerks and transcribers.

The real estate calm, plus the experience gained by the transcribing force in turning out work, cut into the overdue deeds and mortgages to such an extent that today the office was only two weeks behind in delivery, the best record for four years.

All the transcribers are paid $5 a day. The appropriation made in the 1928 municipal budget was for $100,000.

Most of the 100 on the list to be dropped are advanced in years. Invariably they were recommended for the jobs by politicians. A plan is being worked out so that each ward will lose the same number of employes.

4 PLEAD GUILTY IN PANNONIA HOLDUP

Expect Similar Plea from Two Others in Beneficial Association Robbery Plot

SOUGHT TO HIDE SHORTAGE

Four men concerned in a holdup of directors of the Pannonia Beneficial Association, 709 N. Franklin st., last Monday night, pleaded guilty today.

Before Judge James Gay Gordon, Jr., in Quarter Sessions Court, Room 453, City Hall, they entered the plea to ten indictments, involving conspiracy, attempt to rob, assault and battery, and carrying deadly weapons.

Two others pleaded not guilty when arraigned, but later their attorneys announced they would enter guilty pleas later.

Those who pleaded guilty are John Calabrese, twenty-nine, 1641 S. 15th st.; Nicholas Piccolo, twenty-three, 748 S. 10th st.; Joseph Perri, eighteen, 113 Montrose st., and Frank Gallow, twenty-seven, 763 S. 7th st.

Herbert W. Salus, lawyer for Thomas Cirucci, twenty-eight, 611 S. 9th st., was not in court when his client entered his plea. Salus announced later that Cirucci had made a mistake and would change his plea.

Joel L. Schlessinger, thirty-one, 827 Reed st., who is said by the police to have confessed instigating the holdup, also pleaded not guilty. Edward A. Kelly, his attorney, said Schlessinger would modify this by pleading guilty to conspiracy, and not guilty to the other charges.

Schlessinger was secretary of the Pannonia Young Men's Association. He told police he engineered the holdup, not for the purpose of robbery, but to recover books and papers which showed a shortage in his accounts as secretary of the Young Men's Association.

Schlessinger did not participate in the holdup. The other five, all masked, entered the meeting room, all carrying pistols and one a sawed-off shot gun. It is charged they stole more than $800.

CITY LOAN OVER-SUBSCRIBED

More Than Ten Million Offered on $7,500,000 Issue

The $7,500,000 City of Philadelphia loan, for which bids were received in the Mayor's reception room in City Hall today, was over-subscribed by nearly fifty per cent.

The nineteen bids submitted totaled $10,475,000. For the first time in a long period, no bids were submitted by syndicates, due, it was explained, to the fact there is a six per cent. money market prevailing at present.

The bonds are in two issues: one a $5,500,000 fifty-year issue, due June 1, 1978; the other a $2,000,000 loan due June 1, 1943. The bonds bear four per cent. interest.

The Sinking Fund commissioners, with an offer of $1,-750,000 at 100.05, submitted the largest single bid, and the only one above par.

S. Davis Wilson, deputy comptroller, pointed out there is no immediate need for the money, but that the sale was in the nature of a test of the validity of the loans involved. He also said there is $9,000,000 in the city treasury at present.

Mr. Wilson also said that with this surplus it would not be necessary to sell bonds for the Ridge av. spur of the Broad st. subway.

STULTZ AND GIRL LAND AT TREPASSEY FOR ATLANTIC HOP

Pontoon Equipped Monoplane Friendship, Groomed for London Flight, Reaches Base from Halifax

LINDBERGH-LIKE BLONDE COMPLETES
CREW OF THREE

(By Associated Press)

Trepassey, N. F., June 4.—The monoplane Friendship, groomed for a trans-Atlantic flight, landed here at 1.28 Philadelphia daylight time today. It left Halifax where its flight from Boston was interrupted by fog yesterday, at 8.36 A. M. Philadelphia daylight time.

Map shows the route of Wilmer Stultz and Miss Amelia Earhart in the monoplane Friendship from Boston to Halifax, N. S., and Trepassey, N. F.

The Friendship had been so exactly to her course and schedule in the flight from Halifax that the pilot, Wilmer Stultz, brought the ship down within ten minutes of the time he had announced as he took off.

The plane, carrying Miss Amelia Earhart, of Boston, and Lew Gordon beside Stultz, is a three-motored Fokker equipped with pontoons. Leaving Boston yesterday morning, the fliers stayed over night at Halifax because of dense fog encountered.

They are scheduled to leave here at the first favorable opportunity to fly to some port in England, probably London or Southampton.

(By Associated Press)

Halifax, N. S., June 4.—The monoplane Friendship hopped off this morning for Trepassey, Newfoundland, on the second leg of a contemplated flight across the Atlantic to London, England.

A perfect take-off from the eastern passage airport on Halifax harbor was made at 8.36 o'clock Philadelphia daylight saving time. Trepassey is 500 miles in an air line.

The Friendship landed here yesterday after a secret start from Boston.

Wilmer Stultz, who was pilot for Mrs. Frances Wilson Grayson on her first attempt to fly the Atlantic last year, is pilot of the plane. The co-pilot is Miss Amelia Earhart, amateur aviatrix, and director of Denison House, Boston's oldest settlement centre. She is of fair complexion and bears a striking resemblance to Colonel Charles A Lindbergh, whose trail-blazing path across the North Atlantic she hopes to follow. Louis Gordon, of Texas, is flight mechanic.

Miss Amelia Earhart (left), who seeks to be the first woman to span the Atlantic by airplane, photographed at Boston with Wilmer Stultz (center), pilot, and Lou Gordon, mechanic, just before they took off in the monoplane Friendship on their flight. They landed at Halifax yesterday and flew today to Trepassey, N. F., from which point they plan to hop off for England.

Miss Earhart was wearing a brown sweater, tight-fitting brown knickers and high-laced boots when she appeared with her two companions for breakfast. She wore no hat. She was busy with her camera while the additional fuel was being pumped into the tanks.

Miss Earhart seemed a bit nervous during the considerable delay caused by the refueling. She strolled about taking frequent snapshots. Among them was one of the cottage in which Commander Richard E. Byrd had lived for a time.

The knot of people on the float at the air station waved adieu as the plane, three motors roaring, got under way. Stultz had said briefly: "Thank you all—hope we make it."

Stultz said that both of his companions were qualified to take the stick while he operated the radio but that he did not intend to keep in continuous communication.

The fuselage of the Friendship is painted a bright orange with its name in block letters painted in black on either side.

The rudder bears the number "NX-4204." The top of the wing is painted gold and the engine housings are aluminum. Across the bonnet of the central motor is the word "Fokker" in black script.

The plane, equipped with pontoons, is a tri-motored Fokker, purchased from Commander Byrd. The expedition is backed by the Mechanical Science Corporation, represented by the New York publisher and explorer George Palmer Putnam.

With no advance publicity, the plane took off from Boston Harbor yesterday morning for Trepassey. Running into fog off Halifax, Stultz turned back and landed in the harbor here.

The flight is the first attempted by a plane equipped for landing on water, and is expected to prove the practicability of airplane service to Europe.

"It is understood that the backers of this enterprise are interested primarily in scientific experimentation in air transportation over water," said a statement from Mr. Putnam.

"For the first time in trans-oceanic flying a tri-motored ship is equipped with pontoons making it possible to land anywhere in water. It is this type of equipment that Commander Byrd has favored from the first as the inevitable development for long distance commercial flying over water."

Commander Byrd also issued a statement at New York in which he said:

"I believe that the flight of the three-engined plane that will fly with one engine dead, which is equipped with floats for landing in water, is the next step in trans-Atlantic flying and is a sensible pioneering effort. I wish the pilot and crew good luck and every success, and have confidence in the courage and ability of the personnel."

He explained that he had not announced the sale sooner because it was made "with the understanding that regardless of circumstances it was to be kept secret."

The take-off in Boston, shortly after dawn, was made without benefit of newspaper reporters. Even Miss Earhart's mother and sister were not present, being informed of the take-off by telephone. A fourth member of the party, Lou Gower, who had intended to accompany the party to Trepassey to aid in refueling and servicing the plane for her ocean flight, was left behind. Difficulty was experienced in taking off and he got out of the plane. Minus his weight the big Fokker finally got off the water.

The attempt of this expedition, the first to be made this summer for the eastward passage, is a change from last year. Then the slogan was "get across" and any equipment, mostly land planes, single motored, was used. Commander Byrd was the first to fly with a full crew and a tri-motored plane, but the America was not equipped for landing on water.

No lives have ever been lost in ocean flying where flying boats were used. The Navy's NC No. 4 was the first to fly the Atlantic from Newfoundland to the Azores, followed by Commander de Pinedo, who, although forced down, was rescued by a nearby ship. The late Commander John P. Rodgers and his crew floated safely for several days after being forced down by lack of fuel on their flight to the Hawaiian Islands.

The Friendship has a wing spread of seventy-one feet and is powered with three 220-horsepower Wright whirlwind motors. Its weight, with crew, fuel supply and pontoons, is slightly in excess of 12,000 pounds. It is equipped with a 600-meter sending and receiving radio equipment and emergency radio equipment for sending messages in event the plane is down with motors silent. Only 500 gallons of gasoline were carried on the flight from Boston, but she is to be loaded with from 900 to 1,000 gallons of gasoline at Trepassey. In event the gasoline supply runs low one of the motors can be put out and the two remaining are capable of keeping the plane in the air. The registry number of the plane is NX-4204.

(By Associated Press)

New York, June 4.—The Friendship will pause at Trepassey, Newfoundland, only as long as the weather requires, George Palmer Putnam, one of the backers of the flight, said today.

"With the present weather conditions the plane should reach Trepassey in five or six hours from Halifax. Whether the crew of three will go on this afternoon or not, I don't know. I should think, however, that they would snatch a little rest and then wait for the first favorable break in the weather."

Mr. Putnam said that it was estimated that the plane, with moderately favorable conditions, could maintain a speed of 100 miles an hour and on this basis he estimated that from 20 to 24 hours would bring the Friendship to its goal in England.

The plane, he said, is equipped with two radio sets, one with a range up to 1,000 miles and tuned to the 600-meter wave length. An emergency set could summon aid should the ship be forced to land on the water, its radius is between 50 and 100 miles. The call letters of the plane are "WOX." Stultz is a radio operator.

"Should the plane be forced down en route to Europe," said Putnam, "it should be able to float indefinitely unless an unusually strong storm is encountered. The gasoline tanks would be emptied and the side motors could be cut off with a hack saw to give the ship great buoyance.

"We have tried to embody in this equipment every suggestion of Commander Byrd, gleaned from his extensive experience."

GIRL ON FLIGHT STUDIED IN PHILADELPHIA

Amelia Earhart, Once Student at Ogontz School, is Curly-Haired Blonde

IS A SOCIAL WORKER

MISS EARHART READ BOOK A DAY DURING VACATION FROM HERE

Amelia Earhart is recalled at the Ogontz School as the girl who read a book a day during a summer vacation to improve her knowledge of literature.

This record was recalled today by a member of the teaching staff after ten years. Miss Earhart entered the school in the fall of 1916, and continued through the spring of 1918. Her home was in Kansas City at the time.

"A very brilliant pupil, interested in every phase of student life," said the teacher, of Miss Earhart. "She was interested in literature, and that was the intensive manner in which she sought to satisfy this interest."

Miss Earhart was not graduated from the school.

Boston, June 4.—Tall, slight, with curly, yellow, bobbed hair, Miss Amelia M. Earhart, thirty, who is co-pilot of the London-bound monoplane Friendship, bears remarkable resemblance to Colonel Lindbergh, whose air trail she is following.

"She looks more like Lindbergh than Lindbergh himself," declared Brynjulf Standenaes, Norwegian artist, who made life portrait studies of Lindbergh.

Miss Earhart was born in Achison, Kansas, and was graduated from Hyde Park School in Chicago and attended the Ogontz School in Philadelphia.

Through 1917 and 1918 she served with the Canadian Red Cross. After the war she studied medicine and sociology at Columbia and a year later registered in the University of Southern California. Here she took up aviation as a sport.

She presents an appealing, boyish figure in leather and khaki flying clothes. Her eyes are serene or zestful according to the circumstances that confront her. She is a good hand with the motors as well as the polished controls of the Friendship's cabin.

How Miss Earhart came first to be likened to Lindbergh no one at the Denison House, the social services centre where she is employed, seemed to know, but Miss Marion Perkins, chief executive there, said that many persons had remarked similarity of facial contour and expression.

Her preparations for the flight were secret. For three weeks preceding yesterday's take-off, she stayed at a local hotel under the name of Dorothy Binney, the maiden name of Mrs. George Palmer Putnam, wife of the New York publisher who is one of the backers of the flight.

She has been flying since 1918 and enjoys the distinction of having been the first woman to be granted an air license by the National Aeronautics Association. She received her certificate as pilot in 1923 after a few months' flying. In her final test flight at Los Angeles she gained an altitude of 11,000 feet. At present she is a member of the staff of the Denison Airport at Squandum. Miss Earhart's friends describe her as a hard worker with a quiet and kindly sense of humor. She is interested in almost all outdoor sports, likes to dance and to go to the theatre, but doesn't drink coffee nor smoke cigarettes.

Her mother and sister, who live in Medford, had not been informed of her purpose and received their first information of the projected flight from newspapers. Today the mother was reported in a state of nervous prostration, but to Miss Earhart the adventure was scarcely more than a lark.

"It won't amount to anything," she told her companions just before the take-off. "I'll be over there soon and I'll come back on the earliest boat to get back to my work again."

———

(By Associated Press)

Mineola, N. Y., June 4.—Mrs. Wilmer Stultz, wife of the flyer who will pilot Miss Amelia Earhart's Fokker monoplane from Newfoundland to England, said today that plans for the flight had been started more than two months ago.

Mrs. Stultz arrived here last night after driving her own automobile from Boston. At first she refused to talk about the trans-Atlantic expedition, but today she disclosed how preparations had been hastened in absolute secrecy.

"My husband left for Detroit early in April," she said, "ostensibly for the purpose of testing out Commander Byrd's Fokker monoplane. He flew the ship back to Boston and not long afterward, about a month ago, the news leaked out that Commander Byrd had sold the plane."

She said that gasoline consumption tests had shown that the Friendship could carry far more than enough fuel for the hop.

The opinion of the backers and the crew, she said, was that this was the first "sensible trans-Atlantic flight" yet undertaken because of the fact that the plane is equipped with pontoons.

$22,532 FOR HOOVER IN WEST VIRGINIA

Revised List of Contributions and Expenditures Filed with Campaign Funds Committee

$2,000 FROM CONGRESSMAN

(By Associated Press)

Washington, June 4.—A revised list of contributions of $22,532 and expenditures of $18,586 in the Hoover Presidential primary campaign in West Virginia was filed with the Senate campaign funds committee today by Harry C. Woodyard, Hoover manager in that State.

Woodyard said he believed this to represent all the Hoover contributions, and that the apparent balance remaining was obliged in one way or another. Another $1,000 to meet bills not presented as yet would cover everything, he said.

Included in new contributions listed were $2,000 each by Representative Frothingham, of Massachusetts, and Mrs. Mary A. Frothingham; $1,000 from "Mr. Patton, of California," and $1,000 from John A. Bartlett, assistant Postmaster General.

Woodyard said these contributions had been received through James Good, of the Hoover national organization.

The witness was pressed for the basis of a newspaper interview he gave in West Virginia as to expenditures made for Senator Guy D. Goff. He said he had no specific knowledge, but had based his assertion as to large expenditures on "my general experience in politics" and what was going on in the State.

As to the advertising campaign in the State, Woodyard said it was his judgment that the Hoover paid advertising was "more extensive" than that for Goff. He added, however, that his observation of Goff "organization" activities in the counties made him judge that there were large outlays. He told Senator Bratton, Democrat, New Mexico, he meant "groups of Republicans when he said organization."

The help given the State organization by the National organization, Woodyard said, included a check from former Senator Calder, of New York, for $500.

Clyde B. Johnson, of Charleston, W. Va., who described himself as an "anti-Smith" Democratic candidate for delegate-at-large, told the committee he knew nothing of expenditures for Senator James A. Reed, of Missouri, in West Virginia, beyond the fact that he had paid for the armory in which Reed spoke in Charleston in April, costing $100. He was not a "Reed man," Johnson said, but was merely "against the New York Governor."

Senator Steiwer, Republican, Oregon, chairman of the committee, went through the vouchers to find that a total of approximately $3,700 had been paid to the advertising firm of Mays-Williams for newspaper advertising, although Woodyard, on his previous appearance before the committee, had estimated the advertising bill would be almost that much a week.

"We didn't have the money," Woodyard said in explanation.

A. C. Herreld, of Sutton, W. Va., manager of the Reed campaign in the State, said his activities had been confined almost entirely to reducing the number of candidates for Reed delegates. "It was a question of too many delegates," he said.

Herreld said there was "no Reed publicity," and that he has paid all his own expenses in traveling about the State on the delegate matter. The cost would be less than $1,000, he said, but he had kept no record, and did not think the State law required him to report.

Attention of the committee was directed to anti-Smith political advertising in West Virginia newspapers.

"Do you know anything about those?" Senator Steiwer asked.

"No, I do not," Herreld said.

"Were there any Reed contribution?" asked Senator Mc-Master, Republican, South Dakota.

"Not a cent."

The committee took up the suggestion of Senator Heflin, Democrat, Alabama, that it inquire into circumstances under which the Washington, D. C., Daily News published a life of Governor Smith in its editorial columns.

It was told by Lowell Millett, editor of the paper, that instead of being paid for that publication, as Hefllin's statement implied, the Scripps-Howard papers had paid $6,000 for "a life of Smith and a life of Hoover." These two were the respective candidates supported by the Scripps-Howard papers for the Democratic and Republican nomination, Millett said. If Hoover was nominated, he added, the papers would support him, even against Smith. If the Republicans nominated somebody else, "like Dawes, say," they would support Smith, should he be nominated.

BELIEVE NOBILE ON FRANZ JOSEF LAND

Russians Think Amateur Radio Operator Picked up General's SOS

PLAN RELIEF EXPEDITION

(By Associated Press)

Moscow, Russia, June 4.—The Soviet Russia Nobile Rescue Commission, which has been investigating a report by a radio amateur that he had picked up a message believed to be from the missing dirigible Italia from Franz Josef Land, today held a growing belief that General Nobile's expedition may have landed at that place.

The radio amateur at Voznesensk, in North Dvinsk Province bordering Archangel, confirmed reports of the message, giving the full text, although apparently garbled. It read:

"Italia Nobile Franz Josefs S O S S O S S O S S O S Terri Teno Ehn."

This message was received on a 33.35 wave, corresponding to the Italia's radio outfit, the amateur operator stated.

The Relief Commission has decided to send an expedition to Franz Josef Land.

Franz Josef Land is an archipelago lying east of Spitzbergen and north of Novoe Zemblya, running between eighty degrees and eighty-two degrees north and forty-two degrees and sixty-four degrees east. It is a high glacier covered land, reaching an extreme elevation of about 2,400 feet.

The islands are volcanic. Bear and fox are the only land mammals. It is thought there may be a connecting island chain between Franz Josef Land and Spitzbergen.

The possibility that the dirigible may have landed at Franz Josef Land is strengthened by wind conditions about the time the Italia lost contact with Kings Bay, the wind blowing in an Easterly direction.

MAN SLAIN BY GANG IN SPEEDING MOTOR

Woman Sees Murder Near 5th and Callowhill Believed Renewal of Underworld War

---

Shot down at Randolph and Noble sts., near 5th and Callowhill, by two men in a roadster, Stephen Bozzo, thirty, Marston st. near 27th and Morris, was killed at 1.45 A. M. today, in what police believe to be the re-opening of gang warfare in this city.

The man, an awning maker and salesman, was struck once

in the head and once in the chest. Five bullets were fired from the car as he stood on the southeast corner of the intersection. The car then sped west on Noble st., turning north on 6th st.

The murder was witnessed by Mrs. Eva Babyuk, 505 Noble st., who was retiring, and heard the brakes of the motor squeal and then the shots. She looked from her window and saw Bozzo fall, and the roadster speed away. It was painted dark with cream or yellow stripes.

The shots were heard by Hetrick, Terry and McLoughlin, policemen of the 3d st. and Fairmount av. station, who ran to the scene and found Bozzo huddled on the edge of the sidewalk, with blood flowing from the wounds. He was taken to Northern Liberties Hospital, but was dead.

In his pockets police say they found $90 and two bankbooks, one with his own name and one with the name Julia M. Bozzo, his sister. Police went to the Marston st. address, but were informed he had not lived there for six months. Police learned that his wife, Anna, twenty-seven, was living with her parents, Mr. and Mrs. Enrico Cangro, at 2115 Morris st.

McMenamin, a detective, went to the house and was informed the woman was ill and could not be told of her husband's death. Police learned Bozzo had not worked for a year and had been connected with a South Philadelphia gang. The couple have two children, both boys, aged seven and eight years.

When police arrived at the scene, Mrs. Babyuk was leaning from the window, screaming, and pointing to the direction taken by the fleeing car. She was taken to the station house and questioned.

"I was preparing to retire," Mrs. Babyuk told McMenamin, "and had just opened my window when I heard two shots. I looked out and saw the roadster, slowing down at the crossing. Then three more shots were fired from the car, but I did not see who had been shot until the car moved away. Then I saw the man's body lying on the sidewalk. It was so dark I could not see whether the man had been in the car and was pushed out on the far side, or whether he had been walking on the sidewalk."

3

LATEST NEWS*

Latest Stock Market Prices on Financial Page

PILOT HURT IN AIRPLANE CRASH AT BERWICK

Berwick, Pa., June 4.—Hyman Wintersteen, pilot, was slightly hurt and two passengers escaped injury when their airplane was wrecked in taking off from the local airport. Just after clearing the ground the plane lost its "balance" and crashed on one wing. The plane was badly damaged.

WILKINS AND EIELSON LEAVE FOR AMSTERDAM

Berlin, June 4.—Captain George H. Wilkins and Carl B. Eielson, who flew across the top of the world, left Tempelhofer Airdome by the regular passenger plane for Amsterdam today. They will go to London on Wednesday.

ROB 13TH & CHERRY STORE
Four Men Take Cloth, Escape in Automobile

Four men, driving an expensive sedan, ransacked the storeroom of Benson Bros., wool merchants, southwest corner of 13th and Cherry sts., at 3.30 A. M. today, and, according to police, obtained several hundred dollars' worth of cloth.

Eckert, a policeman, was informed by a passing automobilist that "a job was being pulled at 13th and Cherry," and he ran from 13th and Arch sts. to the Benson establishment, catching a fleeting glance of the robbers' automobile disappearing north on 13th st.

Police found the Cherry st. door forced open and the room in disorder, with bolts of goods scattered on the floor. They also found a checkered cap, which they believe was dropped by one of the thieves.

* Editor's Note.—The "Late News" box appears on the First Page. It is sometimes called "Stop the Press News," in that items may be printed therein without making a new plate.

BLIND STOREKEEPER SAVES HIS THREE CHILDREN AT FIRE

Arouses Sleeping Family Who Flee in Night Clothing

A blind storekeeper discovered flames in the kitchen of his home, 1710 N. 42d st., at 6 A. M. today and aroused his three children who fled in their night clothes.

Joseph Teblum, thirty-eight, was smoking on the steps in front of his fish and produce store, when a passerby informed him of the fire.

Teblum rushed upstairs and awakened his son, Harry, seventeen, and his daughters, Ethel, fifteen, and Neva, nine.

While the children were fleeing, Teblum telephoned for firemen and the flames were extinguished before serious damage was done.

Teblum believes their cat caused the fire.

Teblum has been blind since his recovery from influenza nine years ago.

COLD WATER FIGHTS RECITED IN WIFE'S PLEA FOR SUPPORT

Camden Vice Chancellor Allows Woman $10 a Week

Mrs. Phebe Stewart, wife of a poultry farmer near Woodbury, testifying to prolonged cold water fights with her husband in Chancery Court, Camden, today, obtained from Vice Chancellor Leaming a temporary order for $10 weekly support.

The Vice Chancellor said that unless the wife sold her car he would reduce the amount of support.

Mrs. Stewart alleged cruelty, abandonment and non-support by her husband, Leonard, to whom she has been married thirty-one years. They have four married children.

She said she and her husband had lived happily until four years ago. Then, after an argument over his drinking, she said, her husband left the house and built a shack on the farm, a hundred yards from the house. There he has lived ever since.

She said he kept a gun, a large supply of eggs, and buckets of water in the shack. Whenever she attempted to enter the building he repelled her with eggs and threw water upon her. As a last resort, she said, he threatened her with the gun.

The husband declared the most memorable water battle, last April 18, started when his wife threw a basin of water upon him. He retaliated with a bucketful, to which she answered in kind.

17-YEAR LOCUSTS SWARM CONNECTICUT SECTIONS
Make Appearance on Schedule Forecast by Scientists

(By Associated Press)

New Britain, Conn., June 4.—The vanguard of the brood of seventeen-year locusts predicted by scientists for Connecticut this year has emerged from its underground quarters and is swarming in large numbers near this city.

The insects, varying in size up to two inches in length, emerged through the upper earth crust by boring holes half an inch in diameter. Empty shells of the insects scattered about indicated that. True to form many had quickly changed from larvæ to adult condition and had taken wing.

The entire life of these locusts is only a few weeks. During this period, eggs are laid in slits made in twigs of trees, when they are matured the larvæ burrow underground to remain for seventeen years.

Owing to their brief period of life after leaving the ground, the locusts, scientists say, can cause but little damage.

SEE RADIUM SUIT AGREEMENT
Mediator Says Attorneys Will Draw Up Contracts of Settlement

(By Associated Press)

Newark, N. J., June 4.—The first conference of opposing counsel in the suits of five women seeking damages of $1,250,000 from the United States Radium Corporation,

The Bulletin Time Table of Radio Broadcasts is on Page 30.*

*Editor's Note.—This line appears regularly at the bottom of the First Page to help readers locate the Radio Programs. They begin on Page 188 of this book.

held to discuss the terms of settlement proposed by Federal Judge William Clark, acting as unofficial mediator, ended today with success apparently in sight.

Judge Clark announced that the attorneys would draw up contracts to be signed by the litigants, and would meet again in his office late in the day for further discussion and final agreement.

The terms proposed by Judge Clark, who announced he was acting as a private citizen moved by the plight of the women and the delays in bringing their litigation into trial court, included a lump sum settlement of $10,000 on each; annuities of at least $600 for medical expenses; annuities of $600 as pensions, and payment of medical and legal debts incurred in the past.

With capitalization of the annuities, and including the payment of expenses, it was estimated each of the women would receive approximately $50,000.

WORLD NEWS IN BRIEF*

California to Australia fliers pass Equator on hop from Hawaii to Fiji Islands.

Monoplane Friendship flies from Halifax for Trepassey, N. F., on second leg of Boston to London flight.

Chang Tso-Lin wounded when train in which he was fleeing was bombed near Mukden. Several others killed. Pekin quietly awaits Nationalists' occupation.

Ice breaker Braganza wins past ice field where Citta di Milano failed in search for missing dirigible.

ACCUSED AS MOTOR THIEF
Narbeth Man Also Suspected of Burglary Attempt

Joseph McCourt, twenty-one, Montgomery av., Narberth, arrested in Bryn Mawr on disorderly conduct charge, was held today in $1,500 bail for court by Magistrate Still-wagon, on charges of stealing an automobile and attempted burglary.

*Editor's Note.—Summary appearing at bottom of First Page.

Lower Merion police had compared a peculiar automobile tire tread mark left at the scene of an attempted burglary at Narberth with a similar mark left by an automobile which McCourt is alleged to have stolen in Bryn Mawr.

McCourt was arrested in a restaurant at Bryn Mawr, yesterday, a few hours after police had been called to investigate an attempted burglary in the home of John Albrecht, Maplewood road, Narberth. After hours of questioning, police say, McCourt admitted the charge.

JUNIATA HONORS FISHER

Governor Fisher today received his fifth honorary degree of Doctor of Laws. The honor was conferred upon him by Juniata College at Huntingdon, Pa., by Dr. Martin G. Brumbaugh, former Governor of this State.

OFFICIAL WEATHER FORECAST*

Rain tonight and Tuesday, with little change in temperature; fresh easterly winds.

(Weather Table, Pages 66 and 67 of this volume)

THE BULLETIN'S THERMOMETER

A. M.					Today.					P. M.
8	9	10	11	12	1	2	3	4	5	6
64	66	66	66	65	66	66	66	66		

P. M.						Last Night.						A. M.	
6	7	8	9	10	11	12	1	2	3	4	5	6	7
74	73	72	71	70	68	66	64	64	64	64	63	62	63

High, 98, 1925; low, 50, 1910; normal, 69

Last year, high, 65; low, 54; humidity, 87

Humidity, 9 A. M., 79; 1 P. M., 83

*Appears on Page 1.   Complete weather tables appear daily on Page 3.

CHANG IN MUKDEN; HIS TRAIN BOMBED

Fate of Pekin in Doubt as Northern Dictator Flees Into Manchuria

TRIES TO HOLD CONTROL

ASKS U. S. WITHDRAWAL

(By Associated Press)

Shanghai, June 4.—The Nanking Nationalist Government has asked the United States to withdraw its troops from North China.

In answering the American note of May 18, regarding protection of American property and lives in North China, the Chinese version of the Nanking reply issued today stated the Nationalists intended to use only well disciplined troops in Pekin and Tientsin "thus assisting in the protection of Americans."

The reply concluded by asking the withdrawal of the American troops "in order to improve the traditionally friendly relations between the two countries."

Mukden, Manchuria, June 4.—The return of Marshal Chang Tso-Lin, Manchurian war lord, to his stronghold in Mukden after two years of rule as dictator of North China, was marked early today by the bombing of Chang's special train as it entered the suburbs of the Manchurian capital.

Several of those aboard the former Dictator's special train were killed, two officials were injured and Chang Tso-Lin himself suffered slight facial injuries.

The bombing has caused some tension between the Chinese and Japanese as the Japanese declared the Chinese aboard the train fired at random and mainly directed their fire at Japanese gendarmes guarding the railway. The latter replied and for forty minutes there was an exchange of shots.

At least two suspects were arrested and were reported to have been summarily shot, while several Mukden officials also are said to be under arrest.

Japanese reports say that the bombs were of Soviet manufacture. At the start of the Southern Nationalist campaign, which resulted in Chang's defeat, the Southerners were in alliance with the Soviets. The Southern campaign later took a more conservative form and the Soviet agents were expelled from all but a few radical strongholds.

Two bombs were dropped on the train as it was passing under a railway bridge at 5.30 A. M. The bombs blew up the eleventh coach and set fire to four other coaches which were destroyed.

Among the wounded were Wu Chun Sheng, Governor of Heilunkiang Province and the Minister of Agriculture of the former Pekin regime. They were in the car next to that of Chang Tso-Lin.

Some of Chang's Mukdenite troops who had been driven toward Pekin by the Nationalist advance which led to his evacuation remained at the Northern Capital, insuring an orderly withdrawal of Pekin troops.

It was thought that several days would elapse before Nationalist troops completed their military occupation of Chihli Province and entered Pekin.

(By Associated Press)

Pekin, June 4.—The withdrawal of Chang Tso-Lin's Manchurian troops overland from Northern China is meeting with some resistance by the Nationalist Allies. Today there was skirmishing between the Shansi Nationalist troops and the retreating Northerners between Liuliho and the Hankow Pass.

WILL WED BROKER

Engagement of Miss Victoria Frelinghuysen Announced

(By Associated Press)

New York, June 4.—The engagement of Miss Victoria Frelinghuysen to J. Grenville Bates, Jr., of Morristown, N. J., is announced by her parents, former Senator and Mrs. Joseph S. Frelinghuysen.

Miss Frelinghuysen is a graduate of Miss Spence's School and a member of the junior league. She was introduced to society three years ago. Mr. Bates is a member of the brokerage firm of Taylor, Bates and Company, and holds a seat on the New York exchange. He attended St. Paul's School of Concord, N. H., and the Episcopal Academy at Philadelphia. He is a member of the Union Club.

SMOKER SETS BED AFIRE

Man Burned, Two Others Routed at 4th and Green Sts.

A man was burned about the face and hands and two others were forced from their home when a lighted cigarette set fire to a bed in a second-story rear room over a junk dealer's store at 403 Green st., early today.

Michael Martuck, forty-two, a P. R. T. watchman, fell asleep in his bed with a burning cigarette in his hand, he told fireman.

Peter Michael, and his wife, Frances, both fifty-two, were forced to leave.

ADVANCE FIVE P. E. DEACONS

Bishop Garland Confers Priesthood and Ordains Four to Diaconate

Five men now in deacon's orders were advanced to the priesthood and four other men were ordained to the diaconate by Bishop Thomas J. Garland at exercises today in the P. E. Memorial Church of the Advocate, 18th and Diamond sts.

The deacons advanced to the priesthood are:

The Rev. Joseph Rockhill Clair, in charge of All Saints', Williamsport; the Rev. Albert William Eastburn, "Padre" of Philadelphia "Toc H"; the Rev. Jesse Hutchinson Hawkes, assistant at Advocate Church, here; the Rev. Robert Colsher Hubbs, assistant at St. Bartholomew's, New York; the Rev. William Powell, in charge of St. Joseph's Mission, Gladwyne.

Those to be ordained to the Diaconate are Charles Harold Harrison, Arthur Trent Helms, Frederick John Gibbs Kepler, Hugh Latimer Willson.

DRIVER GETS 60 DAYS IN JAIL

Atlantic City, June 4.—John R. Goslin, Randolph st. near Venango, Philadelphia, has been sent to jail for sixty days in default of $200 fine for driving while intoxicated on White Horse pike, near Absecon. He was arrested by State police yesterday.

POLAR FLIER KNIGHTED

"Sir George H. Wilkins" Now Name of Arctic Aviator

London, June 4.—It is now "Sir George H. Wilkins." The intrepid Australian captain, who flew with Lieutenant Carl B. Eielson from Alaska to Spitzbergen, was granted knighthood by King George as part of the honor list issued on the Monarch's sixty-third birthday anniversary.

CUTS THROAT WITH RAZOR

Man Feared Losing Apartment After Period of Idleness

Harry Hait, forty-five, 3028 Berks st., cut his throat with a razor shortly after 5 A. M. today, leaving a note in which he told his wife, Lena, that no one but himself was to blame for his action.

The note also stated that he left all his possessions to his wife and daughter, Mary, eight.

According to the police Hait had obtained work three weeks ago after a nine months' search. They learned from his wife that he had been depressed by the fact he could. no longer afford to keep up the third floor apartment in which they lived. He is in the Woman's Homeopathic Hospital. His condition is serious.

THE 'CLEVER' SPECULATOR

President Hill, of the American Tobacco Company, apropos of speculation, said in an interview:

"There's nothing I hate to see so much as a young man speculating. A broker remarked to another broker one day:

" 'Young Jones is certainly a clever lad, and hasn't he learnt the market well? He's been speculating close on to a year now, and he's got some of his father's fortune left.' "

TRAINMEN DEFEAT W. G. LEE

Head of Brotherhood Is Deposed After Service of 19 Years

(By Associated Press)

Cleveland, O., June 4.—William G. Lee, for nineteen years head of the Brotherhood of Railroad Trainmen, today was defeated by twenty-four votes for president of the organization by A. F. Whitney, general secretary-treasurer.

The vote was Whitney, 486; Lee, 462.

LINK NEW TUBE TO CITY HALL

Steel and Concrete Construction Work There Starts Soon

Steel and concrete construction work will start soon at the City Hall end of the S. Broad st. subway. This work is well under way in the Kater st. end of the tube.

Engineers stated that when the steel erection has been carried to Locust st., the work on the Locust st. subway can be started. The Philadelphia Rapid Transit Co. is authorized to order this work without competitive bidding, and has $10,000,000 to begin the project.

The Broad st. connection under City Hall is now visible to riders on subway-surface cars which pass over it. Excavation has been carried on forty-five feet below the surface.

BLACK CAT CAUSES WRECK

Bus Driver Swerves to Avoid Animal and Hits Motor

Swerving his bus to avoid running down a black cat that ran into his path at Haddon av. and Cuthbert st., Westmont, Albert Denton, 445 Carteret st., Camden, crashed into two automobiles.

No one was injured, although both cars were badly damaged. They were driven by George Knowles, 82 Elgin av., Westmont, and Joseph Lombardi, 120 Rhoads av., Haddonfield. The accident happened last night.

VARE BACK FROM SHORE

Senator-Elect Recovers From Pleurisy—Going to Washington

U. S. Senator-elect William S. Vare returned here today from his summer home in Atlantic City, where he has just recovered from an attack of pleurisy.

He goes to Washington later in the day to attend to business there, and will leave here next Friday with the Pennsylvania delegation to the Republican National Convention, for Kansas City. He is a delegate-at-large.

"I am feeling fine now," Mr. Vare said. "After a thorough physical examination, my physicians informed me there is no organic disorder anywhere."

WOMAN STRUCK BY MOTOR

Seriously Injured While Crossing Broad St. at Poplar

Mrs. Katherine Baumon, forty-eight, 2525 S. 64th st., was struck and seriously injured while crossing Broad st. at Poplar, at 12.30 today, by an automobile driven by W. C. French, Church Lane.

She was taken to the Hahnemann Hospital with a fractured right hip and a fractured skull. French was arrested.

TRAIN KILLS MAN

Victim Struck by Pennsy Express Near Delair May be From Phila.

An unidentified man was killed by a westbound Pennsylvania Railroad bridge express west of Cresson Boulevard, near Delair, N. J., at 8.45 A. M. today.

The man was between forty and forty-five, weighed about 140, wore a blue serge suit, black striped shirt and brown soft hat. A gold pencil, $2.06, and a card bearing the address of 328 N. 8th st., this city, was found in his clothes.

FIRE STARTS IN DRYDOCK

Thirty Workmen Driven From Kensington Plant by Flames

Thirty workmen were forced to flee when a pipeline running to the former Cramp drydock, Beach and Palmer sts., Kensington, burst and caught fire at 8.15 A. M. today, damaging a barge in the dock.

The drydock is now owned by the Keystone Shipbuilding Co. The men were grouped around the barge when the pipe burst, setting fire to the wooden barge.

Firemen extinguished the flames within fifteen minutes, with little damage. The barge is owned by the Standard Oil Company.

HOOVER SENTIMENT GROWS AT CAPITAL

Administration Leaders Refrain from Anything That Would Hurt His Chances

SMITH LIKEWISE GAINS

BY DAVID LAWRENCE

Washington, June 4.—The Republican Presidential race has developed into a contest among three outstanding groups— those who are friendly to Herbert Hoover, but who prefer President Coolidge; those who insist that the President would decline if nominated, and hence Hoover should be chosen, and those who are absolutely opposed to any Administration candidate.

The Democratic race is almost entirely centered on Governor Smith, who appears already to have sufficient votes to force the necessary two-thirds in the early balloting at Houston.

Appraisals of the strength of Governor Smith as a vote-getter have had their effect on Republican leaders, who declare that this is not a year for a dark horse or a compromise candidate but a year for the strongest possible ticket.

The position that President Coolidge will play in the whole Republican situation is as yet undetermined, though members of the Cabinet are positive in their declarations that Mr. Coolidge would not accept if nominated.

Mr. Coolidge is deeply interested in the platform and of course would feel hurt if the convention nominated any candidate who was opposed to the Coolidge policies, including the McNary-Haugen veto.

Opinions differ, of course, as to who the nominee will be, but in the Administration group there is at the moment a feeling that Hoover will win out. This means that the draft talk has been continuously squelched in Administration quarters.

Outside of Washington, however, the reports of a sentiment for the drafting of President Coolidge are based upon what the party in convention assembled might do, apart from any wish that Mr. Coolidge might have in the matter.

Naturally in Washington the average office holder is not likely to go counter to the wishes of the President, and a good many of the people here recognize that the constant talk of drafting Mr. Coolidge is only another method of aiding those who are anxious to stop Hoover.

Indeed the drift to Hoover runs strongly in the Capital, particularly in the executive branch of the Government.

If President Coolidge is to be drafted, the impetus will have to come from outside the official group altogether.

BRYAN'S DAUGHTER ENDS BIG CAMPAIGN

Mrs. Owen Rivals Commoner in Electioneering by 500-Speech Stump Tour

SEEKS SEAT IN CONGRESS

Jacksonville, Fla., June 3.—If she has not broken the long-standing campaigning record of her father, the late William

Jennings Bryan, established in 1896, Ruth Bryan Owen, candidate for the Democratic nomination to Congress from the 4th Florida District, has come very close to it in the campaign she will close here tonight, her supporters assert.

The Great Commoner is said to have traveled 18,000 miles to deliver 600 speeches in twenty-seven States in 1896 after the winning of his first nomination as Presidential candidate with his famous "cross of gold" speech.

While his daughter's travels have been confined to the comparatively narrow limits of the 4th Congressional District, which, however, is among the largest and most populous Congressional district in the United States, she has covered more than 8,000 miles in her flivver, which she has christened "The Spirit of Florida," and made more than 500 speeches in four months. This mileage does not include train trips, some of them running from one end of the district to the other, a distance of nearly 500 miles.

It is estimated that during this period Mrs. Owen has talked to an aggregate crowd of 260,000 persons, exclusive of the radio audience, estimated at 100,000 persons, who heard her from Station WQAM, Miami.

Mrs. Ruth Bryan Owen

According to a survey of the district made by the Jacksonville Journal, co-operating with leading editors in each of the eighteen counties of the district, and published by that paper last Thursday, Mrs. Owen will carry the nomination by a majority of more than 20,000 votes.

Mrs. Owen was a Red Cross nurse during the World War,

having served with Gen. Allenby's army against the Turks. She was promoted from ward nurse to surgical nurse and then to operating room nurse. After the armistice had been signed and before the "boys" could come home, she acted as an entertainer at encampments. Her husband, who was a Major in the British army, died shortly before last Christmas as the result of wounds sustained during the war.

Mrs. Owen is the mother of four children.

WAS 'BABY' DELEGATE

Vineland Woman Was Youngest in 1924 Democratic Convention

The "baby delegate" to the National Democratic Convention of 1924 is wondering now if she will retain that distinction at the convention this month, to which she will again be a delegate.

She is Miss Thelma Parkinson, of Vineland, N. J., an active party worker in Cumberland county. It is true she is four years older now than when she was the "baby delegate" in 1924, but as she still is only twenty-eight she feels there is a chance she may again be the youngest delegate.

Miss Parkinson was graduated from Smith College in 1921, after which she took up welfare work. Soon she turned to politics, and in 1922 Governor Silzer appointed her to fill a vacancy on the Democratic State Committee. Later she was elected to a full term, and in 1923 she was appointed a member of the Cumberland County Tax Board, the first woman in New Jersey to hold such a position.

BLESSES NEW CHAPEL ORGAN

Cardinal Officiates at Overbrook—Gift of Albert M. Greenfield

A program of ecclesiastical splendor surrounded the blessing of the organ at the new chapel of St. Charles Borromeo Seminary yesterday by Cardinal Dougherty.

The instrument, one of the largest four-manual organs in the country, is the gift of Mr. and Mrs. Albert M. Greenfield as a tribute to District Attorney John Monaghan for his humanitarian work in the city.

Notables of the religious, industrial and executive life of the city listened first to a warm tribute by the Cardinal to the generosity of the donor and then to the first concert on the organ, played by Firmin Swinnen, Belgian-American organist.

The exercises were attended by Mr. and Mrs. Greenfield and Mr. Monaghan.

CHESAPEAKE CITY BANK MAN DIES

Elkton, Md., June 4.—Walter G. Pratt, twenty-eight, cashier of the Chesapeake City Bank, died today at Union Hospital of pneumonia. He was the youngest son of Frank G. Pratt, deputy clerk of the Circuit Court. A widow, three brothers and two sisters survive him.

REPUBLICANS BEGIN CONTEST HEARINGS

73 Seats in Kansas City Convention Disputed Before Committee

FLORIDA IS FIRST HEARD

(By Associated Press)

Kansas City, June 4.—Setting out to put their house in order for the National Convention next week, Republican leaders here today were confronted with a series of family disputes over who should have a say in the selection of the party's Presidential nominee.

It fell to the National Committee to fill the role of judge and peace maker with disputes over seventy-three of the 1,089 convention seats demanding its attention.

At the call of the National Committee chairman, William M. Butler, men and women members of the committee had assembled for the start of hearings which were expected to

4

take up much of the week. Their decisions, which may have an important bearing on the final choice of a nominee, are subject to review in the event any of those who lose out press their claims before the convention credentials committee, to be named next week.

The Democratic South, always a fertile field for factional strife among Republicans seeking control of the party machinery in that section, again had furnished the National Committee with most of its troubles. All the contests to be adjudicated during the week are from Southern States, except one involving the two delegates from the non-voting island of Porto Rico.

The contests attracting the most attention from party leaders are those from Louisiana, Mississippi and Texas, where the entire delegations are in dispute, and from Florida, where nine of the ten convention seats have been the subject of bitter controversy.

In addition, the National Committee had on its hands disputes involving three district delegate seats from Georgia, two from Kentucky, and one from Tennessee with indications that contests for six other seats—the four at large from South Carolina and two from the Tennessee district would not be pressed.

Veteran party leaders, who could recall vividly the heated battle over convention seats in 1912 when Taft and Roosevelt were at odds and the effect it had in splitting wide open the party convention then, were quick today to realize the bearing the committee's decisions might have this year. Fewer contests were filed than in 1912 and many past Presidential years, but for the most part they are closely allied with the candidacy of Herbert Hoover, and conceivably might contribute to his nomination or failure to master the necessary Convention strength to go over.

In Louisiana, Mississippi and Texas, the Commerce Secretary is supported by National Committeemen who were instrumental in shaping up one of the contesting delegations. In Florida, the Hoover cause has been championed by a slate of delegates, named in opposition to one drawn up by George V. Bean, the National Committeeman.

Following the precedent of taking up contests in alphabetical order, the Florida dispute had priority today, with the Glen B. Skipper faction seeking to oust the Bean forces.

Next on the calendar were the contests from the First, Fifth and Seventh Georgia districts, each with one delegate. They were the outgrowth of rows between rival local leaders, none of them generally regarded as hostile to Hoover.

7,000 SEE PARACHUTE JUMPS

'Bob' Murphy Fails Twice to Break Record for 'Free Fall'

More than 7,000 persons at the William Penn Airport, Roosevelt boulevard and Red Lion road, watched Sergeant "Bob" Murphy, former service instructor in parachute jumping, make two attempts to establish a world's record for a "free fall" before opening his parachute at the airport yesterday.

The present record is a drop of 2,400 feet before permitting the parachute to open. Murphy made his first leap from a height of 4,000 feet but found the air conditions were unfavorable for making the attempt and released his parachute soon after leaping. The plane was piloted by Captain Fred Lorillard, former Royal Air Force flier.

Murphy made his second attempt in the evening.

INSANE PATIENT ESCAPES

Man Described as Violent Flees from Byberry Hospital

Police throughout the city today were on the lookout for a patient, described as violently insane, who escaped from the Byberry Hospital during the night.

The man is 5 feet, 10 inches tall, weighs about 150 pounds and was wearing dark trousers, a grey and white sweater and black shoes when he disappeared. He wore no hat. His name is Edward Blasky, twenty-eight.

BAKERS MEET AT READING

350 of State Association Opens 20th Annual Convention

(By Associated Press)

Reading, June 4.—Master bakers of the State opened their 20th annual convention today at Galen Hall, South Mountain, with 350 visitors registered.

With an address of welcome by Mayor J. Henry Stump and response by James B. Dwyer, Erie, the convention got under way. The address of the president, Gerald R. Williams, Scranton, commended members for co-operation.

PRESIDENTIAL CAMPAIGN OF 1856

No. 1

(By Associated Press)

Eighteen times since 1856 the two major political parties of the United States have met in quadrennial convention to name candidates for President and Vice President.

Since that year, the first in which the Republicans held a national nominating convention, the nominees of the Republican party have been elected thirteen times and those of the Democratic party have been successful five times. The Republicans have held the Presidency for fifty-two years, and the Democrats for twenty.

The first national nominating convention of the Republican party was held in Philadelphia on June 17, 1856. John C. Fremont was nominated for President and William L. Dayton, of New Jersey, for Vice President. The platform affirmed belief in union of the States but did not declare for freedom of the slaves.

The Democratic party met at Cincinnati June 2-6, and nominated James Buchanan, of Pennsylvania, for President and John C. Breckenridge, of Kentucky, for Vice President.

Buchanan and Breckenridge won, in November, the party's last victory until 1884.

THOUGHT JUSTICE IN U. S. WAS 'EASY'

English Youth Confesses Stealing Motor Here— Faces Jail, Then Deportation

HAD DIARY OF 'CAREER'

A dapper twenty-year-old English youth, speaking in a refined accent, pleaded guilty today in Quarter Sessions Court, Room 453, City Hall, to stealing an automobile and admitted that his idea that American justice was "easy" had led him to commit the crime.

The youth, Leslie Taylor, of London, was arrested last Wednesday in Jersey City for stealing a car belonging to Louis E. Trautwein, 1348 Hunting Park av., this city, from in front of the latter's home the preceding Sunday. After hearing the case Judge Gay Gordon, Jr., turned the defendant over to E. M. Hackney, chief probation officer.

"I am going to send you to jail and show you American justice is stern," said the court, "and after serving time there you will be deported. Your case will be further investigated however, before you go to prison."

The defendant, who claims he is a cousin of Charlie Chaplin, said he had entered the United States from Canada and intended going to Hollywood eventually. In his possession was found a diary which described his travels, many all-night card games with monetary success, and numerous escapades. Luck failed him, however, in this city, he wrote.

"I have become fairly convinced," read a further entry, which apparently led him to the automobile theft, "that justice in America is in no way to be compared with justice in England. Punishment here is slight and much more time is required to inflict it."

HELD FOR STEALING TIRE

Bryan D. Taylor, eighteen, Walnut st., near 33d, was arrested on a charge of attempted larceny at 2.30 A. M. today by a night watchman at 58th and Addison sts. The watchman, Morris Wergleis, said he watched Taylor remove the spare tire from an automobile.

BROKE RECORD

CAPTAIN ARTURO FERRARIN

Italian flier, who, with Major Carlo Delprete, set a new world's endurance flight record, staying aloft 58 hours, 34 minutes. The old record of 53 hours, 36 minutes was set by the Americans, Stinson and Haldeman in March.

TELLS PEACE WORK OF LEAGUE COUNCIL

Senor Aguero, at Fiftieth Session, Reviews Progress in Better Understanding Among Nations

WELCOME SPAIN'S RETURN

(By Associated Press)

Geneva, Switzerland, June 4.—Immense practical progress in achieving good understanding among the Nations is the fruit of meetings of the Councils of the League of Nations, said the Council president, Aguero y Betancourt, opening the first public meeting of the current session of the Council today.

Observing that it was the golden anniversary (fiftieth session) of the Council, Senor Aguero sketched its history. He said that in earlier days those who govern the destinies of peoples hardly knew one another or only met at official interviews but that now a new era had been created thanks to the League.

He voiced satisfaction that Quinones De Leon, of Spain, who sat on the first Council, will soon return in consequence of Spain's decision to return to the League, Senor Aguero added:

Co-operation with Latin-America in health questions was approved by the Council, which adopted a resolution asking interested countries what they were ready to contribute to proposed studies of leprosy in Latin-America, in the way of facilities for investigation and financial support. This committee of investigation includes Dr. H. S. Cumming, Surgeon General of the United States Public Health Service.

FAILS IN BUSINESS, STARS IN KITCHEN

Wife Made Him Do Household Tasks, Man Replies to Her Suit for Divorce

DID THEM FOR LOVE

Los Angeles, June 3.—If a husband is a failure in business life, try him out as the family cook; fire the maid and chauffeur and let him do their work; dispense with the laundry man and, in general, turn the errant spouse loose to make himself useful about the place.

Some such program is doubtless being advocated in many local homes, following the divorce case testimony adduced this week from Kenneth Gulick McClurg before Judge Raymond I. Turney.

McClurg's wife, the former Lillian Stanford, is attempting to divorce him on grounds of infidelity and cruelty.

Originally well to do, McClurg asserts that he was dominated by his wife. They spent almost all his fortune under her direction, he says. Then he set about to look for work. First he started a garage, but it was a failure. Then he looked for work in a department store, but failed to make the proper connections.

OFFERING EVIDENCE

KENNETH G. M'CLURG

Former New Yorker, demonstrating in a Los Angeles court how he was forced to do housework for his wife, Mrs. Lillian Stanford McClurg, English heiress. She is suing for divorce. (Associated Press photo.)

"When my wife learned of this failure she was furious," McClurg told Judge Turney. She discharged the servants. Some one had to do the work and she told me that I was to be the one.

"From then on I was a servant to her. I rather liked the work itself, but her attitude was intolerable. For two years, from 1925 to 1927, I submitted to it. At first I didn't resist because I loved her. When I did begin to resist it was too late."

During those two years, the testimony shows, McClurg lived an amazing life. Every meal that was cooked in the household was produced by the docile husband, and he was a good cook, even Mrs. McClurg admitted that. Dainty omelettes in the morning, tasty salads for luncheon and juicy steaks cooked to a turn at night.

Between meals McClurg was not idle. When the dishes were washed and put away he straightened the house, then washed and mended his clothes. On the frequent occasions when Mrs. McClurg and her mother wished to go out, he doffed his gingham apron, assumed the role of chauffeur and patiently drove them about, in fact, as one of the neighbors observed, he would have made a model wife for some girl who appreciated his ability.

MOTORIST LOSES $40 DEBATE

Cheltenham Policeman Arrests Pittston Man Who Resents Warning

It cost Richard S. Scully, a Pittston business man, $40 and a delay of over two hours last night to lose an argument with a Cheltenham policeman when the latter stopped Scully to warn him about the way he was driving in heavy traffic.

The policeman, Smith, told Magistrate Refsnyder, in the Ogontz police station, that Scully was weaving in and out traffic on Old York road at City Line. When he stopped Scully's automobile Smith said Scully became abusive and defied him to make an arrest.

In the argument that followed Scully started to fight. When he was subdued Smith placed handcuffs on him and drove to the Ogontz police station. Scully was fined $25 for resisting a policeman, $10 for disorderly conduct, and $5 costs. He paid.

LINK WATER WASTE TO ROW

170,000 Gallons Lost as 4 North Wales Fire Plugs Are Opened

Norristown, June 4.—Montgomery county authorities are investigating the waste, through the opening of four fire plugs, of more than 170,000 gallons of water in the borough of North Wales, causing crippling of industries and great inconvenience to householders.

The plugs were found open and nearly run dry yesterday. County detective John B. Stevenson said the vandalism had some connection with the recent controversy between the paid and volunteer fire companies of North Wales.

SAVES 2 BOYS FROM CLIFF

Youth With Rope Rescues Climbers Above East River Drive

A tall red-haired youth rescued two boys from a high cliff above the East River drive, south of the park trolley bridge last night, but hurried away from a large crowd which had watched the rescue.

The boys, Lester Lover, twelve, 4729 N. 11th st., and Aaron Spector, nine, 4716 N. 11th st., were playing at mountain climbing among the rocks when they reached a narrow ledge and discovered that they were unable to get down.

While motorists, who heard them cry for help, went for firemen, the youth borrowed a rope, climbed the rocks, and lowered them to safety.

Obituaries

WALTER W. GALE

President of Publishing Company Dies at W. Phila. Home

Funeral services for Walter W. Gale, president of the Confectioners' Journal Publishing Co., will be held after the return of his son, Paul H. Gale, from France.

Mr. Gale died Saturday night at his home, 4711 Windsor av. His son was informed by cable and left the detachment of the 28th Division with which he was re-visiting battle scenes in France, to return home.

Born in this city, Mr. Gale was connected with the confectionery industry since 1881, and became connected with the Confectioners' Journal in 1886. He was a member of the Manufacturers' Club and the Poor Richard Club. He also is survived by his widow, a daughter, Mrs. G. McK. Bryan; a brother and a sister.

ALFRED LEE

Librarian at Union League for More Than 30 Years

Alfred Lee, for more than thirty years librarian at the Union League, died suddenly yesterday at his home, 12 Snowden rd., Cynwyd. He was seventy-six.

Mr. Lee was a graduate of the University of Pennsylvania in the class of 1873 and of the Episcopal Academy. He was a son of the Right Rev. Alfred Lee, once Episcopal Bishop of Wilmington, and was once active in the affairs of the Evangelical Education Association. He was a member of the Phi Kappa Sigma Fraternity.

He was married in 1892 to Miss Lillian Blakely, of New Orleans, and is survived by four children, Mrs. Margery Lee Adams and Miss Julia W. Lee, of New York; Mrs. Raymond Nicholson, of Germantown, and Alfred Lee, Jr., of this city. Funeral services will be held tomorrow at 10 A. M., at St. Asaph's Church, Conshohocken rd., Bala. Burial will be in Wilmington.

JOHN JACOB STOER

Business Man Was Member of Old Board of Wharves

Funeral services will be held tomorrow at 11 A. M., for John Jacob Stoer, seventy-four, who died Saturday at his home, 672 Highland av., Merion.

Mr. Stoer was born in Pittsburgh, coming to Philadelphia at the age of fifteen. After engaging in the manufacture of shirts, Mr. Stoer left here for West Virginia, where he was in the lumber business. Returning to this city he became treasurer of the old Philadelphia Times, and later was appointed to the Board of Wharves, which went out of existence with the organization of the present Department of Wharves, Docks and Ferries.

He is survived by his wife, who was Margaretta K. Mugel of Pittsburgh, two sons and six grandchildren.

JOHN FOLEY COUSART

Former Philadelphian Was National Chaplain of The Gideons

Word was received here today of the death of John Foley Cousart, former Philadelphia, and for many years national chaplain of the Gideon Association, an organization of Christian traveling men who place Bibles in hotel rooms.

Mr. Cousart died Tuesday at the home of his son-in-law, Judge Howe, Newark, N. J., and was buried Friday in Hillside Cemetery, near Willow Grove. He was long identified with Calvary M. E. Church, 48th st. and Baltimore av. He was a life member of the Pocket Testament League, and during the World War was stationed at the Philadelphia Navy Yard where he distributed Testaments to sailors and officers.

CHARLES M. SAEGER

Allentown, Pa., June 4.—Charles M. Saeger, retired manager of the Coplay Cement Co., died last night in the Palmerton Hospital, Palmerton. He was seventy-two. On his retirement Mr. Saeger established an estate at Bowmanstown, where he was taken ill two weeks ago while dedicating a community house there for which he donated the site. His widow, two sons and a daughter survive.

T. THOMAS FORTUNE

Editor of the Negro World, New York, died Saturday night at the home of his son, Dr. Frederick W. Fortune, 770 S. 18th st., after an illness of several months. He was seventy-two. Mr. Fortune was a special commissioner to the Philippines under President Roosevelt, and was secretary to General Josiah T. Walls, former Florida congressman. Funeral services will be held Wednesday.

KAUSEL DENIES CHARGES

Accused of Hampering Woman Who Quit Camden Co. Home Post

Theodore M. Kausel, superintendent of the Camden County institutions at Lakeland, denies charges made by Miss Kate M. Brusstar, whose resignation as matron of the County Detention Home became known Saturday.

In resigning, to take effect June 15, Miss Brusstar charged she had been "hampered and persistently annoyed" since the Board of Freeholders created Kausel's office at the beginning of the year. She also charged that "wormy sugar" and soap that "would eat the skin off your hands" had been supplied the institution since Kausel's advent.

Kausel said he did not think Miss Brusstar was "a believer in constituted authority." He denied he had purchased any soap for the institution and declared the sugar was the "best."

THOSE VAST ROOMS

"Why the parlor sofa in the middle of the Grand Central Station?"

"We have loaned the terminal to a movie company for a drawing room scene."

MOVEMENTS OF VESSELS
ARRIVED TODAY

Str. Schenectady, Hurum, etc., via Baltimore, mdse. Moore & McCormack.

Str. Paulsboro, Lockport, La., petroleum. Vacuum Oil Co.

Str. City of Philadelphia, Houston, mdse. Southern S. S. Co.

Str. Nantucket, Savannah, mdse. and passengers. Merchants & Miners Trans. Co.

Str. Kinge Inge (Nor.), Jamaica, fruit. Banana Sales Corpn.

Str. Algria (Hond.), Baracoa, fruit. Di Giorgio Fruit Corpn.

Str. Half Moon, Beirut, etc., via New York, mdse. J. F. Shumacher.

Str. Conehatta Santos, etc., via Baltimore, mdse. Chas. A. Devlin, Inc.

Str. Dalmazia (Ital.), Rabat, mdse. P. Gramigna & Son.

Str. James River, Norfolk, mdse. Philadelphia & Norfolk S. S. Co.

Str. Dora Deepwater Point, ballast. Chas. Kurz & Co., Inc.

CLEARED

Str. John Cadwalader, Baltimore, passengers and mdse. Ericsson Line.

Str. Frances Anne, Baltimore, mdse. Green Line.

Str. San Antonio, Houston, mdse. Southern S. S. Co.

Str. Delaware River, Norfolk, mdse. Philadelphia & Norfolk S. S. Co.

Str. H. C. Folger, Brunswick, ballast. Atlantic Refining Co.

Motorship Sharon, Beaumont, ballast. Atlantic Refining Co.

Str. W. E. Hutton, Smith's Bluff, ballast. Pure Oil S. S. Co.

MARRIAGE LICENSES

AT CITY HALL

Peter L. Thomson, 4439 N. 8th st., and Ruth C. Schmidt, 4439 N. 8th st.

Frank M. Shephard, 1536 N. 23d st., and Elizabeth A. Merkle, 2730 W. Eyre av.

Joseph A. Ferrari, 537 N. 65th st., and Sylvia Desiderio, 1232 N. 42d st.

Eugene J. Thudium, 5632 Ridgewood st., and Harriet L. George, 205 E. Wellens av.

Charles Blackwell, 2141 Lombard st., and Alice A. Ballard, 1511 Pike st.

Paul B. Remmey, 1229 Harrison st., and Edythe G. Holden, 4645 Pilling st.

Howard Krassenstein, 250 S. 56th st., and Lillian Leavy, 6103 Delancey st.

Charles Currlie, 513 Hamilton st., and Jean Somckise, 513 Hamilton st.

Albert R. Opper, 1209 N. 25th st., and Florence T. Donahue, 1758 N. Taney st.

Leon D. King, Bryn Mawr, and Alice A. Oliver, 4419 Aspen st.

Louis Davidson, 2429 N. 8th st., and Anna Waldman, 444 N. 8th st.

John D. R. Kramer, 1131 Cottman st., and Ruth N. Grimm, 7410 Claridge st.

Harold J. Tully, 5703 Woodland av., and Margaret L. Green, 6047 Kingsessing av.

Leonard J. Krane, 4732 N. Rorer st., and Ray Cohen, 2321 S. 10th st.

Walter L. Heim, 2024 Ash st., and Mae Lange, 4534 E. Thompson st.

Michael G. Hunt, 1432 S. Vodges st., and Catharine J. Kane, Collingdale.

Morris Kreger, 2108 Orthodox st., and Betty Spiegel, 1567 N. 5th st.

Carl G. Pfizenmaier, 1400 N. 29th st., and Eleanor D. Hubbs, 3728 N. 19th st.

Russell H. Hays, 6818 Chew st., and Lillian M. Kline, 5827 Critenden st.

Joseph S. Manein, 4423 Silverwood st., and Kathryn E. Cronin, 146 Levington av.

Samuel J. Kenney, 8083 Rowland av., and Frances E. Hant-Weicker, 4602 Horrock st.

David W. Cohen, 449 S. 48th st., and Helen E. West, 5115 Wynnefield av.

John L. Winters, Royersford, and Anna W. Gannon, 1709 W. Erie av.

Frank L. Whatley, 2839 N. 8th st., and Regina R. Palinkas, 2323 N. Reese st.

John Belluscio, 1815 S. Camac st., and Filomena Traverso, 1815 S. Camac st.

Wilbur P. Hall, 16 N. 50th st., and Mary S. Foster, 5415 Baltimore av.

Thomas P. Haviland, 130 W. Johnston st., and Annie T. Cusling, 6607 Quincy st.

Edward T. Schumacher, 2720 W. Somerset st., and Josephine M. Nina, Highland Park.

Ralph K. Gallagher, 849 E. Tioga st., and Naomi J. Hoffman, 1911 E. Madison st.

Stanley S. Masda, 3214 Summer st., and Madeline E. Dugent, 3214 Summer st.

George O. Wagner, 1762 N. Dover st., and Julia L. Rumpp, 878 N. 27th st.

William S. Dutcher, 4019 Castor av., and Cecelia M. Moritz, 3816 N. 6th st.

Francis W. Beard, Pensacola, Fla., and Helen S. Falkner, 59 W. Tulpehocken st.

AT ELKTON, MD.

Nelson M. Ruth, 22, 8802 Eastwick av., and Laura V. Everingham, 19, 6511 Woodland av.

Carl G. P. McLeod, 21, and Ruth M. Williams, 19, both of 1718 N. 23d st.

Joseph R. Morrell, 21, 1924 Jefferson st., and Frances M. Terrentine, 20, 2011 Nicholas st.

David V. George, Jr., 21, 5308 Magnolia av., and Emily D. Grodwell, 18, 215 E. Bringhurst st., Germantown.

George J. Blaher, 27, Folsom, N. J., and Evelyn K. Straub, 19, 2388 N. Howard st.

Howard D. Kreen, 21, 5213 Chestnut st., and Kathryn G. Massel, 18, Aronimink.

Joseph W. Hemphill, 22, and Lucy E. Ford, 18, Wilmington.

Earl J. Dennis, 21, and Hilda M. Williams, 18, Chester.

Clifford Fuhrman, 22, and Margaret E. Savill, 21, Chester.

Henry J. Borger, 32, Chesapeake City, Md., and Rose Albright, 28, Baltimore.

Victor A. West, 25, and Virginia A. Ross, 21, New York.

John H. Stafford, Jr., 22, and Edith B. Golden, 19, Baltimore.

Harry I. Jackson, 46, Palmyra, N. J., and Helen S. Leap, 34, Wenonah, N. J.

John W. Kline, 22, and Alice E. Whiteman, 19, Hillside, Pa.

Joseph A. McKernan, 29, and Eleanor I. Coater, 25, Bridgeport, Pa.

Peter A. Mills, 29, Bridgewater, Va., and Evalyn F. Palmer, 20, Hartley, Del.

Beauford A. McIntire, 21, Richmond, Va., and Laura W. Palmer, 18, Hartley, Del.

AT WEST CHESTER

Sam Childres and Madge Hampstead, Philadelphia.

Harry Laspe, Camden, and Ethel Heineman, Philadelphia.

Clement Smyrl and Grace Tutolo, East Lansdowne, Pa.
Linwood J. Gillan and Katherine Kelleher, Kennett Square.
Thomas C. Baker, Londonderry, and Nellie Strickland, Parkesburg.

AT CAMDEN

William C. Gibbs, 24, Downington, Pa., and Daisy Bussard, 21, 911 N. 7th st., Camden.

William R. Feairheller, 30, 1658 Hawarth st., Philadelphia, and Bernice E. Schmeirer, 23, 1143 Princess av., Camden.

Francis S. Nelson, 26, 603 Chestnut st., Camden, and Rose M. Rudolph, 24, 538 Mt. Vernon st., Camden.

George F. Jordan, 21, 1122 Mechanic st., Camden, and Florence M. Johnston, 18, 1268 Lonis st., Camden.

Ralph E. Wood, 30, and Edith Strang, 24, both of 608 Clinton st., Camden.

James Carter, 21, 212 N. 11th st., Camden, and Edna Morell, 17, 1661 S. 7th st., Camden.

AT NORRISTOWN

Paul F. Markley, Fort Monmouth, Oceanport, N. J., and Helen E. Stubbs, Ocean Grove, N. J.

Ellwood Hollinger and Katherine M. Kline, both of Reading.

NIBBLES AT THE NEWS

New York—Mrs. James A. Stillman would love to be the first woman to fly from this country to Europe, but she has her family to think of. She so writes in describing a flight she had with Thea Rasche and perhaps, she concludes, maybe after this she can get a job as a reporter. "Wouldn't I just have fun!"

Buenos Aires—No circus stunt can beat this. A pilot looping the loop was thrown from a plane and parachuted to safety. His observer was left behind. The plane fell crazily, and the observer righted it just in time to land nicely.

New York—"Long may she wave!" Such is the headline over an item describing a woman of seventy-three walking seventeen miles to get a permanent coiffure.

5

WEST PHILA. CLERGYMEN DENOUNCE DANCE MARATHON

Call Arena Spectacle 'Degrading' and 'Immoral'—Money Divided

West Philadelphia clergymen denounced the "marathon dance" which ended at the Arena, 45th and Market sts., shortly after Saturday midnight, when the "contestants" agreed to split up the prize money. "Disgusting," "degrading," and "immoral" were some of the characterizations used by ministers in sermons yesterday.

"The intelligence and moral fiber of our age have reached a very low ebb when young men and women for a prize of gold are willing to shuffle over a dance floor, hour after hour, for days and nights, until they fall from sheer exhaustion," said the Rev. Howard Bell, of the West Hope Presbyterian Church, Preston and Aspen sts.

"We thrill to the exploits of Lindbergh, but disgust fills our hearts at the useless and disgraceful effort known as the dance marathon," said the Rev. A. J. Lewis, Belmont Avenue Baptist Church.

Others who denounced the exhibition were the Rev. R. R. Famous, 43d Street Methodist Episcopal Church, 43d and Aspen sts., and R. Humphries, Centenary Methodist Episcopal Church, 41st and Spring Garden sts., and F. K. Keeler, secretary of the Pennsylvania Railroad Y. M. C. A.

The contest ended when the police ordered the spectators from the Arena, under the Sunday laws. Two couples were then competing for a $1,000 prize. Under the agreement each dancer took $250, or approximately $2.35 for each of the 108 hours consumed. Three "solo" dancers, who continued after their partners dropped out, divided a prize of $500, each taking $166.66, or a little over $1.50 an hour.

The couples dancing at the windup were Joseph Gleason, twenty, 229 N. Ramsay st., and Fern Kaplin, eighteen 2349 N. 30th st.; Joseph Jones, twenty, 229 Mifflin st., and Mae Clark, twenty-two, 878 N. Beechwood st. The soloists who divided the $500 prize are Eddie Close, twenty-seven, 1004 Green st.; John F. Sweeney, twenty-six, 6167 Upland st., and Appella Zandes, twenty-two, 5250 Delancy st.

SMITH AHEAD IN WEST VA.

Official Count May be Needed to Decide Race With Reed

(By Associated Press)

Charleston, W. Va., June 4.—The battle for West Virginia's sixteen votes at the Democratic National Convention remained undecided today, almost a week after the State-wide primary last Tuesday.

So close was the margin separating the delegates supporting Governor Alfred E. Smith, of New York, for the Presidency, and those opposing him under the banner of Senator James A. Reed, of Missouri, that the official count may be necessary to decide the contests for delegate-at-large and some of the district tussels.

The standing today was eleven and a half votes for Smith and four and a half votes for the anti-Smith group. The count represented a gain of one vote for Smith over the last tabulation Saturday.

In the Presidential preference column the count was:

Republican: 2,173 out of 2,306 precincts, Senator Guy D. Goff, 120,519; Secretary of Commerce Herbert Hoover, 106,033.

Democratic: 2,145 out of 2,306 precincts, Governor Smith, 74,869; Senator Reed, 70,777.

2 PRIESTS, TOURING WORLD, VISIT HERE

Dr. Esteban, Head of Augustinian Order, and Dr. Hickey, Assistant General, Inspect Villanova

LEFT ROME IN JANUARY

The Very Rev. Dr. Eustasius Esteban, prior-general of the Augustinian Order, and the Very Rev. Dr. Joseph A. Hickey, former president of Villanova College and now assistant general of the order, who are making a world-wide tour on official visits to the provinces of the order, arrived at Villanova College today.

They started from Rome last January after being received in a special private audience by the Pope. Since then they have visited houses and schools of the order in the Philippine Islands, China, Australia and this country.

They motored here from New York today and were welcomed by the Very Rev. James H. Griffin, president of the college. They timed their visit to coincide with Commencement Week which starts tomorrow.

While in China the two priests visited with the missionaries of their order in the Province of Hunan. From this country they will go to South America and from there to Ireland, England, Spain and thence to Rome.

Dr. Esteban, who is a native of Spain, has been an educator in the order in South America, principally in Chile and Peru, in Mexico and the Philippine Islands. He is an accomplished linguist and speaks Spanish, Italian, Portuguese, French, Latin and English.

Dr. Hickey is well known in this city, having been a professor at Villanova from 1912 to 1925, when he was elected assistant general at the general chapter of the order in Rome. In March, 1927, Pius XI. nominated him as consultor of the Sacred Congregation of the Sacraments.

The assistant general is a graduate of Villanova, but made his theological studies in Rome, where he was made a Doctor of Canon Law. Later he received the order's own degree of Master of Theology from the Collegio Internazionale in Rome. So stringent are the requirements for this master's degree that in the history of the province only four have received it in course.

OPEN DIPHTHERIA CAMPAIGN

78 Public and Parochial School Centres Give Serum Treatment

A campaign to immunize children against diphtheria opened today.

In addition to the health centres where anti-diphtheria serum is distributed all year round, seventy public schools and eight parochial schools were open at 3.30 P. M. today and will be open Thursday for the inoculation of children between the ages of six months and six years.

The treatment, which is under the auspices of the Department of Public Health, will be free. Dr. A. A. Cairns, head of the department, is directing staff nurses and physicians who will carry on the work. Health agencies and private organizations are co-operating.

---

85 ARE GRADUATED FROM DICKINSON

College at Carlisle, Pa., Holds 146th Annual Commencement Exercises

SEVERAL FROM NEAR HERE

Carlisle, Pa., June 4.—Eighty-five seniors and ninety-two law students received their degrees from Dickinson College at the 146th annual commencement today.

Seven honorary degrees were conferred. The recipients were: The Rev. J. Howard Ake, district superintendent of the Harrisburg district of the Central Pennsylvania conference, D. D.; the Rev. Henry F. Lawrence, Atlantic City, D. D.; the Rev. Howard E. Thompson, Cumberland, Md., D. D.; James M. Hoover, missionary of northwest Borneo, L. H. D.; Benjamin Gregory, editor of the Methodist Times, London, Litt. D.; John J. Tigert, United States Commissioner of Education, LL. D.; James Moffatt, New York, LL. D.

Commissioner Tigert delivered the graduation address.

Raymond R. Bell, this city, was valedictorian, and Miss Mary Goodyear, also of Carlisle, was salutatorian. Bell is the winner of the James Fowler Rusling prize for the highest scholarship for the four-year course. Graduates from Philadelphia and vicinity are:

Richard V. Zug, Chestnut Hill; Louise A. Loper, Oak Lane; Marian F. Foberg and Addison M. Bowman, Camp Hill; Albert E. Hartman, Fallsington, Pa.; Christopher T. Crook and Mary G. Smith, Chester; Elizabeth M. Rogers, Moorestown, N. J.; William R. Smith and Dorothy E. Chamberlain,

Salem, N. J.; Marguerite P. Evans, Berlin, N. J., and Samuel Lichtenfeld, Wayne, Pa.

The other graduates are:

Raymond R. Bell, Mary and Ruth Goodyear, William C. McDermott, all of Carlisle; Minerva Bernhardt and Claude C. Bowman, both of Harrisburg; F. Fairlee Habbart, Cambridge, Md.; W. Reese Hitchens, Milford, Del.; Joseph E. Green, Helen McDonnell and Howard M. Wert, all of Carlisle; Alfred J. Marcus, Whitestone, N. Y.; G. Worthington Post, New York City; Lawrence D. Dibble, Honesdale; William Arthur Faus, Jersey Shore; Earl A. Forsythe, Hagerstown, Md.; Carl W. Geiger, Wormleysburg; Joseph E. Green, Carlisle; Martha Jane Green, Carlisle; Helen E. Hackman, Carlisle; Mildred E. Hull, Atglen; Mildred F. Laird, Carlisle.

Raymond A. Lumley, Barnesboro; Helen L. McDonnell, Carlisle; Donald J. McIntyre, Harrisburg; F. Douglas Milbury, Milford, Del.; Jessie E. Poticher, Carlisle; Frank R. Robinson, Lemoyne; John T. Shuman, Halifax; Carroll C. Stauff, Tottenville, N. Y.; A. Marian Thompson, Harrisburg; Clara Yoder, Ardsley; Rupert G. Appleby, Singlehouse; Alton V. Arnold, Brillhart; Victor F. Baiz, Wilkes-Barre; Albert J. Bates, Hazelton; James H. G. Buchanan, Lakewood, N. J.; Bernard E. Burr, Carlisle; Robertson C. Cameron, Wellsboro; Betsy A. Cloudy, Neptune, N. J.; Eleanor G. Dando, Williamstown; John A. Dempwolf, York; Chauncey M. Depuy, Jr., Chambersburg; Byron M. Field, Mt. Vision, N. Y.; Janet D. Forcey, Phillipsburg; C. Thurston Frazier, Carlisle; Fred C. Fye, DuBois; A. Rudolph Green, St. Mary's; James G. Haggerty, Lemoyne; Victor B. Hann, Williamsport; Dorothy E. Harpster, Phillipsburg.

R. Merlin Hill, Richmond Hill, N. Y.; John M. Kelly, Montrose; Henry Kiessel, Tenafly, N. J.; Russel T. King, Montgomery; Ralph S. Krouse, Sunbury; John M. McHale, Centralia; Pamela L. McWilliams, Johnstown; M. Kennard Markley, Harrisburg; Arthur Markowitz, York; O. Dixon Marshall, Adams, Mass.; William Vernon Middleton, Baltimore; Alfred D. Mihachik, Brooklyn, N. Y.; Paul D. Olejar, Uniontown; Lillie K. Rhoads, Birdsboro; Dorothy A. Ritter, Shippensburg; Julius Schutzer, Olyphant; Vladimir Sidoriak, Minersville; Margaret R. Slaughter, Wilmington, Del.; C. Eben

Smith, Hanover; Howard G. Stutzman, Tower City; James Elwood Taylor, Rock Hall, Md.; Charles F. Wahl, Harrisburg; Earle H. Wildermuth, Pottsville; Fred E. Sweely, Jersey Shore, Pa.

SISTERS WIN SCHOOL HONORS

Vineland, N. J., Girls Head Washington College Class

Chestertown, Md., June 4.—Two sisters of Vineland, N. J., carried off senior honors at the 146th commencement of Washington College here today.

The two sisters are Miss Diantha Roe, who delivered the valedictory and Miss Elizabeth Roe who delivered the salutatory.

Honorary degrees conferred were as follows: Dr. James W. Cain, of Baltimore, former president of the college, and J. W. Barnes, professor of commerce in Franklin and Marshall College, doctor of laws; the Rev. D. J. Minick, Montgomery county, Md., and the Rev. Omar E. Jones, of Middletown, Del., district superintendent of the Methodist Episcopal Church, doctor of divinity.

Special student prizes were announced as follows: Philadelphia alumni chapter medal for the best all-around man in the senior class, John J. Cavanaugh, Waterbury, Conn.; medal donated by Harry P. Porter, of Baltimore, for the senior showing the best characteristics of a college student, Stanley Long, Federalsburg, Md.; Washington alumni medal for the highest average in four years in English studies, Miss Diantha Roe, Vineland, N. J.; Simpers' medals for declamation, Miss Louise Price, Chestertown, and Miss Catherine Urie, Kennedyville, Md.; Rogers' medals for the best orators in the college, Miss Adrienne Richards, Onancock, Va., and Harry Poole, Williamsport, Md.

THE WEATHER*

The United States Weather Bureau forecast for 36 hours ending 8 P. M., Tuesday:

*Appears regularly on Page 3—giving detailed forecasts and summaries.

Eastern Pennsylvania, Delaware and Maryland—Rain tonight and Tuesday; not much change in temperature; fresh southeast winds.

New Jersey—Rain tonight and Tuesday; not so cold Tuesday; fresh to strong southeast winds.

FLYING WEATHER FORECAST

Washington to Long Island—Overcast sky with rain and low clouds this afternoon; fresh to strong southwest at 5,000 feet. On Tuesday the weather will be mostly overcast with showers, and fresh to strong south and southwest winds.

The following table shows the weather conditions throughout the country as received in reports of the United States Weather Bureau at 8 A. M. today:

City.	Temp. High yesterday.	Low last night.	Rainfall.	Wind. Direction.	Velocity.	Weather.
Atlanta, Ga.	82	68	.38	S	..	Cloudy
Atlantic City	66	58	.04	SE	..	Cloudy
Bismarck, N. D.	72	50	..	E	..	P. cl'y
Boston, Mass.	76	58	..	NW	10	Clear
Buffalo, N. Y.	58	46	..	E	12	Cloudy
Calgary, Can.	70	36	.18	NW	..	P. cl'y
Cape Hatteras	80	72	..	SW	..	Cloudy
Charleston, S. C.	86	76	..	SW	12	Cloudy
Chicago, Ill.	66	52	.02	NE	18	Rain
Cincinnati, O.	64	52	1.22	NE	..	Rain
Cleveland, O.	58	50	.06	E	10	Rain
Denver, Col.	48	42	1.26	SE	..	P. cl'y
Detroit, Mich.	64	50	.02	E	12	Rain
Duluth, Minn.	66	36	..	E	..	Clear
Eastport, Me.	68	48	..	SW	..	Clear
Galveston, Tex.	82	76	..	S	..	Cloudy
Harrisburg, Pa.	70	56	.04	NE	..	Rain
Halifax, N. S.		48	..	NW	..	Clear
Helena, Mont.	60	48	..	SW	..	Clear

	Temp.			Wind.		Weather.
City.	High yester-day.	Low last night.	Rain-fall.	Direc-tion.	Ve-locity.	
Indianapolis, Ind.	58	48	1.62	NE	20	Rain
Jacksonville, Fla.	90	74	T.	S	16	Cloudy
Knoxville, Tenn.	70	62	1.22	SW	..	Cloudy
Little Rock, Ark.	82	66	.52	E	..	Cloudy
Los Angeles, Cal.	76	60	..	S	..	Cloudy
Miami, Fla.	86	80	..	SE	..	Clear
Montreal, Can.	64	50	T.	SW	10	Clear
Nantucket, Mass.	70	52	.01	W	..	Cloudy
New Orleans	80	74	5.18	SW	N	P. cl'y
New York	72	60	T.	NE	..	Cloudy
Norfolk, Va.	76	62	.38	E	..	Cloudy
Philadelphia	77	62	T.	E	2	Cloudy
Phoenix, Ariz.	102	74	..	S	..	Clear
Pittsburgh, Pa.	66	52	.24	E	..	Rain
Portland, Me.	70	50	..	N	..	Clear
Portland, Ore.	76	56	..	NW	..	Cloudy
St. Louis, Mo.	60	52	.64	NE	..	Rain
St. Paul, Minn.	72	50	..	E	..	Cloudy
Salt Lake, Utah	66	48	..	S	..	Clear
San Antonio, Tex.	92	74	..	NE	..	Cloudy
San Francisco	80	62	..	..	Calm	Clear
Santa Fe, N. M.	66	42	..	N	..	Clear
S. Ste. Marie	60	34	..	..	Calm	Clear
Savannah, Ga.	88	76	..	S	12	P. cl'y
Scranton, Pa.	70	52	T.	N	..	Rain
Seattle, Wash.	70	56	..	S	..	Cloudy
Tampa, Fla.	90	74	..	SE	..	P. cl'y
Washington	76	62	.02	S	..	Rain
Winnipeg, Can.	70	46	..	S	..	Clear

CARDINAL ADDRESSES CLASS

Speaks at First Annual Commencement of Mount St. Joseph

Cardinal Dougherty will deliver the principal address at the first annual commencement of Mount St. Joseph College,

Chestnut Hill, this afternoon, and then lay the cornerstone for Fournier Hall, the new college building.

Eight young women will receive diplomas and A. B. degrees from the college, formerly an academy. The exercises, however, will be cloaked in sorrow by the death on May 25 of Miss Dorothea Fenton, of Trenton, N. J., a member of the graduating class.

The graduates are Eleanore Dolan, Lucille Kahman, Marie Keffer, Constance Magee, Helen Greeve, Catherine Magin, Irene O'Connor and Rosemary Stokes.

The Rev. Dr. Edward B. Jordan, of the Catholic University of America, and Dr. James J. Walsh, of New York, also will address the graduates.

Fournier Hall is being constructed in memory of Mother St. John (Julia Alexia Fournier), first Superior of Sisters of St. Joseph, in this city.

HOLD EXERCISES INDOORS

Rain Spoils Plans of Bryn Mawr College Alumnæ Day

Driven indoors by the rain, Bryn Mawr College alumnæ today held their annual exercises in the school gymnasium, concluding with a basket ball game between the alumnæ and varsity teams.

The usual procession, from Pembroke Arch across the campus, took place, with the class of 1903 leading. They were dressed in ultra-modern costume. The class of 1912, attired in blue smocks with loose fitting trousers, and carrying blue balloons, was awarded the prize as the best costumed.

Other classes represented were 1913, 1914, 1915 and 1927. Cups were awarded by Miss Rebecca Wills, president of the athletic association, the class of 1928 winning the trophies for interclass hockey, water polo, and all around proficiency. Swimming honors went to 1929; basket ball, first and second teams, to 1931.

Miss Constance Appleby, retiring physical director, received a traveling bag and a check from the association and alumnæ, respectively.

How's Your Grammar?

Subject of Infinitive:

"Please tell me why the expression 'who did it seem to be?' is correct."

Answer:

The subject of an infinitive is always in the objective case. In the sentence, "I asked him to go," "him" is the subject of the infinitive "to go," and is in the objective case because of this fact. "Him" is not the object of "asked." Therefore, in the sentence, "Whom did you ask to go?" "Whom" is in the objective case because it is the subject of the infinitive "to go." This is seen when the sentence is rearranged: You did ask "whom" to go?

The complement of an infinitive, which has a subject, is in the objective case, because the complement agrees in this respect with the subject; as "Whom" did you think it to be? (You did think "it" to be "whom?")

But if the infinitive has no subject (in the objective case), the complement is in the nominative case; as, "Who" did it seem to be? (It did seem to be "who?")

'PREP' GRADUATES 39

Swarthmore School Exercises Held Today in Auditorium

Diplomas were awarded today to thirty-nine graduates of the Swarthmore Preparatory School at exercises in the school auditorium.

Charles S. Hamilton, Jr., was valedictorian, and Robert L. Fairing, Joseph T. Wilson, Jr., and Freeman T. Synder also spoke. The diplomas were presented by H. Roger Coleman, head master.

The following honors were awarded:

The Haverford Cup, to the boy who has done the most for the school, J. Hartwell H. Hunter, of Media.

The gold medal for attaining the highest scholastic standing for the school year, to Charles Stuart Hamilton, Jr., of Chicago.

The Rensselaer gold medal, to that senior whose standing in mathematics and science is highest, to Joseph Townsend Wilson, Jr., of Pitman, N. J.

The conduct and character medal awarded to that boy whose deportment and moral influence are most praiseworthy, to J. Hartwell H. Hunter.

The Alumni gold medal to the member of any varsity team and having the highest scholastic standing for the year, to Joseph Townsend Wilson, Jr.

The Phi Beta Kappa prize, to the member of the graduating class having the highest standing in Latin, Mathematics and English, to Charles Stuart Hamilton, Jr.

The graduates:

William T. Ardell
Richard D. Barth
John Baxter
Donald F. Brady
Harry R. Critchley
Leroy E. Durkee
Richard C. Egbert
Robert L. Fairing
Joseph W. Frescoln
Richard M. Camber
Louis J. Geist, Jr.
Ralph M. Gotshall
Wm. H. T. Grafner
Chas. S. Hamilton, Jr.
S. Laurence Harris
Robert T. Hodges
J. H. H. Hunter
John W. Kauffman, Jr.
David M. Kling
James J. Lynch, Jr.

Samuel A. McClellan
R. W. McConnell
Charles W. McGarr
William M. Nash, Jr.
Wm. R. Newgeon, Jr.
Robert L. Picard
Melville C. Rawnsley
Wm. R. Reitzell, Jr.
Henry E. Rhein
Arch K. Schock, Jr.
Charles W. Scott
Frank C. Smith
Howard H. Smith
Rodman M. Smith, Jr.
Freeman T. Snyder
John O. Sprowl, Jr.
Arthur Steckler
Joseph T. Wilson, Jr.
Samuel M. Wilson

POLICEMAN'S SHOT KILLS BOY

Held for Involuntary Manslaughter—Fired on Fleeing Car

James T. Condon, a policeman, of the 20th and Buttonwood sts. station, is being held for the Coroner today under custody of Captain Dennis Mulgrew, commander of the station, in connection with the shooting to death of a sixteen-year-old youth in an automobile believed to have been stolen from 19th and Oxford sts.

Joseph Lyons, 21st st., near Brown, the dead boy, is said to have been one of five boys in the automobile when it was hailed by Condon at 19th and Parrish sts., Saturday night. When the car failed to stop, Condon fired.

The policeman was held on a charge of involuntary manslaughter by Magistrate Carney. The boys are in the House of Detention.

David Ward, fifteen, Marston st., near Thompson; Peter Burnett, fourteen, Ringgold st., near Parrish; William Kellcher, fourteen, Thompson st., near 26th, and Adolph Chomentowskik, thirteen, 23d and Myrtle sts., are said to have been with Lyons in the motor.

GIVE 129 DEGREES AT SWARTHMORE

Douglas Orr, Lincoln, Neb., and Margaret Somerville, Washington, Get High Honors

DR. MAX MASON ORATOR

An appeal for less routine and more personal experience in education was made by Dr. Max Mason, president of the University of Chicago, in his address today at the annual commencement of Swarthmore College. Dr. Mason has just been elected secretary of the Research Bureau of the General Education Board.

Degrees were presented to 129 graduates by Dr. Frank Aydelotte, president of the college, at the exercises held in Collection Hall. William M. Powell, president of the Board of Trustees, read the Scriptures.

"The faults of the educational machinery today," said Dr. Mason, "are the faults of our time. There is no lack of power but too much emphasis upon routine. It has been argued that the continued impartment of education stultifies the student and that education is a substitute for personal experience. We cannot all think but we can all try to think."

Douglas Orr, Lincoln, Nebraska, received the Ivy Medal, and Margaret Somerville, Washington, D. C., the Oak Leaf Medal, which are high honors at the college.

The awards of prizes and honors announced at today's exercises are as follows:

The Oak Leaf Medal to Margaret Somerville, Washington, D. C., retiring president of the Women's Student Government Association. The award is made by the faculty to the woman who has been outstanding in loyalty, scholarship and service during the four years in college. She has held numerous class and student government offices and has been delegate for the college to three national conventions.

The Ivy Medal goes to Douglas Orr, Lincoln, Neb. The medal is given to the man in the senior class adjudged by the faculty to have shown the highest degree of leadership based on scholarship and character.

The Hilda Clark Memorial Medal, to Gwendolyn Norton, Washington, D. C. The Sigma Tau Awards: The gold medal for the best average of the sophomore engineering major, to George B. Hoadley, Swarthmore. The silver medal for the best freshman average for engineering majors, to John T. Cohen, Jr., Chester. The Sarah Kaighn Cooper Medal to

Caroline Robison, Lansdowne, as the member of the junior class having the best record for scholarship, influence and character.

Samuel J. Underhill prize, to sophomore with highest scholastic average, to George Hoadley, Swarthmore.

Anson Lapham scholarship, to freshman with highest scholastic average, to James Booser, Ridley Park.

Those who received degrees are:

BACHELOR OF ARTS IN HONOR COURSES

English Literature

Ellis G. Bishop
Alice G. Burling
Alice E. Follwell
Elizabeth B. Moffitt
Douglas W. Orr
Edna M. Shoemaker
Ella V. Walker
Marietta Watson

Social Sciences

Caroline C. Biddle
Janet L. Bowen
Eilene M. Galloway
George A. Hay
Anne Kennedy
Alex. D. MacDougall
Robert L. Silber
Newlin R. Smith
Charles E. Tilton

French

Ruth A. Kerwin
Marian B. Pratt
Henry A. Smith

Mathematics, Astronomy and Physics

Louis K. Clothier
H. M. MacNeille
Edward Sellers
Mary Wright

Education

Gertrude M. Jolls
Mary S. Spiller

Physiology-Zoölogy

William T. Branen
Gertrude B. Sanders

BACHELOR OF SCIENCE

Civil Engineering

Vincent G. Bush

Electrical Engineering

Charles L. Haines

Bachelor of Arts in General Courses—Botany
Myra Conover

Economics

John W. Dutton
Theodore H. Fetter
Thomas H. L. Foster
Martha Gibbons
Albert D. Keller
Lewis J. Korn
Richard Lippincott
Edward C. McFeely
Margaret E. Mackey
Griffith S. Miller
James R. Miller

Thomas Moore, Jr.
Theo. E. Nickles, Jr.
Lute L. Owrey
Henry T. Paiste, Jr.
Malcolm B. Petrikin
Ruey M. Sieger
Theodore Smithers
Raymond A. Townley
Paul M. Van Wegen
Theodore Widing

Education

Gertrude H. Bowers
Mabel E. Hollinshead
Richard A. Samuel

Elizabeth Van Brakle
Margaret B. Williams

English

Mary K. Andrews
Isabelle M. Bennett
Josephine S. Bornet
Dorothy W. Brown
Julie V. Chapman
Margaret L. DeLaney
Esther C. Felter
Frances E. Fogg
Gertrude Gilmore
Florence E. Griffiths
Emlyn M. Hodge
Mary E. Hopper
Elisabeth A. Jenkins
Charles T. Maxwell
Jeannette R. Poore

Frances Porter
Edna M. Rattey
Kath. E. Rittenhouse
Hilah Rounds
Nell A. Rubins
Elisabeth W. Rumble
Charlotte S. Salmon
Florence G. Sellers
Esther Shallcross
Ruth Shellman
Margaret Somerville
Mary T. Sullivan
Ann E. Thompson
Anna E. Willis
Esther H. Wilson

French

Olive V. Deane
Grace E. McHenry
Anne H. Philips

Ruth M. Purvis
Mary L. Robison

German
Louis D. Moyer

History

Harold S. Berry
Elizabeth E. Clayton
Anne R. Herrmann

Ora K. Lewis
Caroline B. Lippincott
Elizabeth L. Vaughan

Latin

Elsie Battin
Emma P. Engle

Alice S. Jemison
Mary F. Langford

Mathematics

Phyllis F. Harper
Ruth E. Kern

Gertrude N. Taylor

Physiology-Zoology

Edna M. Child
Frances E. Dowdy
Charles F. Hadley, Jr.

Marguerite Lukens
Frances W. Ramsey
Helen P. Williams

Political Science

Edna G. Beach
Henry C. Ford

Joseph E. Pappano
Mary H. Terrells

Chemistry
Robert K. Whitten

Civil Engineering
Carl A. Arenander

Electrical Engineering
Walter F. Denkhaus

General Engineering
James H. Colket, Jr.

Mechanical Engineering

Lawrence A. Hunt

Everett U. Irish

MASTER OF ARTS
Mathematics

Dorothea A. Kern

Charles E. Rickards

Physiology
Samuel R. M. Reynolds

CIVIL ENGINEER
James S. Maffitt, III

6

M. E. GROUPS CLAIM CONFERENCE GAINS

Dr. H. P. Sloan, Conservative, and Dr. E. M. Conover, Liberal, Review the Issues

NEW BISHOP LAUDED

Did the conservatives or the liberals win in the Quadrennial General Conference of the Methodist Episcopal Church which has just closed in Kansas City?

The Rev. Dr. Harold Paul Sloan, of Haddonfield, N. J., president of the Methodist League for Faith and Life, the evangelical essentialists or conservatives in the church, reports that: "The Conference was true to every great historic value.

"It affirmed the supernatural; the absolute Godhead, virgin birth, redemptive death, resurrection and ascension of Jesus Christ; His all sufficient saviourhood; the abiding authority of the creeds and doctrinal articles established in the construction of the Church."

The Rev. Dr. Elbert M. Conover, director of the Bureau of Architecture for the Methodist Church with offices in the Wesley Building, 17th and Arch sts., and one of the liberals in the New Jersey conference says:

"Theological contention and discussion is not characteristic of the Methodist Episcopal Church but centres chiefly in the New Jersey Conference and the Philadelphia Preachers' Meeting as is clearly indicated by the fact that Dr. Sloan's petition in the early days of the Conference to investigate professors in the theological schools was refused consideration by a ten to one vote."

Dr. Sloan in listing some of the accomplishments and some of the things the General Conference failed to do says: "The General Conference was broadly catholic in its spirit, firmly evangelical in its faith, and profoundly Christian in its social and racial ideals.

"It put particular emphasis upon the experience of the New Birth and upon the duty of making that experience effective in transformed lives and in a transformed order of society. It asserted that the Christian preacher could welcome all scientific and reverent scholarly investigations assured that the one stupendous fact of Christ would never be denied or reduced by any discovery that might be made.

"The one objective of the evangelical group in which we were disappointed was our effort to displace the present editor of the Sunday School literature. We ran Dr. John M. Canse, of Salem, Ore., but Dr. H. H. Meyer was re-elected by a majority of 77 votes. The new bishops are all men of firm evangelical faith.

"Doubtless it is true that there is still a dangerous situation in Methodism. This is especially true in the colleges and theological seminaries, where the baldest denial of Christ's divinity is being taught; but the reaction has already begun."

Dr. Conover in reviewing the General Conference points out several issues on which he says the conservative evangelical essentialists under Dr. Sloan failed to gain their objectives.

"In their failure to defeat Dr. Meyer as editor of the Sunday School literature they lost in a thoroughly organized campaign aimed at that objective," he says. "Reports of the Book concern indicate that the publications edited by Dr. Meyer have had a most prosperous four years.

"Another objective was the election of district superintendents. This was declared unconstitutional by the Judiciary committee. Dr. Sloan worked to remove the Bishops on the Commission for the Course of Study for Ministers. The result of the vote in committee was 107 to 7 against his contention.

"The appointment of Bishop Richardson is in fine favor with the Progressives. He has opposed the theological discussions and contentions in this part of the country. It is hoped that his presence will conduce to constructive work and the absence of continued theological contention."

FALLS CAUSE 4,524 DEATHS

A veteran of the fiercest fighting in France tripped on a shoe string, fell headlong, and broke his neck. A steeplejack, who had just performed breath-taking feats on a skyscraper, stumbled on a curbstone and was crippled for life. Latest statistics, reported in Popular Science Monthly, show that the average man's chances of being injured by a fall are almost as great as of being maimed by an automobile. Of 22,000 accidents outside of industry, 6,647 were caused by automobiles, and 4,524 by falls. Next came injuries in sports, 4,452. Seventy-three were hurt getting in or out of bed, and sixty-four suffered from falls in bath tubs.

EDITORIAL SNAPSHOTS

The Junior League should survive without distress the blacklist of the daughters of the American Revolution.—Buffalo News.

The style-makers said that women's skirts would be longer. Also we recall that Voliva said the world was flat.—Commercial Appeal.

The man who tells you the faults of others will tell others of your faults.—Chicago Daily News.

Everything gets more expensive. Think what it will cost a sentimental public fifty years from now to buy and preserve the hospitals where the great men were born.—San Francisco Chronicle.

The oil trials are over and the Paris divorce mills have ceased to grind, so those who go to Europe this year probably go for the old reliable reasons.—St. Louis Post Dispatch.

Politics has strange bedfellows, probably the strangest being those who go to sleep on election day.—Dallas News.

Chicago judge says there is too much cooked-up testimony in divorce cases. And some that is too raw.—Miami News.

WOMEN'S CLUB MEETINGS

Tuesday

Germantown Chapter, D. A. R., annual luncheon. Germantown Cricket Club, 1 P. M.

Germantown Y. W. C. A., swimming meet by Germantown High School girls, in the pool of the Health Education Department, 2.30 P. M.

Old York Road Chapter, D. A. R., stated meeting, home of Mrs. August Wagner, Oak Lane. Mrs. Edwin M. Abbott, regent.

Quaker City Ladies' Motor Club, annual outing for crippled children, Woodside Park.

New Century Guild, Junior Section meeting, 8 P. M.

Y. W. C. A., North American Lace Branch, 1001 Glenwood av., Mothers' Club meeting.

Republican Women of Philadelphia County, 24th Ward, 8 P. M., 614 N. 40th st. Political information. Dr. G. H. Hallett, Jr., conducts model election. Miss Martha J. Johnston presides.

Women's Club of Aldan Child Study Section, home of Mrs. William N. Schoch, 122 E. Providence rd., 8.15 P. M.

Women's City Club hears Mrs. Jeanette Emrich, New York, chairman of the Committee of International Friendship and Good Will of the Federal Council of Church of Christ in America, 2.30 P. M.

Old York Road Chapter, D. A. R., 2.30 P. M., home of Mrs. Theodore A. Rowland, 6311 N. Camac st.

IT'S INTERESTING TO KNOW—

That the average elephant weighs between 175 and 200 pounds at birth.

SUBURBAN HOME SOLD FOR $40,000

Elizabethan Residence at Merion Golf Manor Figures in Realty Deal

GERMANTOWN HOUSE SOLD

The detached Elizabethan type house, of stone, plaster and timber construction, now being built at Huntingdon lane and Golf View road, Merion Golf Manor, has been purchased from William H. Wilson, owner and developer, by Charles J. Swain, Jr., who will occupy it.

The property, which is one of a series under construction, overlooking the Merion golf course, was transferred for a consideration announced at $40,000.

The four store and residence properties, 5516-22 Haverford av., have been transferred by P. J. Hogan to H. L. Webb, subject to mortgages of $75,000. The properties, assessed at $6,000 each, occupy a lot 61 feet by an irregular depth.

S. A. Love has sold the two three-story buildings, 1016-18 Cherry st., combined lot 44x69, to K. L. Morgan, subject to mortgages of $16,000. The properties are totally assessed at $20,000.

Cornelius Haggarty, Jr., has sold, through William H. Wilson and Co., the detached Colonial residence between Wissahickon av., W. Cliveden av. and Lincoln drive, Germantown, to Nicholas Connolly. The house, which is of stone construction, contains fifteen rooms and three baths, and is on a lot having a frontage of 70 feet on W. Cliveden av. and a depth of 175 feet. It was held for sale at $35,000.

Alfred Dunlap has sold the new detached stone Colonial dwelling and two-car garage, at the corner of West av. and Vernon road in the Noble Vista development, Jenkintown.

The house, which occupies a lot 95x150, contains twelve rooms and three baths. The purchaser, whose name was not disclosed, will occupy it after alterations. The price was given as $35,000.

The four-story store building, 126 S. 11th st., on a lot 20x88, has been conveyed by Henry T. White to the Lorewood Realty Co., subject to mortgages of $80,000. The property is assessed at $58,000.

The two-story brick building, 3271-73 Woodland av., adjoining the corner property, has been purchased by R. C. Lyons from Harriet L. Jennings. The property, which was held for sale at $125,000, has an assessed value of $86,000.

Contract for the construction of a church building at Chestnut av. and Bethlehem pike, Chestnut Hill, for St. Paul's Protestant Episcopal Church, has been awarded to Cramp and Co., this city. The building, which is to have a seating capacity of 700, will be of stone construction, one story and basement, and will occupy a lot 48x170. It is to cost about $500,000.

THREE FROM NEAR HERE GET SWARTHMORE SCHOLARSHIPS

Camden Youth Among Eight Winners of College Awards

Three students from this vicinity are among the eight recipients of the open scholarships to Swarthmore College, Frank Adyelotte, president of the college, announced today.

They are Carl K. Dellmuth, 426 Chambers av., Camden; John W. Evans, St. Michael, Md., and Thomas A. Wilson,

WIN SCHOLARSHIPS

Three winners from this section of open scholarships at Swarthmore College. Carl K. Dellmuth, 426 Chambers av., Camden (center); John W. Evans, St. Michael, Md. (left), and Thomas A. Wilson, Wilmington, Del. (right).

Wilmington, Del. The open scholarships are awarded for qualities of leadership, character and scholastic ability.

Other boys awarded similar scholarships are W. Raoul Alstætter, Atlanta, Ga.; Robert E. Hadeler, Dayton, O., and Ralph B. Head, Greenefield, O. The T. H. Dudley Perkins scholarship goes to H. Frank Brown, Las Cruces, New Mexico, and the Swarthmore Western Club scholarship to Albert P. Heusner, York, Neb.

The open scholarships have a value of $500 a year for four years and the others provide full tuition for one year.

Dellmuth, who is a freshman at college, has been awarded the scholarship left vacant by the withdrawal of a member of the present junior class. He has been elected class president the first semester of his sophomore year.

Wilson, who lives at 2500 Van Buren st., Wilmington, has been a member of two athletic teams at the Tower Hill School, and is valedictorian of his graduating class.

Evans, the St. Michael boy, formerly of Point Pleasant, is an amateur astronomer as well as an athlete. He was on the football and wrestling teams of the George School.

MRS. M'MICHAEL LEAVES $386,968

File Inventory of Former City Treasurer's Widow's Estate—Mitchell Harrison Left $272,562

MAN GIVES HOSPITAL $1,000

Mrs. Anna E. Fotterall McMichael, widow of Clayton McMichael, former City Treasurer and postmaster, left a personal estate appraised at $386,968, according to the inventory filed with the Register of Wills today.

Assets included 500 shares International Telephone and Telegraph Company, valued at $83,325; 200 shares United States Steel Corporation, preferred, $29,100, and forty shares Electric Storage Battery Company, $31,000.

Mrs. McMichael died last March at her apartment in the Warwick, 17th and Locust sts.

A supplemental inventory of the estate left by Mitchell Harrison, horse breeder and clubman, lists holdings valued at $272,562. The original inventory, filed in September, 1927, listed assets valued at $876,490. Mr. Harrison died last August at his home in Warrenton, Va.

Mark Bartleson, 5912 Belder st., who died May 27 and whose will was probated today, gave $1,000 to the Presbyterian Hospital, and disposed of the remainder of his $30,000 estate in private bequests.

Benjamin R. Simonton, who died May 28 at 4516 Benner st., devised his $6,000 estate to Mrs. Marian Johnson, of the same address.

Harry P. Raper, 248 S. 51st st., who died May 26, devised the larger part of his $83,000 estate to his widow, Mrs. Sallie R. Raper, in trust, and provided that at her death the principal shall be shared by their relatives. The testator also provided a bequest to his sister, Mrs. Fannie R. Crawford.

Patrick Connor, who died April 28 in the Misericordia Hospital, devised his $10,500 estate to his daughter, Anna, and sons, Joseph, John, David and William.

Mrs. Margaret Harrison, 2315 N. Smedley st., who died May 16, explained in her will she had made no provision for her stepsons, Joseph and James Harrison, of New York, because they are amply provided for. She named Mrs. Minnie Port, wife of Nelson M. Port, principal legatee of her $30,000 estate.

Conrad L. Eagle, 2630 E. Somerset st., disposed of his $12,932 estate in bequests to his sons, John H. and Comly S., his daughter, Mrs. Annie H. Miller, and others.

Anton Hartman, who died May 24 at St. Petersburg, Fla., bequeathed his $38,400 estate to his widow, Mrs. Elizabeth B. Hartman, their sons, Frank and James H., and daughters, Mrs. Emma McMullan, Miss Annette Hartman and Miss Dorothy Hartman.

JUDGE McDEVITT ADDRESSES WOMEN

Judge Harry S. McDevitt addressed 800 members of the Catholic Business Women's Sodality of Old St. Joseph's Church, at their annual communion breakfast at the Penn Athletic Club yesterday. Other speakers were Miss Matilda F. Fay, president of the guild; the Rev. George W. Wall, the Rev. Samuel J. Robb, the Rev. John A. Morgan, the Rev. T. J. Coughlin, and Miss Stasia Meskill.

MOTHER AND SON INJURED

Another Woman Hurt in Crash on Frankford Street

A mother, her son and another woman were injured early today when the automobile in which they were riding overturned after a collision with another car at Oxford av. and Horricks st., Frankford.

Mrs. Elsie Stevenson, twenty-nine; Jack Stevenson, three, and Mrs. Catherine Dorn, fifty-five, all of 1140 Sanger st., were cut and bruised and were treated at Frankford Hospital. Frank Stevenson, father of Jack, who was driving the car, was not injured.

The driver of the other car was Joseph Flaherty, twenty-four, Adams av. near Leiper st. Both he and Stevenson were arrested.

DID YOU SEE IN THE BULLETIN—

1—That fifteen States will have no women delegates at the 1928 Republican Convention?

2—That forty-five trees planted by Washington at Mount Vernon still stand?

3—That 1,737 building operations were started in this city during May, with a total cost of $13,583,485, or $1,000,000 more than May, 1927?

4—That Bartram's Garden, after thirty years' neglect by the city, has been restored?

5—That American girls' colleges are more agnostic in tone than the men's colleges, according to the Rev. C. Leslie Glenn, secretary for College Work of the Protestant Episcopal Church?

(These questions are based on articles appearing in Saturday's Bulletin.)

PROBE ATTACK ON MILKMAN

Victim Knocked Unconscious While Delivering in Frankford

Police are investigating mysterious circumstances surrounding the manner in which John Blasch, Jr., twenty-one, 2915 Kirkbride st., Bridesburg, was knocked unconscious while delivering milk in an alley near Dittman st. and Robbins av. at 4.30 A. M. today.

He was struck by a missile while passing a parked automobile, but his father, John Blasch, who was delivering milk with him, said the motor car was not occupied.

TONIGHT'S EVENTS

Y. M. C. A. School of Music, concert, Central Building Auditorium, 8.15 P. M.

Temple Faculty Club, annual dinner, Cedar Brook Country Club, 7 P. M.

Olympic players, comedy at St. Aloysius Hall, 26th st. near Tasker.

Woman's Democratic Committee of Philadelphia, political talk, 1501 Spruce st., 8.15 P. M.

BANK OPENS NEW BUILDING

Financial Leaders Inspect Franklin Trust Co.'s 52d St. Branch

Men of prominence in financial and business circles attended the opening today of the new building of the Franklin Trust Co., northeast corner of 52d and Market sts.

Gifts of flowers received from numerous banking and commercial establishments transformed the first floor of the new building into a veritable bower. H. Ennis Jones, vice president, received the visitors.

As a matter of record of its first day's activity in the new building motion pictures were taken of those who visited the bank. The bank was originally established on its present site in November, 1917. In announcing the opening of the new building G. Addison Harris, Jr., president, pointed out when the West Philadelphia office opened eleven years ago resources of the company were slightly more than $5,000,000, while today they are more than $45,000,000.

FATHER DIES IN SEA DISASTER

Lebanon Girl Learns of Death After Receiving Graduation Gift

Lebanon, Pa., June 4.—While Miss Marian Gotwalt, eighteen, a senior in the high school here, was admiring a diamond ring sent by her father, her grandmother, with whom she lives, received a telegram announcing that the girl's father had been killed in a steamship collision.

The father, Ray F. Gotwalt, was first substitute engineer on the collier Kershaw, which was rammed and sunk off Vineyard Haven, Mass., on Friday. The ring and a letter congratulating her on her coming graduation from high school on June 14 was received on Saturday.

Gotwalt had planned to be here for the daughter's graduation.

HONOR STUDENTS

Miss Martha Riegel (left), salutatorian, and Miss Irene Bachman, valedictorian of the Hellertown High school at the annual commencement.

OLDEST MINER DIES NEAR POTTSVILLE

Pottsville, June 4.—Benjamin Wehry, ninety, of Donaldson, the oldest Civil War veteran in this section, is dead. Up until a few years ago he worked as a coal miner, and was pointed out as the oldest miner in the anthracite fields. His widow, eighty-eight, and a daughter survive.

JAIL UPPER DARBY MOTORIST

Charged with driving while intoxicated, James T. Morgan, Oakley st., Upper Darby, was sentenced today to ninety days in the Gloucester county jail, by Justice of the Peace Harry Friant, of Woodbury. Morgan was arrested at Jefferson, N. J., last night by State police. His driving license was revoked for a year.

HAE YE HEAR-R-RD THIS ONE?
A LIE—BUT IT'S FUNNY

Scene—A dinner table in the North of Scotland. Father at the head of the table, mother at the foot and four children, two on either side.

Father (a large steak pie in front of him)—"Now, bairns, will ye hae steak pie or a penny each?"

Children (in chorus)—"A penny, faither!"

Father distributes a penny each and helps himself and his wife to large portions of steak pie.

(Mattie, the maid, brings in a dish of rice pudding.)

Father—"Now, bairns, will ye a' hae a pennyworth o' rice pudden?"

Harry Lauder

EVENING CHAT

The Bulletin will not publish engagement announcements sent to this office unless confirmed.

AN ENGAGEMENT

Mr. and Mrs. Charles P. Turner, of Garden City, L. I., announce the engagement of their daughter, Miss Helen Morris Turner, and Mr. Harry Coles Bates, son of Mrs. Fannie Barry Bates, of Tarreytown.

Miss Turner is a graduate of the Cathedral School of St. Mary and of Vassar College, and is a sister of Mrs. R. T. Leiper Patterson, of this city.

Mr. Bates is a graduate of Hamilton College and of the New York Law School.

Captain and Mrs. Clement Biddle Wood, of "Camp Discharge," Conshohocken, will entertain at luncheon on Sunday next at "Camp Discharge," in honor of the active members of the First City Troop and their wives, following the annual pistol shoot for the Gold Medal of 1828 which will be held at "Camp Discharge" by the members of the First City Troop.

Mrs. William R. Philler, of Haverford, has issued invitations for a luncheon on Friday, June 15.

Mrs. James Newman Carter, of "Westover," Chadds Ford, will entertain at luncheon at the West Chester Country Club on Tuesday, June 12, in honor of Mrs. William Kemble, of Boston, Mass.

Miss Frances Fullerton Jones, daughter of Mrs. William Jones, of "Dreghorn," St. Davids, will be guest of honor at a buffet supper that Dr. and Mrs. Samuel Sidney Woody, of 4000 N. Front st., will give on Sunday evening, June 10. Miss Jones and Miss Julia Rush, of Wynnewood, will sail on June 15 for Europe.

Mr. and Mrs. Loring Underwood, of Belmont, Mass., have issued invitations for a dinner-dance to be given at their home on Thursday, June 14, in honor of their daughter, Miss Lorna Underwood and Mr. Andrew Galbraith Carey, of Baltimore, who will be married on the following day.

Miss Anne Thomson and Mr. Clarke Thomson, of "Corkerhill," Bryn Mawr, sailed on Saturday for Europe. They will return home in August.

Mr. and Mrs. William Lyttleton Barclay, of East Gravers lane, Chestnut Hill, have taken a cottage at Bay Head, which they will occupy shortly for the summer. Their son-in-law and daughter, Mr. and Mrs. Muscoe R. H. Garnett, of Greenwich, Conn., will be their guests in August. Miss Anne Wister Barclay will sail with her uncle and aunt, Mr. and Mrs. Isaac Starr, of Stenton av., Chestnut Hill, the latter part of August, for a five weeks' trip to Italy.

Former Senator and Mrs. George Wharton Pepper, of Devon, will open their cottage at Northeast Harbor after July 1.

Mr. and Mrs. Reed A. Morgan and Miss Elizabeth Morgan, of Roxborough, have returned from Europe, where they passed the winter.

Mr. and Mrs. Joseph Wayne and Miss Laura Wayne, of Saint Martins lane, Chestnut Hill, returned on Saturday from a several months' trip to Europe.

Mr. and Mrs. Albert L. Hoffman will pass the summer at Mr. A. Rene Moen's estate at Cove Neck, Oyster Bay. Mrs. Hoffman was Miss Elaine Sullivan, of "The Woods," Radnor.

Mr. Gardner Cassatt, of this city, was among the ushers at the marriage of Miss Caroline Thom, daughter of Mr. and Mrs. Corcoran Thom, of Washington, to Major Robert Le Grou Walsh, Air Corps, U. S. A., which took place on Saturday in St. Matthew's Church, Washington.

Mr. and Mrs. William Ellis Scull, of this city, who are traveling in Europe, have left Aix-les-Bains, for Paris.

Mr. and Mrs. C. J. Brooke Young, Jr., St. Davids, are

MISS PAULINE MUNN

Daughter of Mr. and Mrs. Charles A. Munn, of this city and Paris, who arrived in this city last week to be among the bridesmaids at the marriage of Miss Anita Porter Clothier, daughter of Mr. and Mrs. William Jackson Clothier, of "Valley Hill Farm," Valley Forge, to Mr. George Randolph Packard, Jr., on June 23.

receiving congratulations upon the birth of a son, C. J. Brooke Young, 3d, on June 2. Mrs. Young was Miss Anne Louise Johnson, daughter of Mrs. Ferdinand M. Johnson, of this city.

MISS IRVA BAIR

Daughter of Mr. and Mrs. Irvin Bair, of Germantown, whose engagement to Mr. Robert J. Jamieson, son of Mrs. John Jamieson, of this city, was announced recently.

(Vanity Fair Studios, Inc.)

Colonel and Mrs. John S. Muckle, of "Craig Hall," Haverford, entertained at luncheon at their home yesterday, Senor Don Carlos G. Davila, Ambassador from Chile at Washington, and Commander Julio Allard, and the officers of the Chilean cruiser General Basquedano, now at this city.

Mr. and Mrs. Marshall S. Morgan, of East Mermaid lane, Chestnut Hill, will open their cottage at York Harbor the first week in July.

Mrs. Norton Downs, of "Villa Primavera," Chestnut Hill, is spending this week at Atlantic City. Mrs. Downs will open her camp at Upper Dam, Maine, early next month.

Mr. and Mrs. James Starr and Miss Sarah Logan Starr, of "Belfield," Germantown, will open their place at Chester, Nova Scotia, the middle of next month.

Mrs. Arthington Gilpin, of the Touraine, is visiting her sister-in-law, Miss Elizabeth Gilpin, at Chestnut Hill, for several weeks.

Mr. and Mrs. Joshua Ash Pearson and Miss Elizabeth Pearson, of W. Chestnut av., Chestnut Hill, will sail shortly for Europe, where they will pass the summer.

Mr. and Mrs. Hollinshead N. Taylor and Miss Mary Hare Taylor, of "Kenwood," Beth Ayres, will open their cottage in Nova Scotia on August 1.

Mr. and Mrs. Bruce Ford, of "Sugar Loaf," Chestnut Hill, sailed on the Majestic on Saturday for a two months' trip to Europe.

Mr. and Mrs. H. Frazer Harris, of "Harston," Chestnut Hill, will open their camp at Upper Saranac the middle of next month.

Mr. and Mrs. Arthur Emlen Newbold, Jr., of "Laverock Farm," Chestnut Hill, will occupy their cottage at Northeast Harbor, on July 1.

Miss Augusta Willoughby Gage Ellis and Miss Leidy, of the Wellington, 19th and Walnut sts., are occupying a cottage at East Hampton for the summer.

Mrs. Lorillard Spencer gave a luncheon at Newport yesterday for her sister, Mrs. William K. Dick, who is her house guest at "Chastellux." Others passing the week-end there include Mrs. Dick's son, Mr. John Jacob Astor, and Miss Phyllis J. Walsh, of this city.

Mr. and Mrs. Isaac Tatnall Starr, of "Falcon Hill," Chestnut Hill, will open their cottage at Watch Hill, R. I., the end of this month.

Dr. and Mrs. John H. Gibbon, of 1608 Spruce st., who are occupying "Lynfield Farm," their place at Media, for

7

the early summer, will open their cottage at Mount Desert, Maine, the latter part of next month.

———

Miss Olivia M. de B. Gazzam, daughter of Mrs. Joseph Gazzam, of the Coronado, will leave the latter part of the month for West Hampton to spend the summer with her uncle and aunt, Mr. and Mrs. Edward B. Robinson, of New York, who have taken a cottage there for the summer.

———

Mr. and Mrs. Spencer Penrose are arriving in the Ile de France, and will be at the Ritz-Carlton, New York.

———

Mr. and Mrs. Gilbert Harvey, of Mayfair House, Germantown, are leaving shortly for Cape May where they will occupy their new cottage at Madison and Stockton avs.

———

Mr. and Mrs. Robert Martin Williams, of 2019 Locust st., will occupy their cottage at Cape May this week.

———

The marriage of Miss Ruth Brewster Noyes, daughter of the late Judge Walter Chadwick Noyes, and Mrs. Noyes, of New York, to Mr. William Sherman Stevenson, son of Mr. and Mrs. Josiah Stevenson, Jr., of Pittsburgh, will take place on Saturday, June 30, at the home of the bride's mother, at 1010 Fifth av., New York.

———

Professor and Mrs. Thomas Jex Preston, Jr., of "Westland," Princeton, had a family reunion yesterday. Their guests were Mr. and Mrs. Richard Cleveland, of Baltimore; Mr. and Mrs. William Stanley Dell, of Princeton, and Mrs. W. S. B. Bosanquet, of England.

———

Mr. Floyd Yates Keeler, of New York, and North Salem, N. Y., announces the engagement of his daughter, Miss Kathryn Lyon Keeler, and Mr. Leicester Hayden Sherrill, son of Mr. and Mrs. Arthur B. Sherrill, of this city.

Miss Keeler was graduated from Vassar in 1927 and Mr. Sherrill from Harvard in 1926.

The marriage will take place in October.

———

Mr. and Mrs. George A. Dash, of Harwood Park, Upper Darby, announce the engagement of their daughter, Miss Agnes H. Dash, and Mr. Walter A. Zeuner, of Highland Park, Upper Darby. The marriage will take place in the late summer.

———

EVENTS OF THE DAY

———

Mrs. William Jones, a luncheon to meet her daughter, Miss Frances Fullerton Jones, at half after one o'clock at "Dreghorn," St. Davids.

Mrs. Frank Perley Prichard, of 1520 Spruce st., a luncheon and auction bridge party at Belmont Mansion in honor of her daughter, Miss Anne Perley Prichard.

President and Mrs. Frank Aydelotte, of Swarthmore, a luncheon at Swarthmore, to meet the Class of 1903.

Mrs. John B. Thayer, of "Redwood," Haverford, a musicale, to meet Miss Ruth Townsend.

The Women's Committee of the Philadelphia Chamber String Simfonietta, a tea at the residence of Mrs. Austin M. Purves, of Chestnut Hill.

Mr. and Mrs. Julius Oelbermann, of Chestnut Hill, a supper in honor of their daughter, Miss Elizabeth G. Oelbermann, after the class day exercises of the Springside School. The guests will include the graduating class of which Miss Oelbermann is a member.

Mr. and Mrs. Howard Butcher, Jr., of Ardmore, a buffet supper, following the rehearsal for the marriage of their niece, Miss Margaret Tatnall, daughter of Mr. and Mrs. Abram G. Tatnall, of Ardmore, and Mr. Edwin G. Fox, son of Mr. and Mrs. Charles Y. Fox, of Wynnewood, which will take place tomorrow in All Saints' Church, Wynnewood.

TINKER—SWENEY

The marriage of Miss Elizabeth Jane Sweney, daughter of Mr. Maurice Vansant Sweney, to Mr. Franklin Lyle Tinker, son of Mr. and Mrs. William E. Tinker, will take place at half after six o'clock this evening, in the Chapel of the Church of the Mediator, the Rev. Granville Taylor officiating, assisted by Dr. J. Ramsey Swain, of the Woodland Presbyterian Church.

Mrs. John M. Kellogg, of Germantown, will be the matron of honor. Miss Mary Craig Lank, maid of honor, and the bridesmaids will include Miss Martha E. Tinker, sister of the bridegroom, Miss Ruth Anderson, Miss Anne Lefener and Miss Florence Elray, cousin of the bride.

Mr. David Bushrod James, Jr., will act as best man.

A reception will follow the ceremony at the Merion Tribute House.

NOT TOLD BY THE CABLE

Chivalry Among the M. P.'s—Upon the authority of an English patriotic ode we are informed "Britons never, never shall be slaves." Also, in another song, intended to be more humorous than patriotic and addressed to the British tar, "His energetic fist should be ready to resist a dictorial word."

There is truth in these boasts. Every now and then the House of Commons starts investigation into infringements upon the rights of a subject, no matter how humble his rank in life. One of the most sensational debates of recent times is reported in London papers as having taken place a few days ago over insults to a twenty-two-year-old working girl while under police examination. The girl, Irene Savage by name, had been arrested with Sir Leo Money, a middle aged, married man, formerly in government employ, while sitting together on a bench one evening in Hyde Park. The two were accused of "necking" although the technical criminal term sounds more appalling. Police testimony, the only testimony submitted, was so vague the magistrate dismissed the charge and placed $50 cost against the police.

A few days later, a chief of detectives invaded the workshop where the girl was employed and compelled her to accompany him to New Scotland Yard.

The girl's version of her treatment there was brought to the attention of the Commons by Thomas Johnston, a Socialist member. He said that at Scotland Yard Irene was interrogated by Inspector Collins while Inspector Clarke took down the questions and answers.

Collins began by informing Miss Savage that the Sir Leo Money case was not nearly finished, that the police officers who had been implicated in the case at Hyde Park were men of good police record, and he added, "Don't tell lies to us. We know everything and if you tell lies both you and Sir Leo Money will suffer."

Elaborate questions were then put about how she and Sir Leo Money went to a cinema, where they sat in the cinema, how they sat in the cinema, and what happened. The questions proceeded for a long time, whether any presents in money or goods had ever been given to Miss Savage and she admitted she had once got a pair of suede gloves from Sir Leo Money at Christmas time.

She denied any misconduct, denied "kissing or cuddling" in the cinema, or that Sir Leo Money "sat with his arm round her in the cinema."

Then she said in the statement which she gave, a sworn deposition: "I got very tired of the cross-examination and let the statement go at what the officer had written down." It was to the credit of the officers that at this period they offered her tea.

Tea was brought in. There was one spoon. The officer suggested in a friendly, flippant, humorous way that the one spoon would do for them all and that "Irene will spoon with me." Then the questioning proceeded, half-hour after half-hour.

They tried to trap her and asked her whether she had taken any wine that night at dinner, and said that she might be really dazed and might not remember actually what had transpired. This she denied.

They asked her to stand up and show the length of her dress. They asked her what was the color of her petticoat.

A Socialist Member: A damn shame.

They made comments on her petticoat, added Mr. Johnston. He then read the statement which he said Miss Savage had made. She said:

"I was then requested to give full particulars of the clothes I was wearing and what Sir Leo was wearing. They also requested me to stand up so that they could see the length of my clothes.

"There was no woman present. They inquired whether I wore a petticoat, and, if so, what was the color, and they made the statement that it was a very pretty petticoat I was wearing."

Then Inspector Collins said: "You are really a good girl and you have never had a man, have you?" (Socialist cries of "Shame!") "But there are several things one can do without really sinning. Don't be afraid to tell us as we will look after you."

"Then," continued Mr. Johnston, "the demonstration—it's the only word I can use—took place. The officer sat down beside Miss Savage and asked for a demonstration of what had happened in Hyde Park.

"The officer said: 'When we were young we had a good time ourselves. We are only making these inquiries for the sake of the police officers whose conduct is being inquired into.' The police officer put his arm around the girl to demonstrate how Sir Leo might have been sitting.

"After five hours of this"—(loud cries of "Shame!")—"without any opportunity given to that girl to be assisted by a legal adviser, without even a woman police chaperon being present, that girl was then released from what I can only describe as a Third Degree examination." (Cheers.)

When she got home she collapsed. "The officers," she said, "repeatedly warned me that I was not to say a word to anybody that I had been at Scotland Yard or that I had made a statement."

At the close of Mr. Johnston's statement other M. P.'s expressed themselves with great indignation against such police methods and took the Home Secretary to task. Criticisms were only quieted when the Home Secretary and the Director of Public Prosecution promised inquiries should be made into the affair.

QUAINT QUERIES IN VAST VOLUME OF VOICES VARY BUSY ROUTINE OF TELEPHONE GIRLS

Most Persons Are 'Nice,' But Bad News Makes 'Em 'Grouchy'—Did Lindy Land? And What Will the Final Score Be, Please?

What Shall I Wear at a Wedding? Who Was Elected? How Can I Cure a Black Eye? Who is My Hubby's 'Sweetie'?

One of The Bulletin telephone operators—the one with bobbed hair of a hue called Titian, chestnut, henna or russet, and sometimes red—leaned back a moment from the eighth floor switchboard and stretched.

Voices . . . voices . . . voices . . . all kinds of voices

"If I could write a book," she smiled, "about the things I hear over these wires, I'll bet it would be interesting to read.

"Here was an excited man who wanted to know the base ball score, and when I told him it was tied at nothing to nothing in the second inning, he yelled, 'In whose favor?' That happens lots of times."

There was a buzz and a tiny yellow light gleamed on the board. She inserted a plug, then leaned back again for a few seconds' respite from the murmur of voices floating in . . . . deep masculine voices, shrill feminine voices, grim, cheery, rasping, musical, quavering, booming voices.

The tremendous traffic in voices, totaling more than 500,000 calls in a year, consists mostly of business calls and queries about important events. Aside from these, the most frequent query is about—well, what would a body think?

The "inside story" of a "triangle"

"Weddings," laughed the henna-headed girl. "Most of the calls are about what to wear at weddings."

"Evening Bulletin," she sang into the mouthpiece suspended under her chin. "Yes, this is leap year. . . .

"That was a woman's voice.

"About 1,000 calls a day go through this board, besides the direct connections. But on days when big things are happening, like air flights, elections, important sport events and deaths of prominent persons, we are swamped. The day the Bremen landed on Greenly Island we received 1,000 calls an hour.

"Lindbergh's flight was another big rush for us; but it was over quicker.

"Many persons tell us they rely on us to confirm reports they have read or heard, because they know we are careful not to give out anything unless we know it is authentic.

An elite "bawling out"

"Cure for a black eye? One moment, please. I'll connect you with the Information Department. . .

"A woman who had seen a picture of a girl called up to find out the girl's name and address. She said, 'Girlie, I'll let you in on a little secret. That dame is my husband's sweetie, and I know she lives in Jersey City, and her first name is Mildred, and I'm a-going to find out that dame's last name if it's the last thing I do."

"One moment, please. . . . That was a boy who wanted ideas for a birthday present for his mother.

"One night a lady with a very fashionable voice — you know, full of ah's and uh's—'phoned a message for the Society Department. Her name was Mrs. James Spondulix van Spiffington, or something like that, and when I asked her to spell it, she said, in a horrified voice, 'Why haven't you ever heard of Mrs. James

This happens often

Spondulix van Spiffington?' and when I said 'No,' she got awfully 'mad' and 'bawled me out.'

"How to spell Aloysius? One moment, please. . . .

"Why is the whistle blowing? I'll connect you with the City Desk . . .

"Income Tax? One moment, please . . .

"Scores? Don't you mean innings? No? Well, I really couldn't say. Nobody can tell till the game is over . . .

"What do you suppose?" her blue eyes twinkled. "That was some stenographer calling up for her boss about the ball score. She wanted to know how many more scores there would be before the game is over.

A regular summer base ball problem

"Wives call up every afternoon when there are 'big doings' at Shibe Park or Baker Bowl and say, 'Operator, can you tell me when the game is going to be over? My husband's out there and I want to have his supper ready when he gets home.'

"When the A's or Phils are losing, the voices sound grouchy. We are blamed for bad news, it seems.

"But most people are very nice, you know. At least, those that call The Bulletin are.

"There is no difference between men and women in being nice over the 'phone. Women, though, are more persistent.

"Do men ever get 'fresh?' No; they never get a chance. Some times in the evening some young fellow, all dressed up with no place to go, or maybe a lonesome night watchman, calls up to chat. It's easy, though, to disconnect him.

"One moment, please. Thank you!"

URGES OLD FAITHS ON YOUTH

Rabbi Wise Delivers Baccalaureate Address at Bryn Mawr College

---

An appeal to youth to abandon the modern movement toward self expression and return to the religion of their fathers with full acceptance of the moral codes of Moses and of Jesus Christ has been made by Rabbi Stephen S. Wise, of the Free Synagogue, New York.

Rabbi Wise delivered the baccalaureate address to 100 seniors of Bryn Mawr College who gathered with 1,000 of their friends in Goodhart Hall, last night, to hear the first sermon delivered in the building dedicated only the day before.

The Evening Bulletin

Published Daily Except Sunday at Filbert and Juniper
Streets, CITY HALL SQUARE,
Philadelphia, Pa., by the

BULLETIN COMPANY.

WILLIAM L. McLEAN, President.

Robert McLean, Vice President; William L. McLean, Jr.,
Treasurer; Fred Fuller Shedd, Editor; Charles E. Shull,
Directing Editor; William B. Craig, Managing Editor; William Simpson, Business Manager; R. L. McLean, Circulation
Manager.

All communications should be addressed to THE EVENING BULLETIN, Bulletin Building, City Hall Square,
Philadelphia, Pa.

SUBSCRIPTION RATES:

In Philadelphia and Surrounding Towns: 12c. a week
(payable to carrier).

Outside Philadelphia, by mail, in U. S., Canada or U. S.
Poss., 50c. a month; $6.00 a year.

Foreign Countries, $1.50 a month.

Mail subscriptions accepted only when prepaid. Remit by
P. O. Order, Express Money Order, Draft or Registered Letter.

Bell, LOCUST 4400. Keystone, Race 5701.

Entered at Philadelphia Postoffice as Second-Class Matter.

APRIL, 1928 CIRCULATION

Net Paid Daily Average 551,409 Copies

The Bulletin circulation figures are net, all damaged and
unsold copies have been omitted. WILLIAM L. McLEAN,
President.

MEMBER OF THE ASSOCIATED PRESS

The Associated Press is exclusively entitled to the use for republication of all news despatches credited to it or not otherwise credited in this paper, and also the local news published herein.

MONDAY, JUNE 4, 1928

AN UNGRACIOUS REPLY

Refusal of the State's Sanitary Water Board of information desired by the City's Counsel in the Schuylkill pollution cases was ungracious, but it is not a serious stop to the City's program of action.

So far as it can be judged by results, the information possessed by the State Sanitary Water Board is not of much importance. Either the board is not inclined to enforce the law or has not been sufficiently active to acquire the information, easily available along the Schuylkill, competent to secure the enforcement of the law. It is a notorious fact that the law has been continuously violated. But the policy at Harrisburg has always been to "negotiate" with the offenders against this particular law, and it may be that it has never considered it necessary to gather up evidence necessary to convict and punish.

The City is not stopped from making its own survey. There is data of a survey made some years ago, now in the hands of the Bureau of Water. And a new survey will not be a very troublesome undertaking. Even though it may involve some additional time and cost, it will be a worth-while foundation for the City's course, which, it is assumed, will be pursued steadfastly, regardless of inclination at Harrisburg to confine its endeavors for Schuylkill purification to moral suasion.

DISGUSTING 'SPORT'

Fortunately, the "Sunday" law lent its aid to decency and enabled Superintendent MILLS, of the police force, to put a stop to the disgusting "dance" marathon, for which no adequate corrective could be found elsewhere.

Having had one experience with such an affair, it may be assumed that it will be enough and that the discretionary power vested in the licensing authority will be used to prevent a similar scheme again getting beyond the reach of law.

Although revenue from admissions, concessions and in other ways is said to have netted the promoters a "good thing," the attendance has not been either in quantity or quality, of a sort to indicate any popular interest which merits further recognition. As a betting field, it did not differ much from the dog race proposition which City Solicitor ASHTON frowned upon because of its tendency to promote gambling, and altogether it was of the kind of "sport" which the community can very well afford to ban in the future.

ATLANTIC CITY'S NEW BRIDGE

The new Albany avenue bridge across the Thoroughfare at Atlantic City now adds to the full utility of the broad highway which leads across the meadows from Pleasantville to the City-by-the-sea and over which there is a constant and heavy flow of traffic despite the relief afforded by the alternate route over the Absecon Boulevard. For all the region south of Chelsea, to be connected soon with Ocean City by way of Longport, the Albany avenue route is the most desirable in avoiding the traffic delays in passing through the congested section of Atlantic City, such as south-bound motorists meet if they take the Absecon Boulevard route.

One of the main reasons for the construction of the latter route was the desire to avoid the grade crossings of the three railroads which one has to pass on the Shore Road in going from Absecon to Atlantic City, via Pleasantville and Albany avenue. Elimination of these grade crossings, on one of the most heavily traveled motor roads in South Jersey, should be the next objective, as the wonder is that accidents, which have occurred there from time to time, have not been more numerous. Their presence is a continuing menace to motorists that should be removed.

UNFAIR TO THE POLICE

Patrolmen who are called on to hand over part of their pay to cover a margin of cost of uniforms over and above the part of the cost paid by the City have just cause of complaint. It is not fair for the City to fix an allowance for uniforms and then fix a price in excess of the allowance. There is no more justification for making a policeman pay for his uniform than there would be in making a buck private in the army of the United States go down into his jeans for the O. D. that covers his manly bosom.

What a policeman wears underneath his uniform is his own business. It may be crossbar, or wool, cotton or silk. He is entitled fully and freely to drape himself with whatever quality, style or color of garment he may prefer, before drawing on the outer habiliments. But when he goes on duty the City insists that he shall wear clothing of specified weight, materials, quality, color and cut. They are a part of his job. The uniform is as much the mark of official authority as the shield, the stick and the other impedimenta of keeping the peace. And as a token of the public service in which he is engaged the public should fairly bear the cost.

It is also the practice to make the patrolman bear the cost of upkeep and repair of uniforms. This is justified by the argument that otherwise he may be careless about them, and subject them to hard usage and unnecessary risks. The plea is not wholly specious. But, in all fairness, when a policeman, in pursuit of his official business, suffers damage to his uniform in violent encounter, it does seem as if it might be regarded as official damage, incurred in the public behalf, and properly chargeable to the City.

CANADA'S CORDIAL ASSENT

Canada's reply to the Washington invitation to become a party to the multi-lateral anti-war treaty is remarkable for a heartiness of tone and cordiality of expression such as has characterized no other response to the American initiative. Although the Dominion has been insistent on recognition of its status as an independent entity in the international field, it makes no attempt to hedge around its approval by qualifications derived from its sovereignty. It considers the KELLOGG proposals as affording, through their directness and simplicity, a notable opportunity to ensure lasting peace to the world and hastens to add its endorsement.

The single point on which the note dilates is the compatibility of the war-repudiating covenant with the obligations of League membership, in which connection Canada restates its opposition, constantly manifest at Geneva, to the League as a super-state with obligatory sanctions. Having joined the League with the expectation that it would become a useful agency for international peace, Canada finds its adhesion to the KELLOGG proposal absolutely consonant with its purpose in going to Geneva.

Canada's approval of the KELLOGG plan, following closely as it does those of the Irish Free State and New Zealand, ought to have much influence with London, in spurring it promptly to make effective that adherence already pledged in the CHAMBERLAIN note. The United States is grateful to acknowledge, in addition to the cordial endorsement of its plan for universal peace, this new proof of the warm friendship and sympathy of the Dominion for itself.

LAWYERS HIT THE EXPERTS

The New Jersey State Bar Association rises to smite the present procedure in relation to the expert testimony of psychiatrists and other medical witnesses. The Legislative Committee struck straight out from the shoulder in declaring that such witnesses frequently gave biased and prejudiced testimony in favor of those who employed them.

There is nothing new in the charge, which leading alienists like the late Dr. CARLOS F. McDONALD have reiterated, more in sorrow than in anger. But it comes with all the greater force from lawyers, since the public attributes to counsel for the defense in notorious murder trials the chief responsibility for trying to befog an untrained jury with conflicting technicalities on abnormal mental conditions. Yet the New Jersey State Bar Association takes a forward stand in advocating legislative action to provide the remedy which public opinion deems most effective.

Their plan is that in any case where expert evidence becomes necessary, the trial court shall appoint a commission and fix the compensation of the witnesses, who shall be punishable for contempt of court if any of them shall accept any other fee or reward. The definite recommendations of a State bar, following the lead of eminent jurists and the American Bar Association, is convincing proof that the revolt against the scandalous abuse of expert evidence is approaching a climax where the law's conservatism must give way. If lawyers do not want biased and prejudiced expert witnesses, and the medical profession frowns on them, the remedy cannot be long delayed.

INDUSTRIAL ARBITRATION

The Commerce Committee of the American Bar Association, after prolonged study and the patient hearing of authoritative representatives of capital and labor, publishes the proposed Federal statute to enforce voluntary contracts for the arbitration of industrial disputes in the field of interstate commerce. A most significant feature of the accompanying report, which will come up for discussion at the annual meeting in July, is the fact that the only dissentient to the legal enforcement of arbitration contracts was WILLIAM Z. FOSTER, whose radicalism is based upon the principle of industrial war.

The proposed statute aims only to apply to voluntary agreements to arbitrate disputes between labor and capital the fundamental principle of the common law for the enforcement of all contracts voluntarily entered into and not the result of fraud, duress or coercion, or against public policy. This procedure would plainly provide a middle ground between compulsory arbitration, which is repugnant to the Constitution, and the deplorable industrial warfare which takes the form of strikes and lockouts.

WILLIAM GREEN, president of the American Federation of Labor, told the committee that it was fundamental with that great body to encourage stabilization through co-operation between labor unions and organizations of employers. Arbitration is certainly a most important aid to this beneficent end. But as the law now stands agreements to arbitrate are revocable at will by either party, unlike all other contracts.

COLLECTING STATE TAXES

Policy of the Auditor General's Department in using every resource of the law to force the prompt payment of all taxes and fees due to the Commonwealth bore abundant fruit in the collection of $12,000,000 more for the general fund in the year ending May 31, 1928, than in the corresponding twelve months ending May 31, 1927.

The enormous task of settling the taxes payable by corporations has always been the most formidable work of the department. Collections were complicated by the numerous appeals, many of which were obviously dilatory. Improvement in this regard required firmness, tempered by sufficient elasticity to concede the justice of meritorious representations. The result of this rule applied to all the revenue-producing activities of the Auditor General's office is that there is a record balance exceeding $35,000,000 in the general fund for the multiform uses of the Commonwealth.

SLANTS AT THE NEWS

Rhododendrons everywhere.

If Sundae why not Mundae?

Back to the one-cent postal card.

June house-building starts with a rush.

Annie Laurie and the lamb's Mary were both real.

8

And a concrete floor isn't the easiest thing to dance on, at that.

———

Gotham is already talking of a second tunnel under the Hudson.

———

Why does a motor car have such an affinity for every roadside pole?

———

"Cake failure has a reason," says a culinary sharp. Yes, indeed. Usually the cook.

———

Of course where a subway is to end has nothing to do with where it can be started.

———

Maybe Gen. Atterbury and Col. Lindbergh will extend that air line to Honolulu.

———

Naturally the Coolidge summer vacation at Brule will make Superior, Wis., feel that way.

———

Senate probers who found Tammany's big Chief had gone fishing must have had a sort of fellow feeling for him.

———

Chap who asks how many farmers are going to tour Europe this summer doesn't dare ask how many will spend next winter in Florida.

———

Indictment of 101 citizens of Melrose Park, Ill., for prohibition violations puts that town in the running with Cicero for Chicago suburban honors.

———

CHEMICAL FOOD

Report comes from Berlin that a German chemist believes he has discovered an artificial food, if what he produced by his experiments with wood can so be called. The chemist, Dr. Friedrich Bergius, was trying to imitate in his laboratory the process by which nature makes coal in the course of tens of thousands of years. By accident, as so many other discoveries have been made, he noted that the wood he was using altered not to coal at one point in the experiment, but a structure resembling grain and grass. It is the belief in Berlin that food for cattle can be made by the Bergius process, and if for cattle, for human beings also.

One does not know whether to regard the report as a threat or a promise. Compressed foods are already made and "ersatze," or substitutes for real food, were extensively used in Germany during the war. But no lines can be observed forming to buy compressed foods and no German has been discovered who continued to use ersatze when real human provender could be had after the war. Perhaps the day will come when the earth is so crowded that people will be thankful for artificial food, but that time seems still far off and most people will have only sympathy for the men and women who will then be eating chemical meals.

For most people do not eat just to live. Eating is necessary to keep alive but the majority of people also get pleasure from eating. Anticipation of a good dinner breeds a pleasurable physical and mental feeling. Placed at a table bountifully spread with food to their liking, the mouths of healthy, eupeptic persons will involuntary "water." That is no mere figure of speech, for the salivary glands are excited by the expectation of the food and the dishes are savored by the system before they are tasted. And the feeling of satisfaction that pervades the person who has enjoyed a well-cooked dinner!

Chemical food taken from the pocket as substitute for a real dinner! Ugh. Yes, that Berlin report is a threat, not a promise.

A CHURCH TERCENTENARY

Guest clergymen from Holland participated in opening the celebration in New York yesterday of the 300th anniversary of the founding of the Reformed Church in this country. In 1628, Rev. Jonas Michaelius was sent from Amsterdam to New Amsterdam to create a congregation for the Dutch and the Huguenot Walloons who had come to the new world as early as 1614 but had not had regular religious instruction. German adherents of the Reformed Church early came to Pennsylvania on Penn's invitation. After 1709 there were many arrivals, particularly of those expelled from the Palatinate.

Until 1782, the Amsterdam classis had jurisdiction generally over the Reformed Church in this country and gave liberally to John Philip Boehme and Michael Schlatter in their work among the settlers in Pennsylvania. Ten years after the separation from Holland, the Dutch Reformed Church, now the Reformed Church in America, was officially organized. The German Reformed Church, separately organized, later took the name of the Reformed Church in the United States.

In Philadelphia, there are four churches of the earlier, or Dutch denomination and twenty-seven of the other. More than a half-million people in the United States are communicants in the Reformed Church and represent some of the oldest and finest of the colonial stock.

AMBITION

Tell me, you who hurry by,
Are you happier than I?
With your minds all set upon
Gold and Fame, so hardly won.
Will the clamor of the throng
Calm your hearts the lone night
    long?
Will the plaudits of the crowd
Heal your grief when you are
    bowed
By Sorrow?

Know you not that Fame is empty;
Those who clap go on their way,
Seeking ever fresh adventure,
Caring not for yesterday?
Tell men, then, when none re-
    member,
Is your life to be an ember
That will sadly glow and vanish
As your dreams you vainly banish,
Searching ever for the mirage
Of Success?

Some there are, I pray; I'm one;
Failures, maybe, every one.

Yet, in one sense, richer far
Than the mighty ever are.
Since the lesson we have learned,
Happiness, content, are earned
By unselfishness and love.

These are real, and always lasting,
When the other joys are passing.
They will still be true and fine,
Love, and Faith, and Work will
    shine,
Seeming dearer, day by day,
As we struggle on the way
Of Living.

Build, then, something that will
    live;
Something more than Gold can
    give;
Something that besides your Fame,
Will do honor to your name
And at last, the battle won,
You'll have left a task well done!
                    JANE DRURY.

ONE HUNDRED YEARS AGO

(From the United States Gazette of June 4, 1828.)

The township of Charlestown, Chester County, Pa., has been so divided that the post office at the General Pike, long known by the name of Charlestown Post Office, is now in Schuylkill Township, and therefore the name is not appropriate. The Postmaster General has changed its name to Phoenixville Post Office.

Lewis W. Richards is reappointed postmaster. Phoenixville Post Office is on the route from Philadelphia to Lancaster, via Valley Forge, Kimberton, Yellow Springs and Morgantown, &c.

POINCARE'S TASK

Stabilization of Franc and Settlement of War Debts Remaining Parts of French Premier's Program

France's new parliament has met for a session that will make history. The emphatic vote of confidence which the country gave M. Poincare is regarded everywhere as making definite the success of his plans for arresting the fall of the franc and bringing about a drastic reform of the management of government finance by breaking finally with the endless emission of short term government securities.

The election was hardly over when Premier Poincare took advantage of the mandate given him by the approval of his program to ask bids for a five per cent. loan designed to refund short-term bonds. From the point of view of the inflow of new money, it was an enormous success, but after ten billion francs had been subscribed the Premier declined to accept any more cash, announcing that until June 8 only certain old short term issues, reconstruction reparation and Treasury bonds would be received for the new issue. The public response has been encouraging, billions of the old issues having been turned in.

The first part of M. Poincare's financial problem may thus be considered solved. Now he and this Parliament must take up the two big remaining problems, the final stabilization of the franc at a fixed ratio to gold, and the settlement of the

American and British war debt claims. August has already been indicated as the probable date for stabilization. There is as yet no lead from the Premier or any of his prominent supporters as to their war debt policy. An indication of his difficulties may be seen in the fact that the leader of the strongest group in the Chamber, the Republican Democratic Union, and its representative in the Poincare Cabinet, is an outspoken champion of the view that France owes the United States nothing. He is M. Louis Marin, whose famous speech in the Chamber in January, 1925, asserting that France had already discharged its obligation in blood, made an international sensation. But it is not expected that M. Poincare will fail of a majority if, as expected, he decides that a settlement of the debt question is essential to France's permanent financial stability and international credit.

Until his entire financial program has been developed, M. Poincare, according to current political opinion in Paris, will not lack a substantial majority. His difficulties will come when other issues press to the front. His backing on financial questions is essentially non-political. But politics in France has not been adjourned until the solution of the financial problem. Party politics of intensive kind was played among the Deputies-elect prior to the opening of Parliament in a way that has caused considerable revisions of the political classification of the Deputies as contained in the first list furnished by the Department of the Interior. This made the Republican Democratic Union the strongest group in the Chamber with 158 members. The radicals, non-Socialist, Socialist and Communist, were given 278 seats. The two middle groups, composed of so-called Republicans of the Left and Republican Radicals, had 154 members. The Royalists and Alsatian autonomists, who elected three members, made up the rest of the 612 seats.

On this calculation M. Poincare could have counted on a solid bloc of 312 votes, more than a majority, furnished by the Republican Democratic Union and the middle groups or Centre, independently of any votes from the Left, where he has, nevertheless, assurance of some support on financial issues at least.

The Republican Democratic Union, sometimes referred to in press despatches to this country as the Nationalists, is described by the Paris correspondent of the Manchester Guardian, possibly with some exaggeration, as of a conservatism besides which the most extreme of British die-hard Tories "fade into a pale pink." Exultant over their big lead over the other groups the Union leaders began to demand larger representation in the Government.

As soon as the election results had been made known, M. Poincare declared that, although precedent demanded that the Government of the day should resign at the opening of the new Parliament, he intended to carry on with his present Cabinet. That Cabinet, having been taken from the membership of the old Parliament with its Radical majority, had a preponderance of Radicals. M. Poincare showed himself indisposed to yield to Nationalist pressure; he wanted no weakening of present Radical support of his financial program, and, presumably also, in view of the fact that normal tendency of French public opinion is toward moderate radicalism, did not want to risk the future of his Government by tying up too definitely on the conservative side. He preferred the "Radical mask," an unfriendly critic says.

News of M. Poincare's attitude caused rumors of many defections from the Republican Democratic Union, and it was asserted that fully a third of those assigned in the election returns to this group would be found further toward the Radical side when it came to the voting. The organs of the "Left" or Radical and Socialist alliance, even began to contend that the April election had really been a Left victory. Deals for new groupings of the Deputies-elect immediately began. One attempt made was to form a group of the men elected for the first time, so that they would be encouraged to act independently of the old hands, committed to old party combinations and strategy.

The chief effort made, however, was to weld all the deputies of moderate tendencies into a solid Center group, the members of which would be the permanent supporters of M. Poincare. The two present middle groups have altogether 154 members and accessions from the Union would make the Center, instead of the Union, the biggest block of votes in the Chamber. Numerous meetings were held, but it was found impossible to rally the middle group members behind any one individual.

The man most in view for the new Center combination was Andre Tardieu, who figures in M. Poincare's Cabinet as a non-partisan, belonging to none of the established groups. M. Tardieu, who was French High Commissioner in the United States after this country entered the war, was the right-hand man of M. Clemenceau at the Peace Conference and has written one of the most authoritative accounts of the negotiations. He was regarded as the heir of the Clemenceau political influence and a likely future Premier. Circumstances, however, have caused him to play almost a lone hand in French politics since the Armistice.

A second aspirant for leadership of the Center group is Henri Franklin-Bouillon, one of the principal critics of the Versailles treaty. He was an influential member of the main Radical party, in which he led a movement last year to agree to a political truce or moratorium, lasting at least five years, in which all parties should join under M. Poincare's leadership to bring about financial and economic stability, and fight surversive Red agitation. The regular Radical leadership opposed his plan, and it was defeated at the party congress.

M. Poincare's present Cabinet is a strong one, representing every important group in the Chamber except the Socialists. It includes the ex-leader of the regular Radicals, former Premier Herriot, and the two chief leaders of the Republican Socialists, another constituent element of the old Left Cartel, Paul Painleve and Aristide Briand. M. Poincare himself, Senator Barthou, a former Premier, and M. Marin represent the Union, and George Leygues and the Minister of Commerce, Maurice Bokanowski, a recent visitor to this country, belong to the middle parties.

MEN AND THINGS

Women Are Eligible to 49.1 Per Cent. of the Popular Vote, But Only About One-third Make Use of Their Franchise

President Coolidge's popular vote four years ago was 15,725,016, out of a total of 29,091,417 votes cast. It has been estimated that there will be 28,500,000 women eligible to vote for President next November. So that any party or candidate who could carry the women's vote of the country would be able to sweep the election. That is, providing his rival did not capture the men's vote solidly. In the latter case the men would have it. The census authorities say that there are 58,000,000 men and women in the United States eligible to qualify as voters, and the women count only about forty-nine per cent. of the total.

Like many statistics, these figures are to be liberally discounted to get a reasonable view of the situation. Out of the 58,000,000 eligible to qualify as voters, it is not likely that there will be 33,000,000 votes cast, even taking an outside figure. In 1916, the total of the popular Presidential vote was 18,473,446. In 1920, just after the franchise had been extended to the women by amendment of the Federal Constitution, the total popular vote was 26,674,171, an increase of over eight million votes, with perhaps six or seven million of them being women.

———

Professor Hugh L. Keenleyside, of Syracuse University, who has written of the "American Political Revolution of 1924," looks backward for bases of comparison and calculates that between eight and nine million women voted in the 1920 election.

Popular Presidential vote figures are always subject to more or less variations because of the fact that the ballots are not cast directly for President, but for the electors, and, while the general custom is to take the highest vote cast for an elector of the winning candidate as the popular vote of each State, the formula is not always followed. Professor Keenleyside accepts 26,711,183 as the total vote for 1920. In the four national elections preceding that of 1920 he finds that the eligible male voters had an average of participation approximating 67 per cent. Applying this percentage to the number of male eligibles in 1920, which he fixes at 27,245,000, would indicate that 18,254,150 men voted, leaving 8,457,033 votes cast by women.

There were twelve States in the 1916 election in which the women enjoyed the franchise in the Presidential vote, and the plea that President Wilson "kept us out of war" was used with particular appeal to the feminine heart. It is a reasonable assumption of the Syracuse professor that the men continued to vote approximately in the ratio in which they had been voting in previous Presidential elections, while the women were increasing their interest in the polling.

According to his calculation, based on the assumption that 67 per cent. of the eligible male voters marked their ballots, the number of women voting was 35.1 per cent. of the total number eligible.

35.3 PER CENT. OF WOMEN VOTED IN 1924

Assuming that men continued to vote at the fixed ratio, and applying his formula to the 1924 election, Professor Keenleyside finds that in the Coolidge-Davis-LaFollette contest, 19,253,000 men and 9,852,883 women voted, or 35.3 per cent. of the total number of women eligible, an increase in four years of only two-tenths of one per cent.

Simon Michelet, who is another expert with election figures, gives the women a little more credit. He figures, with 42 States—excluding Arkansas, Georgia, Louisiana, Mississippi, South Carolina and Texas, statistics from which were not reliable—that the women cast 37 per cent. of the votes in the 1920 election, and that 43 per cent. of the eligible women voted. Taking his figures and assuming that the participation of women at the polls remains at the 1924 percentage, there will be 10,577,565 women voting next November, with 19,949,057 men, on the basis of their previous 67 per cent. participation, or a total of about 30,000,000 votes.

According to several expert statisticians who have been toying with this phenomenon of American politics, the men, so long accustomed to the franchise, are not increasing their percentage of participation. What is more they are not expected to make any marked increase, while the potential of the women's vote is being continually developed. Particularly in the last four years, the continuous get-out-the-vote movement has been making a special appeal to the eligible women, and the more hopeful ones are predicting that their percentage of 1924 will be largely increased.

MOUNTAIN STATE WOMEN LED IN 1920

Simon Michelet is one of the most persistent electoral analysts in the country and his figures are as reliable as any, although it must be remembered that in the apportionment of the vote between masculine and feminine electors at the polls, the figures are estimates, based in some instances on actual count of the check lists and the extension of the ratio to the vote of the entire State. But there is no official distinction of male and female in the voting record.

Mr. Michelet finds a great variation throughout the country in the participation at the polls by women. According to his analysis, the women of the Rocky Mountain States made the best showing in the 1920 election. He credits them with having cast 41 per cent. of the total vote in that group, and having cast 56.25 per cent. of their eligible vote. There are only about 170,000 more eligible males in the Mountain States than there are women, so that if the women boost their ratio much higher they will be outvoting the men. But in those Mountain States are some of the first suffrage States in the Union, which may account in large measure for the good showing made by the women in 1920 and preclude such a rate of increase in the feminine vote as may be shown in some of the other States.

ANALYSIS OF VOTE IN PENNSYLVANIA

In New York and Pennsylvania, according to Mr. Michelet's estimates, the women's vote in 1920 was only 30 per cent. of the total 34 per cent. of the eligible women voting in New York and only 28 per cent. in Pennsylvania. But since the 1920 elections the activity of the women in arousing their sex to the importance of the ballot has been persistent, the organized political forces have appreciated the wisdom of getting out the women as well as the men, and the women's vote in Pennsylvania this November will be far in advance of the participation eight years ago. There were 905,035 votes cast for Governor in the election of William C. Sproul in 1918. Four years later in the election of Gifford Pinchot there were 1,464,672 votes cast. In 1926, when Governor Fisher was elected, there was a total of 1,503,635 votes. There are no means of determining the exact percentage of this increase to be credited to the women. But it would not be surprising if there were over 600,000 votes cast by Pennsylvania women in the November election.

———

A striking commentary on the processes of democracy in the utilization of the rights of franchise is in the fact that while the official figures, as given in "Smull's" show the total vote in the Fisher election of 1926 to have been 1,503,665, the official registration for that election, according to the same authority, was 2,955,676. Scarcely more than fifty per cent. of the registered vote came to the polls on election day. The greatest vote that Pennsylvania ever cast in a Presidential election was in 1924, when a total of 2,144,719 votes were recorded, President Coolidge, with 1,401,481 votes, having received the greatest endorsement at the Pennsylvania polls ever given any candidate. But even then there were over 800,000 registered voters in the State who did not cast their ballots.

———

1,252,372 WOMEN REGISTERED

The registration of 1926 was composed of 1,703,304 men and 1,252,372 women. It would not be surprising if that margin of less than 500,000 were cut down by the activity of the women's leaders in the registration for next November. But even at the 1926 figures there is a potential in the women's vote in the State sufficient to warrant the earnest appeal of the rival parties and their candidates in the Presidential campaign.

According to the 1926 registration figures, the million and a quarter women who were on the voting lists were divided as follows: Republican, 962,212; Democratic, 282,989; Labor, 1,842; Socialists, 5,829.

The political quinduncs will have ample opportunity for calculating the comparative response of these million and a quarter women to the rival appeals of Secretary Hoover and Governor Smith, should they be the candidates of their respective parties, or to the contesting pleas of wets and drys, or any one of the various other issues that may develop in the campaign.

———

Pennsylvania cannot be said to be an exceptional State, save in its normal Republican preponderance. New York, New Jersey, Massachusetts, Ohio and many other States have all experienced a similar activity in the past few years in the development of feminine interest in politics. In actual qualification for voting, the women are closing up on the men and are showing themselves capable of a more zealous appreciation of the value of the franchise than the men have been showing for the last generation. Each year the women's vote is becoming a greater potential, to be reckoned with in the calculations. And while it has been the general experience, since the extension of the suffrage that most women vote just like the men, and to the extent that there is a political difference within the home, there is no distinctive sex alignment, no party or candidate can now afford to ignore the feminine reaction to its appeal.

EVENING STORY
'Neighbors'

Laurinda Davis tucked the last strand of hair under her garden hat and peered out through the screen door at the open stretch of sunny garden. Her eyes touched professionally on the iris bed, which needed the grass pulled away from roots, at the tea-roses, which should have their warm covering of leaves taken away now, at the violets that were crowding in upon the lilies-of-the-valley in her coveted wild corner. The peonies were up two inches and the hyacinths, tulips and daffodils were ready to bloom. Spring had called in the warm weather suddenly and everything in the garden clamored for attention at once.

Laurinda sang as she went down the garden path. As she reached the rim of her new pool she pulled on protecting gloves and took her trowel from the pocket of her apron. It was a call to battle, this yearly fight against weeds and pests, and it drew her to the soil in a way that tea and bridge invitations could in no manner stop. She had always had a garden and when she moved into the red brick house with its long sloping lawn in the fall the first thing she had done was to have rows of bulbs planted ready for spring.

"I'm glad those lilac bushes that run around our fence line, are high enough to hide the view," she had giggled to her grave-eyed husband only that morning. "Just think, John, what our high and mighty neighbors would think if they should look out of their windows and see me working in the dirt. You'd better send Hitchens around on the terrace to put up a good appearance cutting the grass this afternoon so I can sneak out and do my work, I have some bulbs that must go in the ground today."

"All right," he laughed. "Still the Craigs must like things of that sort or they wouldn't have so much in their own garden."

"Show place!" Laurinda sniffed ungenerously. "She belongs to the Garden club I hear, and the membership in that seems entirely composed of those who do not do their own gardening. A lot they know of the joy of digging up worms."

She paused in her digging and looked up at the strip of red tile roof visible through the lilac bushes. The Craigs had been rather a thorn in her side since she had come to the brick house. They moved in a much older crowd socially than the Davis' and at the Art league meetings, Women's club, Symphony concerts, etc. In the winter they were away in Florida, Laurinda and John had only seen them at a distance, and Mrs. Craig had not been to call.

"High and mighty," she muttered to the bulbs she was planting. A collie dog strolled out across the lawn next door. "Even their old dog is stuck up. If I ever have a dog it's going to be a friendly one, if it does bury bones in the hot-bed."

The morning was exceptionally hot. Streams of perspiration rolled down Laurinda's face as she knelt with her trowel near the iris bed, but she kept on tenaciously. As she neared the lower line of the terrace she saw a trailing line of wildflowers in the vacant lot below her hedge, and she immediately slipped through the bushes to transplant them into her own yard.

Below the Craig yard there was a similar plot of ground surrounded by a straggling hedge, and as she stopped to sink her trowel into the loam Laurinda heard the sharp sound of a hoe coming from that direction. It drew near, and standing up finally she met the smiling eyes of an old woman in a faded dress and ragged hat.

"Good afternoon."

"Good afternoon. Aren't these wildflowers gorgeous?"

"Yes. I brought some of them into my garden, too. Wouldn't you like to see them?"

"Yes, indeed." There was a timid pride in the old woman's voice, and Laurinda went graciously in between the hedge to admire the mass of delicate flowers. "Why, it's lovely in here. It must be an old-fashioned garden when it is in bloom. And aren't those apple trees down in the corner marvelous?"

"I like it." The woman was pleased. "So few people care for gardens, especially old-fashioned ones nowadays. I'm real glad you like mine." She seemed to warm visibly to Laurinda, and she led her along the paths, pointing proudly to rare plants that were just beginning to thrust frail tendrils through the ground, promising her seedlings and offering her advice.

A quaint little house stood at one end of the lot, and she took Laurinda there. It wasn't at all what Laurinda expected to be the home of such a woman, as it was all one room in a studio effect, furnished with a few good early American pieces. But tea was made and served in as comfortable a fashion as one could wish over a lacquered kitchen table, and the cakes had been baked, so the old woman said, in the coal range that stood in a lean-to at the back of the house.

"I love to cook." She said it so apologetically that Laurinda laughed.

"I should, too, if I could make cakes like this."

"If you come over some time I will show you how."

"Will you? I would love to learn. I have always wanted to, but my cook frowns every time I go in the kitchen."

"Your cook?" the woman leaned forward and looked at Laurinda closely. There seemed a mixture of timidity and gladness in her eyes. You aren't—aren't Mrs. Davis?"

"Why, yes."

"Well, my dear, I can't tell you how glad I am to have you for a neighbor. I am Mrs. Craig and live up there next door to you."

Laurinda couldn't hide her surprise. "You are? Why I thought—but this house—"

Mrs. Craig smiled, "I was chased out of my kitchen, too. This is my escape, and this is my own particular garden where I do as I like. Withers can care for that formal affair on the upper terrace; no one goes there anyway."

They laughed together in perfect understanding, rocking back and forth over their kitchen table.

"Do you know, dear, I heard you were such a society belle I imagined you wouldn't be interested in an old woman like me. I don't go calling any more, or I might have found out otherwise. Most of the girls nowadays have only the one interest. I never dreamed that you were different."

Laurinda smiled. "And I thought you were too proud to even notice me. I only wish I had come down through the back hedge sooner."

That night she told John about it, radiantly. "Just think —we are going to cook down on that old range and fuss around in the garden. And oh, John! Mr. Craig likes to fool around with cars, too. That's where he spends most of his time in their garage, and she said for you to be sure to go over; that he would love to have you."

"Well honey, it looks as though it was going to be all right, after all." Laurinda had grown up in the neighborhood where they had lived before, and had come to depend more upon the friendships cultivated around a bridge table. John had realized her need in the brick house, and sympathized with it. His heart was as light as her own as he cut through the hedge after dinner on his way to the Craig garage, and he turned to wave his hat gaily over his head as Laurinda disappeared down the lower terrace.

(THE END.)

A YOUNG GIRL'S CHIC

MAKING THE MOST OF OURSELVES

So often in the summer a young girl in her early teens is allowed to "run wild," as far as clothes are concerned. It is true that it is much better for her to be outdoors, wearing sports clothes, than to be sitting all dressed up, on a hotel veranda. Yet it is a bad idea to let a girl dress in any old thing in the summer time. It is inculcating in her carelessness about her personal appearance that will be very bad for her when she grows older.

Too often we see these young girls in pleated skirts from which all the pleats have long ago vanished and soiled and unbecoming middies. Such a combination serves as an all-day costume.

The wise mother should insist that her daughter be appro-

9

COLORFUL EMBROIDERY

Wool embroidery is the distinctive feature of this maize flannel coat made in the popular, wrap-around style, and boasting the long scarf collar so much in vogue this year.

FLOWER PRINTS ARE SUMMERY

In summer time every girl wants at least one flower-printed dress in her wardrobe. This frock has a rose design on a black background. The coat of black crepe makes an attractive ensemble.

priately dressed, even in the summer time. If she is going hiking she should have rough clothes for that purpose which will not be spoiled by mud, and when she comes home she should put them aside.

Everyday sports dresses, simple, sleeveless, one-piece are so attractive in design nowadays and so easy to make and to launder that there is no reason why a young girl should not look attractive all day long, no matter how many outdoor activities are engaging her attention.

HERE COMES THE SUN!

BY EMILIE LORING

SYNOPSIS

Julie Lorraine and *James Trafford*, strangers to each other, get off a train when it stops at a filling station, in pursuit of a small dog which had jumped off the train. The train pulls out, leaving them stranded in the wilderness. They find food and shelter in a lonely cabin near the railroad. Julie was on her way to visit an aunt, who is afflicted with the match-making mania. Trafford, a young mill-owner, is running for the office of State Senator against a man named Cheever. Though he suspects Cheever of political crookedness, Trafford is conducting an anti-mud-slinging campaign. A severe storm compels them to spend the night in the cabin. There is a terrible crash of thunder and Julie runs into Trafford's arms. Just at this moment Cheever, owner of the cabin, enters. He sees the situation in the wrong light and threatens to create a scandal unless Trafford promises to withdraw from the campaign. Julie has a sudden inspiration and announces that she and Trafford are married. After Cheever leaves they decide to have a ceremony performed and have it annulled after election. They are married by the justice of the peace. Then, hearing that Cheever has been injured in an accident and is expected to die, they decide that it won't be necessary to announce the marriage. After the marriage they separate, Julie going to "Shorehaven," the home of her aunt,

Martha Marshall, and Trafford to his home near by. At Shorehaven Julie meets

Dallas Carfax, to whom her aunt has planned to marry her off. Another guest at Shorehaven is

Billy Jaffrey, novelist and platonic friend of Julie. It is rumored that Trafford is engaged to his mother's ward,

Pamela Parkman, who lives with them. Hearing that Cheever has recovered from his injuries, Julie gives Trafford permission to announce their marriage if necessary. At a tea-party at Trafford's home Cheever appears and Trafford discloses the secret of his marriage. Julie refuses to believe Trafford when he declares his love for her. Pamelia Parkman sees Julie kissing a letter and accuses her of a mercenary motive in marrying Trafford and of tricking him into marriage. Julie risks her life to save her dog from drowning. The rudder of her boat breaks just as she is about to go over some dangerous rapids. Trafford arrives on the scene just in time to save her life at the risk of his own. Julie finds a dog that belongs to a pal of Cheever's bleeding from many wounds. She gives first aid. The man, who has had a falling out with Cheever, advises Julie not to let Cheever "put anything across."

'MUST A MAN APOLOGIZE FOR KISSING HIS WIFE?'

"I won't stop for tea, Julie," Carfax said. "Billy asked me to drop in and tell you that the fishing trip was on for Monday—"

"Monday! I can't—did he say morning or afternoon?"

"Morning, of course, with a picnic lunch at the old mill. He thought it would help you bear the suspense of waiting for election returns. How's the battle going, Jim?"

"It is almost over. I'm speaking tonight and then I'm through."

"Tonight! But we are to dine at Shorehaven!"

"Sorry, Julie, but Cheever has staged a last rally. Take my regrets to Aunt Martha, Carfax."

"I will. Good-bye, Julie. I'll see you at dinner?"

The girl avoided the question in Carfax's eyes. She appeared absorbed in the cup she was filling.

"Ye-es. Don't forget to tell Aunt Martha that Jim is not coming."

When Trafford returned from accompanying his guest to the door he snapped off the lights and plunged the room into flame-tinted dusk. He leaned an arm on the mantel and steadily regarded the girl by the table.

"Was Carfax annoying you, Goldilocks?"

Cap to dynamite. Julie's self-control blew up.

"Annoy me! What has happened to you all? First you smash our friendship and now—now—" her voice broke; tears dimmed the blaze in her eyes. She made a precipitate dash for the door. Trafford caught her by the shoulders.

"I can't let you go like this, Julie. You are right, something has happened to our friendship. You haven't looked at me for a week. You have dodged me every chance you could get. We seem to be drifting farther and farther apart and I won't have it."

"It is your own fault. You glare every time I play with Billy and—"

"Then my glare must be almost continuous. What other sins have I committed?"

Julie warmed to her grievance.

"You know how I hate sentiment—that I only came to Brick House to help—and you take advantage of that and spoil everything by telling me that—"

"That I love you? Forget it, if that is what is wrecking our friendship. Put it out of your mind."

"I can't! I think of it all the ti—" she held back the word too late. Trafford caught her close with an exultant laugh.

"Do you, my Sleeping Beauty? Then put this memory with it!" he whispered huskily before he crushed her lips beneath his.

For a dazed instant the girl's eyes remained closed. Then she rallied and twisted herself free. Her face was white as she defied him.

"I won't speak to you again until you apologize for that."

Trafford's eyes and voice were recklessly triumphant.

"Must a man apologize when he kisses his wife? This one won't. I shall do it again at the first opportunity."

The color scorched to the girl's hair, then drained away. There was an incredulous gasp in the voice in which she warned:

"If you do I—I shall run away with Billy."

* * *

Arrayed in silk shirt, khaki knickers, and hip boots, with a rakish tilt to her soft felt hat and a basket slung over one shoulder, Julie cast her line into deep water in the dark depths of which she had seen a darting shadow. Beside a huge boulder and beneath an overhanging tree-root the trout pool lay still and mysterious, undisturbed by the rippling song, the never-ending murmur of the brook which leaped and plunged, splashed and eddied its way through the woods on its pilgrimage to merge into the pond.

Julie cast tentatively for a while then reeled in her line.

"This pool is a total loss. Why did Billy recommend it?

Bille-e-e! Bille-e-e," she called. She listened. From up-stream Jaffrey sent his robust and not unmusical voice ahead of him in the one song of his repertoire:

"'To-re-a-dor, To-re-a-dor, For thee a fond heart waits. For the-e-e a fond hear-a-art waits!'"

Julie looked up the brook and laughed. Down the middle of it came Jaffrey slipping and sliding over rocks which invited by their mossy greenness and betrayed by their wetness. He puffed from leg and voice exertion as he joined her.

"Unlimber your rod, Marble-heart. Dal and Pam are to meet us at the old mill. They are to motor over with the lunch. Catch either of those two children of luxury tramping. We'll cut through the woods. Quit, you rascal!" he protested as the black spaniel in close proximity shook the water from his coat.

At the girl's whistle the dog dashed ahead of her into the trail. She drew deep breaths of piney fragrance as she and Jaffrey trod lightly in Indian file. They crossed a small clearing where the grass was waist high, where fire-weed blazed and goldenrod swayed in the breeze. A cloud of brown butterflies winged upward at their approach and settled back upon the blossoms. They crossed a bit of corduroy road and came out upon the bank of the pond near the old mill. Jaffrey looked up and down the shore.

"Pam and Dal haven't come and I could eat raw dog, I'm so hungry."

"They may expect to meet us at the upper mill."

"They wouldn't have to walk a step if they stopped there. I'll bet a hat they are waiting for us to find them. We don't go. This is the best place on the shore for a fire."

"Go after them, Billy. Don't grumble, that's a dear. I'm starving."

"I'll go. Do you know what I think? That the man-eating Parkman on her way here detoured to district headquarters to entice Trafford out for lunch with her."

Julie paused in the process of tying up her rod.

"Billy, is Pamela really in love with Jim?"

Jaffrey grinned. "She may be but she means to marry the man who is successful today. Somewhere she has heard that classic 'As Maine goes so goes the country.' She figures that if she starts here, no matter how humbly, she's bound to land in Washington. She has the lady-of-the-cabinet bee in her bonnet."

"But Jim is married."

"Permanently? I wasn't born yesterday, Marble-heart. When Pamela told the story of the runaway dog I suspected in a flash that you and Trafford were the girl and man who had rushed to the rescue. The suspicion settled into conviction when I read of the sale of the prize-winning spaniel. Your expression of shocked surprise betrayed you. Haven't I known you all your life? Haven't you rushed to the aid of someone or something ever since you put up your hair? Did you think that I believed that war-time-romance explanation? It was a pretty bit of fiction but not color-fast."

"Billy, I'll confide—"

"Don't! What I don't know I can't tell. You and Jim met somewhere—love isn't a matter of time, it is a matter of ignition. Apparently you picked up a hang-over germ of that married-in-haste war epidemic. That is the stand I have taken against the flood of conjecture in the village. And I'll say right here, Julie, that whatever happened I'd trust The Trafford anywhere, in any situation, in spite of the fact that at present he is seeing me as through a glass, darkly. I don't mind. I'm flattered pink to have him jealous of my red head and super-waistline." He indulged in a gratified chuckle.

"As for you, I never know where your big heart will land you, you are a curious combination of child and woman, but I do know that you are straight and true as God makes a woman."

Tomorrow: A Warning.

WHIMS

THE BUTTERCUPS

We know they're very common
    And everywhere they'll grow,
But, we'll say this much for them,—
    Their sunny, golden glow

Is always bright and helpful
    Be the day dull or fair.
Nature knew just where to put them
    When she placed them here and there.

MY NEIGHBOR SAYS:

When washing chamois gloves do not rinse them. The more soap left in them the softer they are when dried. Slip them off your hands, squeeze in a clean towel, blow the fingers out and hang the gloves in a current of air, but never near a fire.

EVERY-DAY POEMS
'I Do'

There is no moment quite so breathless,
So solemn, wonder-filled,
As that one that within its heart
Holds vows, love-stirred, love-thrilled.

Love's moment when the ecstasy
Of binding one to one
Is echoed by far stars and skies,
A new World is begun.

So firm the voice of ministry—
One tremulous, "I do,"
A deep-voiced echo of those words
So old and yet so new.

It is a breathless time, eternal,
Of sacred pledge and vow;
All past, all future linked together,
By two words whispered low.

            —George Elliston.

WHEN BOY SCOUTS HIKE

When Boy Scouts hike,
  There is so much to see!
The lilac trees are all in bloom.
  Spring garlands every tree.
The fields are spread with tender green,
  The birds plan new abodes.
Spring leads the way, with golden mien,
  Across the country roads.

When Boy Scouts hike,
  There is so much to do!
A place to pitch a gypsy tent
  Beneath the spreading blue;
To hunt a spring; to make a fire;
  To spread a blanket down.
This is the ultimate desire
  Of every boy in town!

When Boy Scouts hike,
  There is so much to dream,
When far above their outdoor beds
  The lovely planets gleam!
How fragrant is the yielding ground!
  How good it is to lie
And watch the lazy moon go 'round
  The lovely summer sky!

When Boy Scouts hike,
  How much there is to keep!
What memories of wood and field
  Into their young hearts creep!
They never will forget these hours,
  When, steeped in Nature's joys,
They learned from birds and trees and flowers
  The world God made for boys!

—Anne Campbell.

ENSEMBLE FOR GENERAL WEAR

(By Madame Champcommunal)
Coat of green and brown plaid, and green georgette crepe dress trimmed with same material as coat is made of. An ensemble for general day wear.

WARM WEATHER DESSERT

Summer is the time for gelatine desserts. Try this one:

RASPBERRY JELLY FLUFF

Dissolve one package raspberry gelatine in a pint of boiling water.

Divide the liquid into three equal parts, and when cold put one portion into the bottom of a square mold. When one of the remaining portions begins to thicken beat with an egg beater until light and foamy and add one cup of chopped nut meats and one cup of mixed shredded dates and marshmallows.

Spread this mixture over the one in the mold and cover with the remaining third. Chill on the ice and serve, cut in slices and serve with sweetened whipped cream.

OUR CHILDREN

Vocational Training Should Be Part of the School Curriculum

BY ANGELO PATRI

The children are graduating from school, all kinds of schools.

Where are they to go next? Few of them know. That is our fault for the most part. We are training children without a definite end in view and therefore we are wasting time and energy that is sacred to the growth of childhood and the future of this people. What is to be done?

The situation cannot be remedied in a moment. The schools are what their patrons make them. As long as fathers and mothers believe that learning lessons from books is educating the children for service in life, so long will the schools be forced to follow the program that sends children out with no place to go.

Elementary schooling is not enough to fit a child for entrance into industry, professional work, technical work. Eight years is, in my opinion, too long to devote to elementary training that is to end with a diploma that is to be used as a wall decoration. A boy or a girl can learn to read and write, to use books for reference, to count and measure in the ordinary situations that will face him in less than eight years. Some of those years can and ought to be devoted to the training that will fit the child for some useful work, for some higher school, toward some definite goal.

"Where are you going after graduation, my child?"

"I don't know. Guess maybe I'll stay home. Maybe I'll go to work. I don't know."

This is a bright child who stands well in school. Whose fault is it that he is indefinite, so helpless after all this training? Ours, of course. We have not offered the opportunities for experience that alone determine in the child's mind, his powers and tastes and ideals. We have confined his attention to the course of study in books and have ignored the rest. The fathers and mothers have set that kind of school and seem unconscious of the need for any other.

It is too much to expect that a child can visualize his future, that at fourteen or sixteen he or she can have sufficient self knowledge and experience to determine his life work. The great majority have not. It is for us in the schools to offer such opportunities as will enable the children to test out various life works, various tastes and tendencies they discover in themselves, and know what they can do and what they cannot do, what they like and what they dislike.

Scatter throughout the school course from the sixth year on through high school various activities, various occupations, give the children a chance to use tools, experiment with materials and color, try their powers of organization and management, of service and initiative and when they are being graduated they will not be so vague about the next step. It is wonderfully helpful to know where you are going next and why.

A BOY'S ROOM IN THE ATTIC

Space being at a premium these days, the attic is no longer given over solely to an accumulation of trunks, boxes and last season's sporting paraphernalia. The heretofore wasted spaces

under the eaves are now made into attractive living quarters, clever housewives having discovered the practical possibilities of these formerly neglected corners.

The boy's playroom sketched today illustrates an effective treatment for an attic corner and alcove. The alcove section is just large enough to contain comfortably a built-in desk, which is also used to hold a radio, and a sturdy rush-seated chair. On the wide window sill are a lamp and a few books, while a decorative note is introduced by a narrow shelf above the desk holding a picturesque ship model. A day bed and Windsor chair complete the furnishings of this attractive corner.

A daring color scheme adds further to the effect of this inviting space as the walls are daffodil yellow with lettuce-green woodwork. The furniture is painted green with plum colored stripings and the floor is a deep plum shade enlivened by a bright hooked rug. The covering of the day bed is yellow piped in plum.

MAN'S WEAKEST MOMENT
BY HELEN ROWLAND

A man's wife is usually some other woman's fault. His second wife is often his first wife's fault.

Nine times out of ten, a man marries one woman, when he is trying to forget some other woman.

* * *

That is his weakest moment—when he is feeling sorry for himself! That is when his resistance is feeblest and his running speed is lowest. It is the one moment when he ought to close his eyes and pray for safety, and refuse to look at a woman. Because he can't see straight, and if he happens to get the right girl, it is sheer blind luck.

* * *

The "other woman" in a man's life, is seldom the siren who drives him to distraction; she is just any sympathetic little thing who chanced to come along, when he was looking for consolation.

* * *

A man usually falls fatally in love with one woman, when some other woman has begun to bore him or to quarrel with him. Or when some other woman has found him out, or hurt his vanity or shattered his allusions about himself.

* * *

If any girl wants to find a susceptible lover or a husband ripe for the taking, let her look for a man whose heart or vanity needs mending; for one who is feeling "abused" or "misunderstood."

* * *

Nothing so softens a man's heart, weakens his head and makes him slop over with emotional response, as feeling sorry for himself. Nothing makes him so tender, mellow and impressionable as self-pity.

* * *

When one woman has been nagging a man or telling him the truth about himself, any other woman who doesn't know the truth about him, looks just like an angel of mercy. She is as welcome as a trained nurse on the morning after the ether has begun to wear off.

* * *

When one woman has been suspicious or cold or "cruel," almost any other woman seems a paragon of sweetness and sympathy, by comparison. When one woman has been treating him to a display of temperament or cynicism, almost any other woman's arms look like a haven, and her smiles like pure radium by contrast.

*   *   *

When a man is feeling sorry for himself, his vanity is like a sponge and can sop up all the flattery you may feed him, without spilling a drop.

*   *   *

Almost any woman can marry a man when he is trying to forget "the woman before." It's a shame to take the wedding ring!

*   *   *

Lots of women owe their husbands, not so much to their own skill, as to the bad playing of some other woman, who threw the game into their hands.

BERNARD SHAW BOSSED BY WIFE

At Least He Must Go To Movies With Her When Adolphe Menjou Plays, He Tells Actor

WRITER CALLS ON STAR

In a recent issue of The London Daily Mail there is a most interesting report of the talk between George Bernard Shaw and Adolphe Menjou. Here it is:

Time, Saturday (May 19) midday.

Scene: A suite in the Carlton Hotel, London. Every table and corner of the room banked with exotic flowers. A tall, dark, good-looking man, beautifully dressed, walks nervously up and down. Muffled sounds can be heard from an inner room of a girl trying frantically to be dressed in three quarters of an hour.

The good-looking man who has to be given police protection against his own popularity, for at least five thousand people mob him whenever his movements are announced in advance—he is Mr. Adolphe Menjou—speaks anxiously. "Say! Is he really coming to see me? I just can't believe it. What shall I say to him? Doesn't he hate Americans? I wish I could ask him for his autograph, but I can't can I? Mr. Bernard Shaw calls on Adolphe Menjou!"

The telephone rings.   Mr. Menjou answers it.   "Can I see Mr. Bernard Shaw?   Gee.   You bet I can.   Ask him to come right up."

He walks nervously up and down again, his lips moving. There is a knock at the door.

A tall man with pink cheeks and a large, shaggy white beard enters, almost with a bound.   The muffled sounds in the inner room grow still more frantic.   Three quarters of an hour is nothing like long enough, anyway, for a Hollywood leading lady to be dressed for a real occasion.

Mr. Menjou and Mr. Shaw were at once involved in conversation and here is what they said:

Mr. Menjou: This is the greatest honor of my life.   I would have run to Moscow to have met you.   Just fancy you coming up to see me here in the hotel.   You really ought to go to America; they would be crazy about you.

Mr. Shaw: I am getting too old for that; besides there is no point in it.   All nice Americans go to England and then come straight to see me.   I believe Mr. Chaplin called on me, but, having rung the bell, he got frightened and went away.

Mr. Menjou: Mr. Chaplin is the only genius on the film stage.   It was Mr. Knoblock who first discovered me when I was playing the part of a doctor years ago in a film called "The Faith Healer."   But it was Chaplin who gave me my first big chance in "A Woman of Paris."

Mr. Shaw: I agree, Mr. Chaplin is the only genius in films today.

Mr. Menjou: He is absolutely sincere.   And he is a twenty-four hour man; he works all day and all night, and he never loses his temper.   I have had to go through the same scene with him thirty-five or forty times before he got it right, but it never happens.   Today I can get through a film in fifteen days, and seldom take more than a month.

Mr. Shaw: That is the great point about films.   When I am rehearsing a play I go and see it thirty or forty times— not once do they ever get it *all* right, but each time there are one or two bits which I feel are just right, but it never happens that everything is right at the same performance.   I can keep in my mind's eye each separate bit that has been right at the various rehearsals and so I very seldom go to see my own plays. But in films, I suppose that with a sufficient number of trials you can get it all right?

Mr. Menjou: Absolutely.

Mr. Shaw: But then I suppose you do not always have good directors—some directors may like all the bad bits and cut out all the good bits? That cannot happen on the stage, and so you can never have a real atrocity as you can in a film with a bad director.

Mr. Menjou: I am very greatly interested in the new talking film process. In New York a few days ago I saw a film called "The Tenderloin," in which both the two big dramatic moments—particularly where the heroine is subjected to a third degree examination by the police—were done in talking films. It was tremendous, and after that all the captions seemed dull and flat.

Mr. Shaw: That interests me a very great deal. Two or three days ago a huge wagon with batteries and various kinds of mechanism arrived at my front door in the country. It was this Movietone process, and they wanted me to talk and act in front of it. Well, I made an experiment to see what it could do. I tomfooled around the lawn and said all sorts of things.

These American camera men, full of punch and go, then told me that instead of being able to see it—the result, I mean—within twenty-four hours, they had to send it all the way back to America to get it developed.

Once before I was interviewed on a talking film, I behaved just as though it was on the stage. (Mr. Shaw then got up, walked to the end of the room, puffed out his chest, strode round the room, raising his arm and lowering it.) That was what it looked like when it came out on the film. Everything was exaggerated to a ludicrous degree. They ought to have told me that before.

Mrs. Patrick Campbell has had a film test, but she says that she was no good in it at all. The reason, of course, was that she had not been told to minimize every movement, because it comes out in so emphatic a way on the screen. By the way, would you like to come to lunch? My wife is a very great admirer of yours, and it would be a delightful surprise for her.

Mr. Menjou: What a shame! I have got a long standing engagement which I can't break.

Mr. Shaw: Yes, my wife is a great admirer of yours. A fortnight ago I was in Llandudno, and it was advertised in the papers that your film, "The Ace of Cads"—

Mr. Menjou: A very bad film—

Mr. Shaw: Was going to be shown. I knew it was all up then, and that my wife would force me to go with her. When we arrived, the manager showed us into our seats. I looked round for a moment, I thought that we were the only people in the cinema; then I saw three small children also in the audience. That was all. (At this stage Mr. Menjou maintained his imperturable smile, but with a little difficulty.) I told the manager that this was most extraordinary. In London, I pointed out, people have to queue up a week beforehand to book seats. "Oh, said the manager, "the trouble is that Mr. Menjou is appearing also in 'Sorrows of Satan' just across the road."

Mr. Menjou: You know, Mr. Shaw, we have got an entirely wrong impression of you in America. We imagine you to be an austere man, uttering bits of biting sarcasm. I had no idea that you were such a genial man.

Mr. Shaw: It's a very good thing for me. If I give that impression of being sarcastic, I can then behave in a perfectly ordinary way in private life.

Mr. Menjou: I always thought that your flat in the Adelphi was a kind of prison.

Mr. Shaw: Oh, I've given that up now, and am living in Whitehall Court. Do you know that until I left Adelphi Terrace I had been uncomfortable for thirty years without realizing it. Now I am beginning to know what comfort means.

Mr. Menjou: I am thinking seriously of making a film in England early next year, and am looking for good material for it.

Mr. Shaw: Why don't you do "Arms and the Man?"

Mr. Menjou: I would like very much to discuss it with you when I come back next January. Of course, it is not my business to talk money to you, or discuss details; but if you would care to come over to the studio during the time the film is being made I would be only too glad.

10

Mr. Shaw: Ah, but that would cost you another £20,000! They would be my producer's fees. I always have to ask for such big money as practically to ruin people. Unless you do that they think you are cheap and don't have respect for you.

Mr. Shaw rises to go.

Mr. Menjou: This is a very great honor. Are you really 72, Mr. Shaw?

Mr. Shaw: Yes. And I sometimes feel it.

Mrs. Menjou: You will never look as young as that, Adolphe, if you ever reach that age!

Mr. Menjou: You say that? Why, we have only been married four days.

Exit Mr. Shaw.

MOTORS KILL FIVE, SEVERAL ARE HURT

Philadelphia Boy Crushed As Picnic Truck Hits Wall of Bridge at Collegeville

TWO CHILDREN RUN DOWN

Five persons were killed and several injured seriously in automobile accidents in Pennsylvania over the week-end. One woman died from injuries suffered in an accident several days ago.

Hyman Polinsky, sixteen, 706 Sigel st., was killed when a truck bearing thirty Philadelphia picnickers crashed into the wall of the bridge over the Perkiomen Creek at Collegeville yesterday. Polinsky was riding on the fender.

Five-year-old Elizabeth Ellis was struck yesterday in front of her home by a car driven by Mary Francis. sixteen, 5th av., Collegeville. The Coroner gave a verdict of accidental death. Witnesses said the child ran in front of the car.

Mrs. Harriett E. Focht, eighty-five, of Philadelphia, was killed late Saturday by an automobile in front of the home of her sister, Mrs. Daniel Boyer, Stonersville, near Pottstown. The driver, Robert Fox, twenty-two, Stony Creek Mills, Berks county, was arrested.

Earl Louis Weiss, three, 4372 Dexter st., Roxborough, was killed by a motor car at Painters Crossroad, seven miles from Kennett Square, yesterday, as he followed his parents across the highway to a field, where they were holding a picnic.

William H. Quinter, fifty-two, was killed near his home by an automobile driven by John McLain, Pottstown, late Saturday.

Mrs. Bessie Small, 632 Gerritt st., died yesterday in Mt. Sinai Hospital from injuries suffered when struck by a car at 5th and Reed sts. on May 5. She was on the way to the hospital for treatment for defective vision.

Tony Bonnelli, twenty-two, 1727 McClellan st., suffered a broken leg early today when struck by a trolley car and hurled twenty feet into an excavation at Chestnut and Juniper sts.

TELLS PRINCETON MEN'S PAY

Graduates of 1916 Averaged $5,200 Yearly Salary in 1925

Princeton, June 4.—The average salary of Princeton graduates of the class of 1916 was $5,200 a year in 1925, nine years after graduation, according to a survey by Donald M. Watt, Princeton, '16, now of the Yale Personnel Department. The survey showed that the average salary was $2,800 more in 1925 than in 1920.

Mr. Watt sent questionnaires to all graduates of the class of 1916 and received replies from 184, or 51 per cent. He found investment banking paid the best salaries and that business generally paid better than the professions. Less than 5 per cent. of teachers received salaries higher than the class medium. The survey eliminated salaries received from businesses in which the graduate's family was financially interested.

---

3 DROWN, TWO RESCUED

Phila. Girl and Fiance Saved by Friends in Grenloch Park, N. J.

Two men and a boy lost their lives in drowning accidents near this city over the week-end, and a Philadelphia girl and her fiance were rescued in a lake at Grenloch Park, N. J.

Leonard Rhoades, 346 W. Marshall st., Norristown, drowned Saturday when he was swept away by the current while supporting himself on a tow line stretched from the Franklin st. wharf, Norristown, to a barge in the Schuylkill. His body was recovered.

Bruce McIntyre, twenty-five, Chester, failed to reappear after diving into the Delaware off the Sun Shipyard, Chester. His body was recovered.

A. J. Hembelton, forty-two, Milton, Del., drowned when two rowboats upset on Lake Fanganzyki, near Milton. His five companions escaped.

Miss Sally Barbera, nineteen, 721 South st., this city, and William Herman, twenty-two, 714 Snyder av., were the couple rescued at Grenlock Park. They hired a boat and twenty-five yards from shore Miss Barbera dove in. She became frightened and Herman went to her rescue, but both nearly drowned. They were saved by companions in a boat.

CARDINAL DEDICATES CHURCH

Presides at Ceremony in New Transfiguration Edifice

The Church of the Transfiguration, 56th st. and Cedar av., yesterday was dedicated at a Solemn High Mass celebrated by Cardinal Dougherty.

The new church is in the Romanesque style and can seat 1,750 persons. More than 3,000 persons were in the church when Cardinal Dougherty described it as a "vision of splendor which it would be difficult to duplicate in the whole country."

The dedication was held in connection with the silver jubilee celebration of the rector, Rev. Daniel I. McGettigan, who was assigned to the congregation after the death six years ago of Rev. James J. MacAran, founder of the parish.

Cardinal Dougherty's chaplains were Monsignor Hugh L. Lamb and Monsignor Fenton J. Fitzpatrick. The Rev. Joseph A. MacDonald, and the Rev. Daniel J. Boyd acted as chanters with Monsignor Thomas F. McNally, as master of ceremonies.

THE OLD GARDENER SAYS:

If one wishes to introduce a water-garden on his lawn at small expense, the simplest way is to dig a basin about two and a half feet deep. Eight by ten or twelve feet is a convenient size. If the soil is clayey, it should be made as hard and smooth as possible, and if it contains much sand it will need the application of clay. When this is dry apply a cement. After the cement is perfectly dry put about eight inches of old, well-rotted manure in the bottom and cover with as many inches of muck. After all has been made smooth and level, use several inches of clean, white sand to produce a sightly appearance. It is now ready to fill with water from the hose. A lily-pond should have much sunshine but it should also be protected from the winds, for the leaves that stand high above the water are liable to be injured.

Sir: (1) Thick patches of white clover are coming up all over my lawn. Was told that was the result of my sprinkling wood ashes around during the winter. Is that right? (2) There is a wild growth of orchard grass growing two or three feet tall, leaving a bunch of yellow straw standing in the fall. It's impossible to keep it out of the lawn. Will clover kill it out and would you advise continuing sprinkling wood ashes? (3) How do you obtain liquid manure? (4) Can poultry manure or droppings be used for flowers? In what way?

MRS. J. B. B.

(1) Your mixture of grass seed may have contained clover, though lime, of which wood ashes contains a large per cent., encourages the growth of clover. (2) It is doubtful whether clover, even if encouraged by the application of lime in spring, would crowd out the orchard grass. To eradicate the latter would advise you to dig it out. (3) Suspend a sack of manure in a barrel of water. Use this, diluted to the color of weak tea. To prevent possible injury from too strong a solution, water plants before applying. (4) Use dry, scattered at the rate of one pound to each square yard of soil.

ATTERBURY SAYS AIR-RAIL LINE MAY START OPERATION THIS YEAR

Pennsy Head Talks of Lindbergh, Politics, China and of Troubles Arising From 'Feeding the Kitty' Too Often

---

GENERAL ATTERBURY GIVES HIS THREE RULES FOR SUCCESS

In the course of an interview he granted, General W. W. Atterbury was asked what three things he would say to a young man on how to achieve success. He replied with characteristic brevity:

1—"Work hard."
2—"Play when you play."
3—"Don't worry."

General W. W. Atterbury, president of the Pennsylvania Railroad, now stands forth in two new and striking enterprises, says the New York American.

He is the first big railroad executive to seize upon the airplane as an adjunct in carrying passengers.

He is among the few men of eminence in the world of finance and commerce who has accepted a high political office.

"I regard membership on the Republican National Committee," he said, "as an opportunity to perform a real public service to the country and of doing some good. The proceedings of this committee, in their ultimate effect, are of large importance to the business, industrial and social life of the people.

"For example, take the matter of legislation. Its effect should be the intimate concern of every citizen. The time to take a hand in the affairs of the country is in the formative stage. If we do not do so, then we have no right to complain, if later on things do not go to suit us. I regard this new post as one of the gravest responsibilities I have ever assumed."

With a twinkle in his eye, General Atterbury referred to the association of Colonel Lindbergh with his air-rail project, whereby passengers are to be whisked from coast to coast in forty-eight hours. General Atterbury said:

"We decided to go into the air-rail line only after the most serious weighing of all the factors. We were particularly impressed with the network of airlines spreading over Europe.

"Naturally in looking for a technical adviser on airplanes and flying we wanted the best—Colonel Lindbergh. Our officers felt very much gratified that he would undertake this work, for his participation in it will give the public added assurances that the prime consideration we have in mind is safety. That is, of course, in addition to the very great pleasure that we have in being associated with a young man so deservedly honored by all the world."

BY 'AIR-RAIL' SOON

It was recalled that when Lindbergh spanned the ocean from New York to Paris, General Atterbury promptly named his crack train to St. Louis "The Spirit of St. Louis," in honor of Lindbergh's great feat.

"Now in a very short time," so General Atterbury said, "one will be able to step up to the ticket window at the Pennsylvania station here, and buy an 'air-rail' ticket to Los Angeles. He can board the 'Spirit of St. Louis' at the station, sleep all night as it rolls luxuriously along, then alight and take a plane at Columbus, O. Then a daylight air hop to the Sante Fe railroad, thence by rail for another night. Then the next day by airplane, one descends from the skies at Los Angeles.

"This service will be started at the earliest moment, consistent with safety," said General Atterbury. He was asked if it would be ready within the year. He replied:

"In a much shorter time than that we hope. Safety is the prime consideration. We do not know when an all-air line will be feasible. We do not think it will be feasible until night flying becomes as safe as day flying. However, we expect to cut the time to the coast considerably under forty-eight hours. The schedule will develop always with the consideration of safety to our passengers in mind."

WON'T DISPLACE ROADS

General Atterbury has no fears that the advent of the airplane and the pressure of competition by the motor car will enforce ultimate amortization of the railroads. He was asked:

"Do you envision railroads ultimately reduced to haulers of freight as a result of the age of flying and motoring?"

General Atterbury replied:

"Not in your day or mine."

General Atterbury disclosed he is an ardent devotee of a greater foreign trade for the United States as one of the things which will enable maintenance of the country's unusually high standard of living. In this connection he told this story:

"When I was a youngster there used to be a poker game played at a table with a slot in the centre. Into that slot went a certain percentage of every pot. It was the 'kitty' that went to the house. Well, you know, if the players played long enough the 'kitty' got all their money.

"We are in the same position as regards foreign trade. If we stop sending out our manufactured products in exchange for raw materials and stand aloof, we merely consume all that we have. This exchange is like putting new money in the game.

"I am glad the President signed the Jones Shipping Bill. I am for any reasonable measures that will put the American flag back on the high seas."

General Atterbury has no fears of the economic results or any other results of a shorter work week, wherever it is possible. He said:

"On the results of a shorter work week, giving a man more leisure, I am an individualist. It's every man's right and privilege to devote his leisure to what he likes. Whether it would mean more time for study of the arts, greater culture or merely frivolities, I can't say. That is up to the man himself, but if we help him to appreciate the finer things of life he will probably turn some of his leisure to those things."

3,000,000 IN CHINA STARVATION ZONE
One-third Doomed to Die in Stricken Area of Shantung Province
LIVE ON ROOTS AND GRASS

BY REGINALD SWEETLAND—Special Cable to The Bulletin

Shanghai, June 4.—Three million souls today face starvation and 1,000,000 of them are doomed to die, according to American observers who have visited the famine-stricken area in Shantung Province to devise relief measures and also to gather enough facts to convince the world of the dire necessity of immediate relief.

Of these people who live in a territory of about 100 square miles, as barren as Death Valley in California, some may be able possibly to scrape along until relief is forthcoming. The next four months should tell.

Roots of trees, shrubs and blades of dried grass constitute the sole food for the millions drifting over the province trying to find nourishment. It is not too much to say that these millions have not had the semblance of a meal in many months.

Other millions have left the province and have gone to Manchuria. Parents have sold their sons and daughters for as little as $5 each for the purpose of buying their passage from the stricken area.

The fact that the Nationalists now control Shantung has done much to raise optimism among the foreigners and Chinese directing the relief campaign. The Nationalist government has informed the China International Relief Committee that it will be given the fullest co-operation in administering the relief fund being raised in the United States.

Considerable criticism was aroused in foreign circles in China concerning the advisability of expending vast sums in Shantung owing to the Civil War disturbances as well as the so-called Japanese occupation of the province. The relief committee answers this by quoting a passage from a letter received here from the American Minister, John Van A. MacMurray, saying:

"In spite of the disturbed conditions occasioned by military activity and banditry it is believed that it would be possible to find, within the large area of the affected sections, districts in which the limited relief might be carried on effectively with a minimum probability of interruption."

With Shantung under Nationalist rule it is expected that the political abuses which aggravated the stricken area, are likely to end. For example, Governor Chang Chung-Chang exploited the province by collecting four years' advance taxes from the farmers, compelling thousands to forsake their homes.

The result was that crops were not planted. This year the seeds were dug up by the starving millions and eaten before they had a chance to sprout. Thousands, peaceful residents of Tsinan, evacuated that city owing to the Japanese occupation, depending upon the starving villagers to support them.

(Copyright, 1928, by The Bulletin and Chicago Daily News Co.)

Swarthmore College Alumni Day Feature—Seated in the flivver of the vintage of 1903, entered in the campus parade by members of that year's graduating class, are Miss Roberta Boak, of Pittsburgh, at wheel, and Miss Carolyn Forstner, 918 Fillmore st., Frankford, undergraduates.

The Hunter and His Kill—Rochester B. Slaughter, a member of the party which obtained specimens of Arctic animal life for the Chicago Zoo and Field Museum, is standing beside a huge polar bear. Notice the size of man and bear.

Evelyn Garcia Tossed a Basket Ball 74 feet, 5 inches, and contributed to Haverford High School's winning of the Delaware county girls' track and field championship.

Sarah Weinstock (left) and Viola Cantor in a Cossack Dance at the Northern Liberties Playground annual circus, at 6th and Noble Sts. Children from the Stanfield and Ferry Road playgrounds also took part.

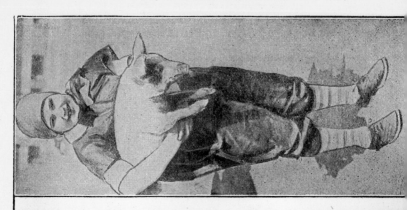

May Day and Mother Goose Features at the Vare Recreation Centre, 26th and Morris sts. Director John J. Dugan, of Public Welfare, is crowning Miss Mary E. Glass, 2036 Gunther st., as Queen of the occasion. Robert Bilson, 1249 S. 29th st., is seen as Tom, Tom the Piper's Son, who stole the pig in the Mother Goose rhyme.

Views of Pennsylvania's World War Memorial at Varennes, France, at the dedication of which Mayor Harry A. Mackey made the principal address on Memorial Day. The inscription on the monument reads as follows: "In honor of her troops who served in the Great War, among whom were the liberators of Varennes, 1918, and in grateful appreciation of their service this memorial is erected by the State of Pennsylvania, 1927."

Members of the Lansdale High School Band — Olive Kaufman, at left, and Margaret Griffiths, at right, played the cornet, and Evelyn Fry, the clarinet.

During the Annual Observance of "Wissahickon Day" under the direction of the Philadelphia Riders' and Drivers' Association, on the upper Wissahickon drive, Fairmount Park. J. Sergeant Price's tally-ho is seen passing the reviewing stand at Valley Green. Miss E. Gwen Martin, daughter of Judge and Mrs. J. Willis Martin, is driving, and seated beside her is Mrs. E. Florens Rivinus (Page 154).

Nancy Strawbridge Claghorn, eight-year-old daughter of Mr. and Mrs. John Winthrop Claghorn, of Chestnut Hill, is shown above.

Pennsylvania Military College, Chester, Confers Degree on Charles E. Hughes at Special Commencement. Left to right: Dr. L. Webster Fox, president of the board of trustees; former Secretary of State Charles Evans Hughes, Commander Richard E. Byrd and General Charles E. Hyatt.

DR. FRAZER RESIGNS AS DEAN AT PENN

Has Been Head of Towne School 16 Years— Other Faculty Changes Announced

MANY GET PROMOTIONS

Resignation of one dean and appointments and reappointments of officers, professors and instructors at the University of Pennsylvania were announced today by Dr. Josiah H. Penniman, provost.

Dr. John Frazer is retiring as dean of the Towne Scientific School, a post he has held for sixteen years. After a year's leave of absence he will devote his time to practical research work and the teaching of chemistry. It was for more time to pursue this work that Dr. Frazer asked to be relieved of his administrative duties.

Edward T. Grandlienard, professor of Civil Engineering, has been named acting dean of the Towne Scientific School. He has been teaching at the University twenty-two years and was elected to his present professorship in 1924.

Dr. Penniman announced the election of two new faculty members. They are Dr. Enos E. Witmer, who will become assistant professor in Physics in the College, and Dr. Florian A. Cajori, assistant professor of Physiological Chemistry in the School of Medicine.

Dr. Charles P. Olivier was appointed director of the Reese Wall Flower Astronomical Observatory. Dr. Olivier, whose election as professor of astronomy in the college was announced some time ago, is coming to Pennsylvania from the University of Virginia.

The promotions, listed effective July 1, and listed by schools and departments follow:

College—To be professors, Frank A. Laurie, Jr., English; Albert C. Baugh, English; Herman J. Wiegand, German literature; Fred W. Beal, mathematics; John Robert Kline, mathematics; Stanley P. Shugert, mathematics; Joseph Hall Bodine, zoology; David Henry Wenrich, zoology. To be assistant professors, Thomas P. Haviland, English; Merle W. Odgers, Latin; Emil Cailliet, French; Otis H. Green, Spanish.

Wharton School—To be professors, Theodore J. Grayson, finance; G. Lloyd Wilson, commerce and transportation; S. Howard Patterson, economics; Clarence A. Kulp, insurance. To be assistant professors, John H. Frederick, commerce and transportation.

School of Medicine—To be associate professor, Edward A. Schumann, obstetrics. To be assistant professors, John Cooke Hirst, 2d, obstetrics; Grayson M. McCough, physiology; James H. Jones, physiological chemistry; Robert L. Gilman, dermatology.

Moore School of Electrical Engineering—To be assistant professor, Knox McIlwain, electrical engineering.

School of Education—To be professor, LeRoy A. King.

School of Fine Arts—To be assistant professors, Harl McDonald, music; James P. Metheny, design; J. Horace Frank, architecture.

School of Law—To be assistant professor, Layton B. Register.

Following are the reappointments on the teaching staff:

College—Assistant professors, Emil Doernenberg, German; Morris S. Viteles, psychology; Edwin B. Williams, romance languages; Charles L. Parmenter, zoology; Percy A. Caris, mathematics; Roy F. Nichols, history; Witt Bowden, history; Edwin M. Fogel, German; Reese D. James, English; Paul C. Kitchen, English; Irwin Boeshore, botany; Samuel G. Bartin, astronomy.

Military Science and Tactics—Professor, Lieutenant Colonel Charles A. Dravo; assistant professors, Captain Russell B. Reynolds; First Lieutenant Hilton E. Heineke; Colonel Robert T. Oliver, Major William R. Dear.

School of Medicine—Associate professor, William C. Staedie, research medicine. Assistant professors, Samuel E. Pind, physiology; Howard C. Carpenter, pediatrics; Stuart Mudd, pathology.

School of Education—Assistant professor, Walter H. Magill.

Moore School of Electrical Engineering—Assistant professor, Charles Weyl, electrical engineering.

CLEMENTON MAN FOUND DEAD

Howard Jaggard, fifty-two, of Berlin road, Clementon, N. J., was found dead in a chair in the kitchen of his home shortly after 8 A. M. today by his wife, Maud. Death was caused by heart disease. Jaggard was a butcher. He had five children.

BUSINESS COMMITTEE NAMED

Four Men Will Serve to Work Out Arbitration Problems

In order to set up machinery for working out business arbitration problems, in keeping with legislation recently passed in Pennsylvania and other States, Philip H. Gadsden, president of the Philadelphia Chamber of Commerce, has just appointed an arbitration committee of four men skilled in this subject.

The committee is headed by William P. Barba, formerly vice president of the Midvale Steel Company, and the other members are Edward F. Beale, head of John T. Lewis & Brothers Company; William J. Conlen, admiralty lawyer, and John H. Minds, of the United Gas Improvement Company.

LETTERS TO THE BULLETIN

RULES

(1) Publication of a letter must not be regarded as endorsement of its sentiments by The Bulletin. (2) Name and address are required as an evidence of good faith, but will not be printed if correspondent so prefers. (3) Letters should be written on one side of sheet and not exceed 200 words in length.

TROUBLE'S WHAT YOU MAKE IT

Did you tackle that trouble that came your way
  With a resolute heart and cheerful?
Or hide your face from the light of day
  With a craven soul and fearful?
Oh, a trouble's a ton, or a trouble's an ounce
  Or a trouble is what you make it.
And it isn't the fact that you're hurt that counts,
  But only how did you take it?
                    —Edmund Vance Cooke.

(Today's thought suggested by Harvey E. Freed, principal of the Lawton Public School. Tomorrow a thought suggested by Henrietta W. Calvin.)

ON CURRENT TOPICS

IN MEMORIAM

Under the sky of cloudless blue,
Under the stars with their greaming hue,
Under the flowers so fresh and fair,
They laid my baby with tender care.
The cold north wind with its piercing breath
Or the snowflakes so pure and fair
Have not yet reached that tiny mound
Or dampened the locks of my darling's hair.
Although my baby I cannot see,
I know he is safe in Heaven with Thee.
In the long and weary nights to come
I shall pray "Thy will, not mine be done."

S. E. GILMORE.

SEES UNFAIR SALE OF POPPIES

Sir: During this Legion poppy sale I was accosted by a "vet" and when I asked him how much he wanted he replied: "Anything you want to give, buddy." I gave him eighteen cents, all the change I had. The next day my wife was approached by a "vet." She gave our little son a dime to buy a poppy. The "vet" passed it back to her, saying: "They are twenty-five cents, madam; genuine American Legion poppies." While she was fumbling for more change a man bought one for a dime.

Now I'd like to say just this to any soldier who would do a thing like that, it is such as you who make people disgusted with "our boys." I am a war veteran (a real one). My father is a Spanish-American veteran and my grandfather a Civil War veteran (still living). I don't blame people for being disgusted with men wearing our uniform, who would do anything so mean.

SERGEANT A. M. RICH.

CONNIE MACK'S TEAM MAY JUMP AHEAD

Sir: Although the Yankees are in front again this year after winning the pennant in the American League by nineteen games last season and then trimming the Pirates four straight in the World Series, experts hold out hope that in three years the seven other teams in the league will be able to give the New Yorkers some opposition. Three years is a long time, and even then there is no guaranty that the Yanks will not still be winning when that time arrives.

The biggest disappointment in the league to date is Washington, which is last. Detroit has not done much better, but has possibilities. Chicago and St. Louis are floundering around, although the latter has been an agreeable surprise. The Red Sox team, under good managing, has surprised, too, while Cleveland has been a revelation so far. This team, with the able assistance of Uhle, a star pitcher, may be the one to overpower the Yanks in the race.

Coming down to brass tacks, then, it looks like Philadelphia. The Athletics may be the team. Cobb and Speaker in the outfield, the return of Simmons, Hauser and good pitching by several reliables have been factors in keeping the team right behind New York. Although the team made a poor showing against New York, yet they may stay in second place until the stretch then jump ahead to win.

NEW YORKER.

HIS POINT FOR OPEN SUNDAY

Sir: I have been amused at the letter concerning open Sunday. The writer of it does not seem to have met many people, for he mentions he had never yet found a truly anxious seeker for the open Sunday. I am living in the city three years and have not found anybody so far who enjoys a closed Sunday. The claim that a man who not only says, but works ten hours a day, has about four to six hours to spend for amusements made me think that the writer never really worked so long in one day. He gives the working man time until 12 to 1 o'clock at night to amuse himself, but I do not think anybody would be physically able to do so for a length of time without injuring his health.

The letter shows very clearly that the writer is not so much interested in the welfare of the people as in the welfare of the church, although this is not in keeping with his profession.

The gentleman advises the working man to amuse himself at night, so that his church will be filled on Sundays. The percentage of the people that would be affected through an open Sunday is very small, and furthermore would have ample time to attend church service as the "places of mad pleasure" would not be opened before 2 o'clock in the afternoon, anyway, and there is hardly anybody who spends his whole Sunday in church. Does a person benefit through something which is forced upon him?

WERNER KAELBLE.

DENIES HUMAN LIFE AT ARCTIC POLE

Sir: No person ever reached the North "terrestrial" (south magnetic) Pole and returned alive. We call it the "North" Pole because it attracts the north magnetic end of the mariner's compass needle, but as like forces repel, it is not a hard matter to understand that it could not be other than a negative or south magnetic pole.

Unquestionably, the earth is a huge magnet. Imagine a globe revolving on its axis with a peripheral speed at its equatorial surface equal to a ball one inch in diameter revolving about 6,000 revolutions per second and you will approach the speed of the earth's surface in space at the equator.

The earth's surface travels in a direction from west to east around its axis, and its enormous speed creates a counter-friction in the opposite direction, or from east to west. All physicists and scholars agree that electricity is the result of the friction of some kind of motion that is caused by crossing or cutting lines of force at angles varying from and at ninety degrees, and that the induction of this current causes a magnetic flux at right angles to its direction of flow, which, traveling in a coil or helix-like shaped conductor, counter-clockwise, presents at the near face end of the helix a north magnetic pole, and at the opposite face a south magnetic (or as we call it the North Arctic) Pole.

The magnetic lines of force emanate from the north magnetic pole (the south, or Antarctic, pole of the earth), and diverging radiantly around its surface in longitudinal lines travel to and enter the south magnetic (or North Arctic) Pole of the earth.

Can anyone with this simple condition of facts doubt that at the extreme Arctic (so-called North) Pole there exists a vortex of such magnitude that anything approaching near enough to reach its influence would be sucked or drawn into and swirled to destruction beyond all hope of averting such a result?

Columns could be written on this text, all of which would only prove more conclusively that no man, ship, airplane or earthly contraption, animal or bird ever reached the "North Pole," the German-Irish crew having demonstrated unquestionably that all instruments of measurement prove fallacious in that district.

If this theory has any basis of fact, it is reasonably certain that there could be no water or other matter at the inverted apex of this vortex, as at that point a most complete vacuum would result in the destruction of all temperature and pressure and matter would consequently cease to exist. All the planets of the universe are undoubtedly subject to the same formulæ, and it is due to their difference in texture, weight and various speeds of motion that they are held in a divinely balanced juxtaposition to each other.

"Thus far and no further," says the Creator, and by placing such limit to our powers and desires of discernment prevents our closer scrutiny of His wondrous work.

A. L. OSGOOD.

SPECIAL QUERIES

BROAD ST.: Passes to the west of City Hall at Market st. If the street was so numbered the building at the southwest corner of Broad and Market sts., numbered by the city 1426 Market st., would bear the number 2 S. Broad st. —(J. G.)

MARRIAGE LAW: In New York State, non-residents may apply for, have issued and make use of license same day, except in case where one or both of the parties are minors. All persons under twenty-one must file notice five days in advance and must produce birth certificates or other proof of age. Persons under eighteen must have parents' consent.—(E. M.)

MOTOR RACES: For dates and admission fees of events on tracks near Philadelphia address the Automobile Association of America, 23 S. 23d st.—(F. W.)

POPULATION: London had a population of 7,476,168 in 1921; New York had an estimated population on June 1, 1926, of 5,924,500.—(E.)

SEA SCOUTS: This is a branch of the Philadelphia Boy Scout Council. To join Sea Scouts applicant must be fifteen Cost of membership, 50 cents annually and, generally, dues of 10 cents a week. Youths living in North Philadelphia may make application for membership to the Sea Scouts, St. Bartholomew's Protestant Episcopal Church, who meet at 1109 E. Hunting Park av., or to the Scouts who meet at the Germantown Boys' Club, Germantown av. and Penn st.—(S. V.)

"BEAUTY'S EYES": By F. E. Weatherly, song set to the music of Paolo F. Tosti begins, "I need no stars in Heaven to guide me." It may be purchased.—(E. O.)

NEW JERSEY MARRIAGE LICENSE: All applications for licenses must be made at least seventy-two hours in advance of the time set for the ceremony. Licenses are issued forty-eight hours after application and must be delivered to the clergyman, magistrate or person who is to perform the ceremony twenty-four hours before the time for its performance. The residence of the parties determines to whom application shall be made. If the woman is a resident of any city, borough, town or other municipality in New Jersey, license is obtained from the Registrar of Vital Statistics, if there is such an officer; if not, then from the clerk of the municipality in which she resides. If woman is non-resident of State, then license is obtained from the Registrar or clerk of section in which man resides. If both are non-residents of the State, application is to be made to proper officer of county or township where ceremony is to be performed.—(K. M.)

ECLIPSE OF MOON: There will be two in 1928. The first, total, will occur June 3, early in the morning, but will be visible in the United States only in the West. A total eclipse occurs on November 27 early in the morning. This will be visible throughout the United States. According to Eastern Standard Time, eclipse begins at 2.24 A. M.; total phase begins 3.33 A. M.; total phase ends 4.49 A. M.; eclipse ends 5.39 A. M. (2) Mars will be nearest the earth on December 15, 1928. At that time it will be 54,300,000 miles distant from the earth.—(M. D.)

SELLING STORIES: Submit them to editors of publications.—(C. K.)

ADOPTION OF BABY: Might apply to Children's Bureau, 311 S. Juniper st.—(C. T.)

PUBLIC BUILDINGS APPROPRIATIONS LAWS: This law approved February 24, 1928, increased the authorization of $165,000,000 already in effect for public buildings to $265,000,000, and otherwise amended the general public building authorization of the Sixty-ninth Congress as embodied in the Public Building construction act of May 25, 1926. Under the law as it now stands the status of the building program is as follows: Appropriations up to $265,000,000 authorized, spread over a term of years. Of this total $15,000,000 is for completed buildings, authorized under the act of March 4, 1913, which could not be finished on account of war-time conditions interfering with the cost limit; $50,000,000 for buildings in the District of Columbia and $200,000,000 for Government building activities outside the District. Under the law as amended $35,000,000 can be expended annually and of this sum $10,000,000 is to be used in the District of Columbia. No information has yet reached the postoffice authorities here as to the amount to be expended for public buildings in Philadelphia.—(A. C.)

BOXING REGULATIONS: For local police regulations governing boxing bouts apply to chiefs of police.—(S. P.)

DEVIL'S POOL: Or Devil's Hole, a small fall of the Cresheim Creek into a basin near where the creek empties into the Wissahickon Creek is said to have received its name from having been a place where the Evil Spirits and the Good Spirits of the Indians are supposed to have gathered to battle.

The spot is also said to have been an Indian place of wor-
shiping the Great Spirit.—(W. L.)

SOLDIER'S WIDOW'S FUNERAL: There is no Government fund for defraying funeral costs of Civil War veteran's
widow.—(F. F.)

STEAMSHIP PITTSBURGH: Made her last trip from
Philadelphia to Ireland in 1922.—(MRS. H.)

FORMULAS

DULL VARNISH: A varnish that does not reflect light is
prepared by mixing a solution of rosin with some liquid in
which rosin is insoluble. A mixture of 3 to 5 parts of sand-
arac, dissolved in 48 parts of ether and $2\frac{1}{2}$ parts of benzole
resembles ground glass when dry. A solution of dammar rosin
in benzol, mixed with ether, gives a dull varnish. Keep away
from heat and fire as these ingredients are highly inflammable.
—(R.)

REMOVING PAINT: Prepared paint remover may be purchased or an effective remover may be made by dissolving one
pound of caustic soda in two pounds of warm water then stir
into two pounds of cold water two ounces of starch and two
ounces of china clay. When the soda solution cools add the
starch, clay and water mixture, stirring all well together.
Apply to the paint and after it remains for a few moments,
paint and paste may be scraped off together. The wood should
then be washed with clean water and then with water and vine-
gar to remove the caustic soda which if left would be dele-
terious to the wood.—(S. A.)

THE MOTOR PATHFINDER

NEW JERSEY LICENSE TAGS: Each county is assigned
a letter to designate cars owned by its residents, as follows:
Atlantic, A.; Bergen, B.; Burlington, N.; Camden, C.; Cape
May, F.; Cumberland, Y.; Essex, E., 1-E. and 2-E.; Hunter-
don, J.; Mercer, L.; Gloucester, Z.; Hudson, H.; Middlesex,
K.; Monmouth, M.; Morris, V.; Passaic, P.; Ocean, O-N.;

Salem, S.; Somerset, I.; Sussex, R.; Union, U.; Warren, W. Each county begins its series with 1001. Tags for non-residents have numeral 4 first.—(MRS. B.)

VINELAND, N. J., FROM 5TH ST. and SNYDER AV., PHILADELPHIA: 58 miles: North on 5th st. and right at Race over Delaware River Bridge, right from Crescent boulevard to Broadway and by Broadway through Gloucester, Brooklawn, Westville, Woodbury, Mullica Hill, Bridgeton, through on Pearl st. to Norma, Vineland.—(W. G.)

WATERVILLE, ME.—578 miles: North on Broad st. and right at Roosevelt boulevard through Morrisville, Trenton, N. J., Princeton, New Brunswick, Elizabeth, Newark, Englewood, ferry to Dyckman st., New York, N. Y., left on Broadway, right on 207th st., and by Fordham rd. to Boston Post rd., by which through Connecticut towns, Narragansett Pier, Saunderstown, Providence, Wrentham, Mass., Walpole, Boston, Cambridge, Somerville, Malden, Lynnfield, Newburyport, Salisbury, Smithtown, N. H.; Portsmouth, Kittery, Me.; Kennebunk, Biddeford, Portland, Brunswick, Augusta, Waterville. —(MRS. W.)

ETHICAL PROBLEMS

SOCIAL CIRCLES FOR LADS AND LASSIES

Sir: Thanks a lot, "M. W.," for your comment. Yes, I believe you must be the type of man we girls admire. Like you with the girls, I'm not wanted by the boys I want—that is, the older ones—and I get so lonesome I hardly know what to do with myself. Here's hoping for the best.

DIANA.

SLOW CLUBS WELCOME OUT-OF-TOWNERS

Sir: Please tell me of the Slow Club chapter meeting nearest my home in Glenolden, the dues, etc.

KITTIE.

(There's the Main Line Chapter, meeting at the Ardmore Y. M. C. A., Lancaster pike. Membership in the Y. M. C. A. is a prerequisite and the dues are 25 cents a month. They start their meetings about 8.30 P. M. All chapters are open to out-of-town members. If you come to the city, suggest the Dramatic Chapter, meeting every Friday evening at the West Philadelphia Public Library, 40th and Walnut sts.)

SHOULD THEY INVITE THE BOYS?

Sir: The other night my chum, sister and I met three boys. On leaving us, they promised to call around, but they all promise, but never do. The problem is, my mother is giving a benefit party for our church. Would it seem bold for us to get in touch with these boys and invite them? How about it, readers?

And boys, why is it at a dance that some girls get all the dances and others equally as good dancers get none? I have experienced this a great deal of late. If a girl is painted up like a doll, she can count on every dance, otherwise she's out. Why?   CISS.

CHARM OF CONVERSATION

Sir: If I may offer my opinion on the subject of conversation I would say that the first requisite is talent. It is akin to the oratorical and its charm is style, the subject matter being of secondary consideration. No matter how well we may be informed upon a subject our impression or reaction upon the listener will be nil if we lack expressive force. If, however, we think clearly and offer a sincere expression the subject matter may often be ignored.

The art of conversation is a give-and-take between two or more persons. With some it ends in argumentation, depending entirely on how aggressive they are, or to what degree mental reaction has taken place. Conversation may be trite or highly intellectual, depending, of course, upon the mental equipment of the conversationalists.

If one would converse well one must find people who converse well. One must rise or fall to the level of the people spoken to. And if one has talent this ability of accommodation will soon be in evidence.   C. J. B.

FOR HER SHYNESS, HAIR AND LIMBS

Sir: Here's my sad story: I'm afraid I'm losing my boy friend. To tell the truth, I don't think I'm enough of a pal for him. I'm shy where he is concerned and he is inclined to be quiet, too. (1) What can I do to arouse his interest? People usually like me when they first meet me, but after the fourth time, I imagine they tire of me. Is there any remedy for this? (2) My legs are skinny. What can I do to make them heavier? (3) My hair is a vivid shade of red. Is there anything to make it darker? (4) There is a young chap who drives me home from Sunday School occasionally. Is it proper to thank him, and if so, what shall I say? (5) Do men prefer femininity in girls instead of boyishness?

GAMMA ALPHA BETA.

(1) There is no positive rule for holding one's "boy friend" or for retaining acquaintances. Traits which attract one person may annoy or even repel another. Still, it pays to be cheerful, and show normal interest in those you come in contact with; to be a good listener is as likely to please as to have a good "line." Both are invaluable. (2) Regular exercise will create muscular strength, and in some cases make legs look larger, but there is hardly anything that will materially increase the size without increasing the weight of the body. Cocoa butter persistently rubbed in by vigorous massage is said to have fattening effect, but nothing will fatten some legs naturally sinewy. If you are under weight, possibly due to violation of some physical laws, you should be treated by a doctor. (3) Seldom are hair coloring preparations satisfactory unless applied by professional hairdressers. Even then they all require constant renewal and a trouble. It is better to go to a professional dyer who will treat hair according to texture and other conditions. (4) "Thank you very much for the ride home." (5) Impossible to give generic answer to such a sweeping question so far as "men's preference" is concerned, but a woman of wide experience says that among her large circle of young women acquaintances those that make the best and earliest marriages are the feminine type.

BOUDOIR HINTS

SUPERFLUOUS HAIRS: Nature must take its course and the only way to eradicate the hairs is by the use of the electric needle in the hands of an expert. Shaving with razor will remove hairs, but must be continued. Next is this advice of a specialist: "Make a mixture of equal parts of lemon juice, ammonia, and peroxide and apply it with a pad of absorbent cotton once a day till the hair is thoroughly bleached. It will still be there, of course, but practically invisible.—(B. H.)

EYE WASH: For healthy eyes, a good daily tonic is a bath of cold water. The normal tear gland furnishes the normal bath for the normal eye. Bathing the outside of the eyelids in cold water is however a wholesome stimulant under normal conditions. When the eyes are tired or "sandy" a prolonged application of hot water is both restful and hygienic. Another advice is take a "nap" and at bedtime bathe the eyes with soft rag dipped in cup of water (having been boiled), into which has been placed a pinch of boracic acid powder.—(A. W.)

CAN YOU ANSWER THESE?

1—*Which is the largest of all oceanic birds?*
2—*To what length do their wings grow?*
3—*How much do these birds weigh?*
4—*What is the color of their plumage?*
5—*Where are they chiefly found?*
6—*How do they show their remarkable powers of flight?*
7—*What other large web-footed bird is found near large bodies of water?*
8—*What is the disposition of a gull?*
9—*What is one of their chief habits?*
10—*What bird is called "The King of Birds"?*
11—*From ancient time, what has the eagle symbolized?*
12—*Why was it chosen as the emblem on the coat of arms of the United States?*

(Answers appear on Page 171)

REPLIES TO 'CAN YOU ANSWER THESE?'

1—The albatross.

2—Sometimes fifteen feet.

3—Often exceeding twenty pounds.

4—White with black bands on wings and back.

5—In warm Southern seas.

6—By sometimes sailing in the air for an hour without the slightest apparent motion.

7—The gull.

8—Quarrelsome and noisy.

9—Following ships for days, searching for any possible scrap of food.

10—The eagle.

11—Might and courage.

12—Because of its qualities and because its habitat extends over the whole of North America.

(See questions on Page 170)

WAR-TIME NEWS BULLETINS 10 YEARS AGO IN PHILADELPHIA

(From the files of The Bulletin, June 4, 1918.)

Additional reports of U-boat raid off coast show it of greater extent than first thought. Passengers of Carolina, torpedoed off New Jersey, are landed in small boats at New York, Atlantic City and Lewes, Del. Sixteen out of thirty-five in one boat drowned in storm. Bathers at Atlantic City carry survivors ashore through surf.

All bright light displays in New York City are ordered discontinued during U-boat raid.

Germans continue slow gains toward Paris. Machine gunners of 3d American Division hold bridge at Chateau-Thierry.

French get cannon to front line and Germans advance into direct artillery fire.

12

PICTORIAL HISTORY OF THE WORLD WAR

—Effects of American Victory—1918

THE MATERIAL RESULTS OF THE AMERICAN VICTORY AT ST. MIHIEL WERE VERY IMPORTANT. AN AMERICAN ARMY WAS AN ACCOMPLISHED FACT AND THE ENEMY HAD FELT ITS POWER. NO FORM OF PROPOGANDA COULD OVERCOME THE DEPRESSING EFFECT ON THE GERMANS.

THE ABILITY OF THE AMERICAN ARMY TO DRIVE THROUGH THE GERMANS' DEFENSE GAVE OUR TROOPS AN IMPLICIT CONFIDENCE IN THEIR SUPERIORITY AND RAISED THEIR MORALE TO THE HIGHEST PITCH. FOR THE FIRST TIME BARBED WIRE ENTANGLEMENTS CEASED TO BE REGARDED AS IMPASSABLE BARRIERS. OPEN WARFARE NOW CAME INTO ITS OWN.

OUR DIVISIONS CONCLUDED THE ATTACK IN SUCH HIGH SPIRITS THAT WITHOUT THE USUAL REST THEY WERE IMMEDIATELY AVAILABLE FOR EMPLOYMENT IN HEAVY FIGHTING IN A NEW THEATER OF OPERATIONS.

ST. MIHIEL WAS AMERICA'S ANSWER TO THE ROLL CALL OF THE NATIONS ON THE EVE OF THE LAST BATTLE OF THE WORLD WAR. AMERICA WAS NOW TO FACE A STILL GREATER RESPONSIBILITY.

355

WHAT IS WRONG IN PICTURE?

Saturday's Answer—Gasoline.

Word Golf

The object of this game is to change one word to another word by a series of "strokes." Only one letter can be changed in each "stroke," which must result in a new word. If you can beat "par" one stroke, you score a "birdie." If you can knock two strokes off "par," credit yourself with an "eagle." If you succeed in three strokes less than "par," hand yourself a "Pterodactyl"—the rarest of all birds.

(Solutions appear below)

SOLUTIONS TO 'WORD GOLF'

(Answers to the problems which appear above)

Fire—Fore, Fort, Foot, Coot, Cook.
Home—Come, Cone, Cane, Cant, Cent, Tent.

----

3 IN MOTOR HURT AT RUNNEMEDE, N. J.

Phila. Driver Escapes as Car Upsets—Several Women Injured in Other Accidents

LINDENWOLD MAN DIES

John Hainsman, forty-eight, of Lindenwold, N. J., died in the West Jersey Homeopathic Hospital at 6 A. M. today, from injuries suffered on May 1 when he was knocked down by an automobile on the White Horse pike near his home.

Louise Brown, thirty-two, of Magnolia, was bruised early today when a car driven by her husband figured in a collision on the White Horse pike at Oaklyn.

Three persons, all Philadelphians, escaped with minor injuries yesterday when the car in which they were riding overturned on Evesham av., near the Black Horse pike in Runnemede.

They are: Herman Woloskin, twenty-three, 3104 Berks st.; Lillian Abrams, eighteen, 840 Ritner st., and Eleanor Shirley, eighteen, 2716 N. Front. Morris Gerallinelli, 1333 S. 6th st., the driver, escaped injury.

Clarence Mudwig, 601 N. 6th st., this city, and Rose Mudwig, 532 Green st., suffered minor injuries yesterday when an automobile driven by Dr. J. J. Manuel, of this city, overturned on the Harding Highway near Bridgeton.

Jammed between two automobiles which figured in a triple accident while he was walking along the River road near Palmyra, yesterday, Manley Barfield, sixteen, Trenton, suffered a broken right leg. He is in Cooper Hospital.

Struck by a hit-and-run driver at White Horse pike and Ormand av., near Oaklyn, yesterday, Bernard Peterson, twenty-four, 103 Elm av., Camden, was thrown from a bicycle and suffered several fractured ribs. He was taken to the West Jersey Homeopathic Hospital.

Alice Smythe, of this city, is in the Atlantic City Hospital with a broken right arm and a possible fracture of the spine. She was injured in an automobile crash near Egg Harbor, yesterday.

----

4 MOTORISTS FINED AT SOMERDALE

Three Philadelphia motorists were fined for traffic violations on White Horse pike by Justice of the Peace Zeigler, Somerdale, N. J., yesterday. They are Nicholas Negri, 708 Buttonwood st., $20 and costs for reckless driving; Isadore Gordon, 5237 Fairmount av., $10 and costs for reckless driving; Harry Short, 1235 W. Venango st., $5 for passing a traffic signal. Harold Lane, Detroit, was fined $10 for wrong registration cards.

FIVE INJURED IN FOUR-MOTOR CRASH ON LINCOLN HIGHWAY

Woman Badly Hurt in Oxford Valley, Bucks Co., Accident

Five persons were injured when four automobiles collided on Lincoln Highway, near Oxford Valley, Bucks county, shortly before midnight.

The injured are: Mildred Moody, thirty-eight, 4337 Brown st., this city, in the Mercer Hospital, Trenton, condition serious; Margaret Duncan, 743 18th st., Paterson, N. J., back injured, head cut; Margaret Pral, 179 Jasper st., Paterson, shock and bruises; Lewis H. Johnson, colored, 1722 W. 8th st., Wilmington, Del., and Frank W. Sieling, Jr., 156 Montgomery av., Cynwyd, cuts and bruises.

Sieling was given a hearing early today before Squire John H. Alvey, Woodbourne, Pa., and sent to Langhorne jail in default of $800 bail.

According to police, Sieling tried to pass a bus on the Lincoln highway, but was forced to the side of the road, striking Johnson's automobile, bound toward this city, forcing it into a ditch.

Sieling's car rebounded into the automobile driven by Rochester Harris, colored, Petersburg, Va., badly damaged it. It was owned by Harry W. Silberstein, 986 Leggett av., Bronx, N. Y. Sieling's car then swerved again and collided with that of Jacob Vandervliet, 16 Park av., Hawthorne, N. J., wrecking it.

COLLINGSWOOD FIREMEN AT CHURCH

The Collingswood Volunteer Fire Department held their annual special services in St. Paul's Lutheran Church, Collingswood, yesterday. At the same time the Rev. I. H. Hagedorn, pastor of the church, celebrated his seventh anniversary. Music was furnished by the Collingswood band.

PHILA. GIRL AND FRIEND THRILLED AS THEY START AIR TOUR OF EUROPE

90 'Planes Leave and Arrive at Tempelhofer Field Daily Amid Traffic Police Signals

---

CATHEDRAL SPIRES AND OLD CASTLES ARE WELCOME GUIDES FOR PILOTS—ALPS BEAUTY ENTRANCES

BY MILDRED JOHNSON

Two eager and enthusiastic American girls, air-traveling over Europe, reported to the travel bureau of the big German air transport company, the Deutsche Lufthansa, in Berlin. They were the writer and a friend, Esther Wanner, reputed to be the first girls to sight-see Europe by air.

A happy group of fellow air-travelers greeted us cheerily, perhaps a little awe-struck that two girls should fly unescorted. Our tickets, from Berlin to Prague, were handed to us by a smiling clerk. It was to be the first stop on a circuitous air tour which would take us visiting to the middle southern countries of the continent.

BY BUS TO THE FIELD

But ten minutes from the centre of the city, and we were stepping from the bus in front of the airport building at the Berlin airport, Tempelhofer Feldt. Besides being the best located airport in the world, its equipment must necessarily be extensive and adequate, as it is, to enable them to carry on the steady traffic of incoming and outgoing planes, amounting in the summer season to ninety a day.

LIKED ADVENTURING IN AIR OVER EUROPE

Miss Mildred Johnson, right, of Manoa, Delaware county, and her friend, Mrs. Esther Wanner, of Portland, Oregon, who unescorted entered upon a sight-seeing tour of Europe from the air, observing aviation progress abroad.

A swift and courteous customs inspection is next on the program, after which we were directed to one of a dozen planes lined up on the asphalt apron all ready to depart. It was one of those big low-wing Junkers monoplanes that never fail to enthuse me.

Snug within the cozy cabin, we took off from the midst of co-ordinated signals of the field traffic policemen, the pilot and able mechanics.

Over a sea of chimneys which stood out prominently through the slight ground haze that covered Berlin, we flew south over orderly rows of cultivated fields of varying shades of green and brown to Dresden. Heavenly skies and a warm sultry atmosphere—clouds lazying along in defiance of our terrific speed.

SHRIEKS AS GIRLS COME ABOARD

Four passengers leave us at Dresden, and in their place come two pretty German girls with two friends; one of the extremely fat type that really should require an excess baggage charge. It is obviously the first flight the girls have had. Such excitement—shrieks of ecstasy, of anticipation, perhaps fear; so many people are fearful, for what foolish reason, I can't imagine.

The terrain turns to wooded hills, interspersed with deep furrowed fields, and fields of green, blending together in a great geometrical masterpiece.

The homes become more frequent. We are no doubt near Prague. What appears as a field of great tall smokestacks looms ahead, but it is really Prague. The fat man and the rest of the party are still in raptures as they step from the plane, and the excited intonations of their conversation lead me to believe they all rather enjoyed their first flight.

A trim uniformed customs officer met us and after looking over our passports, politely explained that it is necessary to have a visa for Czecho-Slovakia. Knowing how serious customs officers usually consider this neglect, the courtesy was much appreciated.

Into the inevitable omnibus we proceed to make our bow to Prague. Frankly we are not impressed. The hotel is cold and reeks with a dank musty atmosphere. The cobbly pavements make walking difficult and the language sounds as though it would take ten years to learn. There is a general depressed expression of the many who stride along beside us, and more than enough dirt litters the streets.

A short sight-seeing trip beneath cloudy skies occupied the next morning, and we proceeded to the flying field again for a flight to Vienna.

PILOTS APPRECIATE CHURCH SPIRES

Due to foggy weather the plane from Berlin, which proceeds to Vienna, was late and, recalling to our minds the hospitality of our old south, lunch was arranged for us by the customs officer of yesterday while we await our plane. Whatever else Prague has not, she has nice customs officers.

The Berlin plane comes bounding over the field, an hour late. After depositing the Prague passengers, we are ushered into the plane. On to Vienna with three other passengers coming from Berlin.

It is a strange and a fine thing, that the looming spires of countless church steeples form the best landmarks for the pilots all over the world. Occasional castles topping forested hills—a beautiful sight from the air—are also excellent guides for the pilots.

The form of the earth becomes rumpled and very picturesque. And now the blue Danube comes along to enhance the picture. If the famous poets and composers who have sung its glory through the ages had seen its rare beauty from the air, I am sure they would have been even more inspired. Following its rich green banks for a short time, we come quite suddenly to Vienna, the city of music, of culture, of beautiful women, but for us the city of bad weather.

For two days thereafter the bus took us from the office of the travel bureau in Berlin to the flying field, only to return us after giving the weather five hours in which to clear sufficiently for us to fly to Venice this time.

The next day we flew. Although a cloudy day in Vienna, the sun was shining brightly just beyond. The landscape, like a chameleon, changed from farming land to forest-covered hills and then to a fairyland of sparkling-white snow-covered mountains. It was the Alps, the beauty of which we have heard much, but to actually see them from an altitude, which magnifies their beauty of contour and color to an unbelievable degree, is simply spellbinding. We had almost two full hours of this grandeur on which to feast our eyes.

Sailing under azure skies we pass over the Alps much too soon and on to fertile green farmlands of Italy. Turning the nose of the plane slightly, we see on the distant horizon innumerable sails of fishing boats bobbing upon the Adriatic.

Leaving the billowy clouds above, we sweep down gracefully to a green stretch on the Lido and come to a stop before an excited group of field and customs men who tell us that the famous Italian flier, Di Bernardi, not a half hour earlier had bettered his own world's speed record, making 310 miles an hour, over a rectangular course from the Lido to Venice and back to the other end of the Lido.

TOMORROW—THRILLED BY RADIO CONVERSATION BETWEEN 'PLANES

(This is the first of four articles by Miss Mildred Johnson describing an aërial voyage of 3,000 miles over five countries of Europe which she and a friend, Mrs. Esther Wanner, of Portland, Oregon, accomplished. Miss Johnson has won public attention in the last two years as the "Apostle of the Air Mail," having traveled 20,000 miles in United States mail planes. Her home is in Manoa, Delaware county.)

DENOUNCES WATER BOARD

Grover C. Ladner, City Counsel, Scores Refusal to Report on Survey

---

The Sanitary Water Bureau of Pennsylvania has been vigorously denounced for its refusal to co-operate with the city in legal action planned against pollution of the Schuylkill by Grover C. Ladner, special counsel for the city, in a letter to the Board.

The letter was sent yesterday to Theodore Appel, chairman of the Board, and asserts the refusal of the Board to furnish information from their surveys concerning the source of pollution would necessitate the duplication of the expensive surveys.

WHAT DO YOU THINK OF IT?

Three Persons Are Asked a Question of Timely Interest

THE QUESTION

What is the most constructive manner in which a person can spend his leisure?

WHERE ASKED

Central part of city.

THE ANSWERS

1. Charles Platt, Prospect av., Chestnut Hill.—"In exercise, such as tennis or golf, which is not too strenuous, but 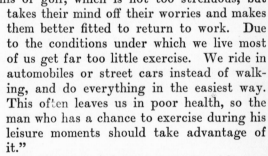 takes their mind off their worries and makes them better fitted to return to work. Due to the conditions under which we live most of us get far too little exercise. We ride in automobiles or street cars instead of walking, and do everything in the easiest way. This often leaves us in poor health, so the man who has a chance to exercise during his leisure moments should take advantage of it."

2. Margaret Johnston, 2625 Parrish st.— "Oh, there are a great many ways, but few of them are ever very seriously considered. The most important of these seems to me to be the development of the mind and this is best accomplished through serious reading. Now when I say 'serious  reading' I don't mean the study of special subjects nor the following of any set program, but I mean reading many different kinds of books and actually trying to understand them. It becomes a habit which is a source of much enjoyment and one that is unequalled for developing both the character and the mind."

3. Edward Mattis, Spring City, Pa.—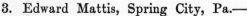

"That all depends upon the season. In the summer the natural thing to do is take part in as many outdoor sports as possible; that builds the health. Then in the winter I think the most sensible thing a person can do is to increase their field of knowledge through the medium of good books. If their time allows it would also be a good plan to take special subjects in one of the universities, but one scheme don't work all year around."

Tomorrow's Question—*Which is the most beneficial to mankind, the radio or the airplane.* (Suggested by Walter Quinn.)

ARCHITECTURAL PRIZES AWARDED

Princeton, June 2.—A design of a town hall in the Georgian style, drawn by William McMillan, of Baltimore, Princeton University art school senior, has been awarded first prize in the contest of the Princeton Architectural Society. Honorable mention was given Alan R. Stuyvesant, of Allamuchy, N. J.

BUSINESS FEVERS

It is about time, says the financial philosopher, to get away from the tradition that Presidential years are necessarily the occasion for business chills and fevers.—American Magazine.

DUCKING A THUNDERBOLT

"Who's that behind us, Fred?" asked the man at the wheel as a car hooted.

"Only a flapper in a roadster," Fred answered.

The driver hurled his wheel over, swerved the car off the road, crashed though a fence, and upset.

"Thank heaven we escaped!" he muttered.—Smith's Weekly (Sydney).

TRAVELS IN NATURELAND

No. 55.

The Viper's Herb That Fled Across the Atlantic

Back about the year 1675 the blue thistle adorned the English hill-sides alone.

Then one day someone called it a viper's herb. The practice had come of looking for some special sign on plants to indicate for just what use they were intended. Someone saw the spotted stem of the blue thistle and its seeds shaped like a serpent's head and announced that it was good for snake bite. It therefore became known as Viper's Herb.

As though in chagrin the plant seems to have fled to the newly-colonized world across the Atlantic. Just how it came here no records show. Perhaps the seeds borne on a wind hid themselves in some baggage.

It is but one of the plant immigrants that have been brought not voluntarily to this country. These immigrants seem to thrive better in many instances than native plants. Viper's Herb is content to grow in dry fields, in waste places and along the road. Its flowers of bright blue grow on curved spikes.

PROFIT AND LOSS

Doctor—"Well, I hope you profited by my advice?"
Patient—"Yes, doctor; but not so much as you did."—Pearson's.

LITTLE STORIES FOR THE BEDTIME

By Thorton W. Burgess

THE SECRET IS DISCOVERED

Longbill and Mrs. Longbill had kept their secret well. They intended to keep it until the time came when four fluffy little Longbills would come from those four eggs and Mother would proudly lead them out into the Great World.

No one knew where that nest was. More than once it had taken a great deal of courage to sit perfectly still. More than once Mrs. Longbill had heard the patter of feet and known that Reddy Fox was within jumping distance of her. To have taken to her wings would have been safety. It would also have meant giving her secret away to Reddy. So she sat tight, not moving so much as a feather, and Reddy had passed on, without knowing that she was there.

Once Lightfoot the Deer had jumped right over her. More than once Redtail the Hawk had sat in a tree right above her. It had taken courage—a great deal of courage—to sit still with enemies so near.

"It will only be a few days more," said Mrs. Longbill, "before these eggs hatch."

"I'm glad of that, my dear," said Longbill. "I certainly am glad of that. No one has discovered our secret as yet and I guess no one will. Hello! Here comes somebody down through the swamp now. I'll slip away from here, so not to be seen."

So Longbill slipped away. Mrs. Longbill sat motionless, but her bright eyes were very wide open and her ears were strained to catch every little sound. Somebody was coming through the swamp and it was somebody large. Could it be that Buster Bear was coming down to the Laughing Brook? Certainly those footsteps were heavy enough for Buster Bear.

A stick snapped. A moment later another snapped. With each snap the heart of Mrs. Longbill jumped inside her, but she didn't move.

Nearer and nearer drew those heavy footsteps. Would they pass by, as other footsteps had passed?

Because her eyes were so far up on her head, Mrs. Longbill could look back and see who was coming. She realized in a moment that it was one of those two-legged creatures, whom she had learned to fear and hate, because each fall they had tried to kill her with terrible guns. Her heart beat fast and fear filled her whole being. Still she remained guarding that precious secret. She wouldn't move until it was absolutely necessary.

Nearer and nearer came that two-legged creature. She knew he hadn't seen her yet. Perhaps he would turn aside without seeing her. He was so close now that in one step more he would step on her. That would be the end of her and of her secret, too. There was no sense in being foolish. With despair in her heart, she took to her wings, almost brushing the face of this two-legged creature as she rose into the air.

"A woodcock!" exclaimed Farmer Brown's Boy, for that is who it was. "A woodcock! That means a nest. I must be careful where I step. That nest is close by, for that bird

"Hello, here comes somebody through the swamp now."

almost touched me as she rose. Ah, there it is! If I had taken another step, I should have crushed those eggs."

Sure enough, right in front of him and almost at his feet, was a little clump of alders with four eggs. There wasn't much of a nest—just a few leaves in a little hollow in the soft ground. Farmer Brown's Boy stooped over and examined the eggs, but he didn't touch them. He took care not to touch them. Then, very carefully, he withdrew.

"That little lady certainly has courage," said he. "She certainly had courage to sit until I was ready to step on her. I am delighted that Longbill and his mate are nesting here this year. I hope I'll have a chance to see the babies. I shall have to keep sharp watch of this nest."

HEALTH: HOW TO KEEP IT

Climate and Form in Cases of Rickets

By Dr. Herman N. Bundesen
President American Public Health Association

It long has been known that the prevalence and severity of rickets vary in different locations throughout the world. It is conceded that there is less rickets in the extreme Southern States than in the Northern States.

C. T. Williams has found that in New Orleans children with marked deformities due to rickets are rarely seen. He studied a group of children to see if he could not find what factors are responsible for the mildness of the rickets in that city.

One hundred children were studied. In twenty-six, active rickets was found. Three of these cases occurred in breast-fed children and the remainder in bottle-fed babies. All of the children with active rickets responded to treatment with cod liver oil, regulation of the diet and sun baths.

Green vegetables were plentiful in the diets of the nursing mothers. This was true during both summer and winter. There was also a strong tendency to have citrus fruits and meats in the diets. Forty-seven of the fifty-three mothers who were nursing had this sort of diet and only three of the fifty-three babies had rickets.

An analysis of the living conditions showed that fourteen per cent. of the residences were exposed to the sun on all four sides, eleven per cent. on one side and two per cent. were not exposed to the sun. Ninety-six per cent. of the children had either front or back yards in which to play.

The findings of Williams showed that severe rickets is extremely rare in this section. In his conclusions Williams suggests that green vegetables have some protective influence, although most green vegetables contain little, if any, vitamin D. The geographic location is probably the factor most responsible for the occurrence of the mild form of rickets seen. Good exposure to sunlight of the tenement houses, low buildings, playground facilities, the types of clothing and the diet, all must be taken into account.

Proper diet for the nursing mother as well as for all children, plenty of sunlight, fresh air and cod liver oil are the measures which are employed. They are productive of good health, strong physique and resistance to disease.

FOR CROOKED, SWOLLEN FINGERS

"I am sixty-one years old and for three or four years I have had pains in the joints of my fingers. They swell up and my fingers are becoming crooked. What can I do for this trouble?

C. K."

You are evidently suffering from "arthritis deformans." Treatment consists first in searching for a focus of infection that is present in the body and moving it. Each joint may require separate treatment. Sometimes vaccines are helpful. Rest, fresh air, passive motion and good food must also be employed. Sometimes surgical treatment is necessary. Tonics containing iron sometimes are beneficial. Outdoor life and moderate exercise will help to build up the general condition.

"What is the drug phenolphthalein? What is it used for, and what effect has it on the system? MRS. A. S."

Phenolphthalein is a drug used in many laxative preparations; it is also an indicator which is used to determine the acidity or alkalinity of a solution. It is somewhat habit forming if used as a laxative with any degree of regularity.

"I have pain in top and sides of knee. Is this rheumatism or arthritis? Is there any difference? What is cause and cure, if any? MRS. N."

It is possible that the pains in your knee are due to arthritis, which means an inflammation of the joint. Rheumatism is a specific kind of arthritis. It would be advisable for you to have an X-ray picture taken of your knee. This would help in finding the cause of the trouble.

Tomorrow—"Care of the Toothbrush."

13

THE BULLETIN TIME TABLE OF RADIO BROADCASTS

(Programs are given in Eastern Daylight Saving Time)

RADIO WEATHER FORECAST

Distant reception from all directions tonight will be weak.

HEADLINERS FOR TONIGHT

7.00—WJZ—Smalle and Robertson, duets.

7.30—WCAU—Snellenburg Instrumental Trio; Royal P. McClelland, tenor; Elizabeth Harrison, soprano.

WJZ—Roxy and His Gang.

8.00—WLIT, WEAF—O'Cedar Shining Hour, Keller Sisters and Brother Lynch, harmony singers.

WIP—Royal Hawaiians.

8.30—WLIT, WEAF—A. and P. Gypsies. South American program.

9.00—WCAU, WOR—Spur Tie Hour. Golf Talk by Johnny Farrell.

WJZ—Riverside Hour; Orchestra.

9.30—WLIT, WEAF—General Motors Family Party. French compositions.

10.00—WLIT, WEAF—The Cabin Door.

WJZ—Works of Great Composers.

10.30—WLIT, WEAF—Time-to-Retire Boys and Orchestra.

11.00—WJZ—Slumber Music.

MONDAY, JUNE 4
6 P. M. to 8 P. M.

6.00—WCAU—"Planting at the Seashore," C. F. Greeves-Carpenter. WJZ—Base ball scores; Manger Orchestra. WEAF—Waldorf-Astoria Orchestra. WGY—Stock reports. WNYC—Market High Spots. WLWL—Dominican Hour.

6.10—WCAU—Mr. O'Naip at the ivories. WNYC—Constance Veitch, 'cellist. WODA—Dodge program.

6.15—WOR—Old King Cole. WHAP—Orchestra concert.

6.20—WCAU—Base ball scores. WGBS—Children's Playground Period.

6.25—WGY—Base ball scores. WNYC—Base ball scores.

6.30—WIP—King Joy Orchestra. WCAU—Janssen's Orchestra. WGY—Van Curler Orchestra. WNYC—German, V. H. Berlitz. WHAP—Stella H. Alexander, pianist.

6.40—WJZ—Program summary.

6.45—WFI—Base ball scores. WJZ—"Dogs," Frank Dole. WPG—Organ recital.

6.55—WFI—Safety Talk. WEAF—Base ball scores.

7.00—WIP—Uncle Wip's Roll Call and Birthday List. Marion Hughes, singing. WFI, WEAF—Talk by James G. McDonald, "Democrat Japan." WCAU—The Storyloguers. WJZ—Smalle and Robertson. WPCH—N. J. Industrial Hour. WNYC—Advanced German, V. H. Berlitz. WODA—Mr. Investor and Mr. Advisor. WLWL—Iselo Ilari, tenor. WOR—Base ball scores. WHAP—Talk, James Hyndman. WPG—Morton Concert.

7.10—WODA—Love's Music. WOR—Shelton Ensemble.

7.15—WCAU—"Famous Crimes," Isaac D. Levy. WEAF—National String Quartet. WLWL—Serenades. WRC—Shopping with Bab.

7.25—WGY—Base ball scores.

7.30—WLIT—Base ball scores. WCAU—Snellenburg Instrumental Trio; Royal P. McClellan, tenor; Elizabeth Harrison, soprano. WJZ—Roxy and His Gang. WEAF—Christopher Ward in a Burlesque Interview with Captain John Smith. WGY—General Electric Program. WNYC—Police alarms. WOR—Levitow's Orchestra.

7.35—WLIT—Sylvania Orchestra. WNYC—Frank Och's, popular ballads. WHAP—Stella Alexander, pianist.

7.45—WEAF—National String Quartet. WNYC—Metropolitan Musicale. WODA—English class. WLWL—Classique Concert Orchestra. WPG—Talk.

7.50—WHAP—Talk, Franklin Ford.

8 P.M. to 10 P.M.

8.00—WCAM—Pauline Freitag, alto. WLIT, WEAF—O'Cedar Shining Hour. WIP—Royal Hawaiians. WCAU—Hornung White Bock Hour. WMCA—Christian Science lecture. WPCH—Investment Talk. WODA—Safety Talk. WGN—Old-fashioned almanack.

8.10—WODA—Tom McGovern, baritone.

8.15—WCAM—St. Lawrence Dramatic Club. WPCH—Sol Cohen, violinist. WHAP—Christian Science reading.

8.30—WCAM—The Euterpians. WLIT, WEAF—A. and P. Gypsies. WPCH—Edna Bennett, song recital. WODA—Clifford Lodge Frolic.

8.45—WPCH—Studio program.

9.00—WCAM—Lapitino Ensemble. WCAU, WOR and 15 stations—Spur Tie Hour. WIP—Little Symphony Orchestra. WJZ and 15 stations—Riverside Orchestra. WPCH—United String Ensemble. WJAS—Concert.

9.15—WMCA—Jewish Entertainers.

9.30—WLIT, WEAF and 30 stations—General Motors Family Party. WCAU, WOR and 15 stations—Durham Hour. Come to the Fair. WJZ—Marimba Melodies.

9.45—WMCA—Jewish Concert. WPCH—Henry Burbig, humorist. WBBM—Wagner's Oriental Room Orchestra.

HER PIES BURN UP, FORGOTTEN.

10 P. M. to 1 A. M.

10.00—WLIT, WEAF—The Cabin Door. WJZ—Works of Great Composers. Genia Faneriova, soprano, and a baritone. WPCH—Osborne's Orchestra. WBBM—Coon Sanders Nighthawks.

10.15—WMCA—Rainbow Inn Orchestra.

10.20—WBBM—Fred Pohlman, tenor.

10.30—WLIT, WEAF and 29 stations—Fisk Time-to-Retire Boys. WCAU, WOR and 15 stations—Keystone Buccaneers. WBBM—Blue Monday Chasers. WGN—Recital.

11.00—WLIT—Walton Orchestra. WCAU—Janssen's Orchestra. WJZ—Slumber Music. WEAF—Park Central Venetian Gondoliers. WMCA—McAlpineers' Orchestra. WOR—Roseland Orchestra. WPG—Silver Slipper Orchestra. WBBM—Tomorrow's Tribune.

11.15—WBBM—Louie's Hungry Five.

11.30—WCAU—Lido Orchestra. WOR—The Witching Hour. WPG—Follies Bergere Orchestra. WBBM—"Lots of Harmony," Jimmy and Larry. WBBM—Sam 'n' Henry.

11.45—WBBM—Royal Canadians.

12.00—WMCA—The Wolfe and the Baer. WRC—Le Paradis Band. WGN—Dream Ship.

12.15—WGN—Country Club Frolics.

12.30—WGN—Radio Vox Pop.

12.45—WGN—Drake Orchestra.

TUESDAY, JUNE 5

6.45 A. M. to Noon

6.45-7.45—WEAF—Tower health exercises.

7.15—WOR—Gym exercises.

8.00—WEAF—Morning service.

8.15—WEAF—Parnassus Trio.

8.30—WEAF—Telephone message talk, Hubert L. Burdick.

9.00—WNAT—Walter Stainthorpe Musical Hour.

10.00—WIP—Menu.

10.15—WFI—Market reports.

10.30—WFI—Ten-Thirty Tidings.

10.45—WEAF—Parnassus Trio. WGBS—Gym class.

11.00—WEAF—Barbara Lowe, beauty talk.

11.10—WLIT—Daily Almanac; announcements.

11.15—WLIT, WEAF and 14 stations—Household Institute.

11.30—WLIT, WEAF—Studio program.

11.45—WEAF—"The Farmers' Wealth," Thomas Shayne.

NOON TO 6 P. M.

12.00—WLIT—Stanley Theatre Organ recital. WEAF—Studio program.

12.15—WLIT—Religious service.

12.30—WLIT—Walton Orchestra. WCAU—Golden Dragon Orchestra. WEAF—Market reports.

12.45—WEAF—Pennsylvania Orchestra.

1.00—WIP—Germantown Theatre Organ recital by Geibel Falconer. WFI—Tea Room Ensemble. WJZ—Park Central Orchestra.

1.30—WFI—Market Reports. WGBS—Scripture reading.

1.40—WFI—Tea Room Ensemble.

1.45—WEAF—Studio Orchestra.

2.00—WPSW—Paul Whiteman's Orchestra (recorded). WLIT—Arcadia Orchestra. WJZ—"Your Daily Menu." WEAF—"Dancing," by Dorothy La Salle.

2.15—WEAF—Parnassus Trio.

2.20—WJZ—Lucille Buhl, beauty philosopher.

2.30—WPSW—Music Box Revue. WLIT—From the Announcer's Viewpoint.

2.35—WJZ—"Gardens," Olive Hyde Foster.

2.45—WJZ—Studio program.

3.00—WIP—Thelma Melrose Davies Vocal Studio program. WFI—Character sketches given by Constance Marie O'Hara; a group of French songs by Grace Smith Green; talk, "What Does Your Writing Show?" by Gertrude O'Reilly; Chopin recital by Loretta Kerk; book chat by Ethel Kooker. WJZ—The Merry Three.

3.15—WEAF—Hudson River.

3.45—WIP—Bible Talk, by George G. Calhoun.

4.00—WIP—"Market Hints," W. R. Whittacre; Emily Kri-
der Norris School of Expression and Stage Art. WJZ—
U. S. Navy Band. WEAF—"Rugs and Their Symbols,"
Helen Eames.

4.15—WEAF—Studio prorgam.

4.30—WLIT—Jane Birkhead, soprano; Ambrose Dluccian
and Bruno Kaminski, violin and piano accordion in short
Polish music recital. WEAF—Women's League United
Synagogue of America. "Children's Rights," Mrs. Jeanette Seidman.

4.55—WCAU—Department of Agriculture Farm Flash.

5.00—WCAU—Theatrical revue. WJZ—The Tea Timers.
WEAF—Chamber music.

5.30—WLIT—Children's Twilight Hour. WJZ—Stock
market closing prices. WEAF—Jolly Bill and Jane.

5.45—WJZ—Ivy Scott, soprano,

6 P. M. to 8 P. M.

6.00—WCAU—Janssen's Orchestra. WFAN—Words and
music. WJZ—Base ball scores. Manger Orchestra.
WEAF—Waldorf-Astoria Orchestra. WGY—Stock reports. WPCH—San Marco, baritone. WLWL—Castle-
ton Instrumentalists. WEEI—Elks Orchestra.

6.15—WGBS—Children's Playground Period. WPCH—
Peggy Vincent, songs. WOR—Shelton Ensemble.

6.20—WCAU—Base ball scores.

6.25—WJZ—Program summary. WGY—Base ball scores.

6.30—WFI—Brass Quartet. WCAU—Golden Dragon Or-
chestra. WFAN—Green's Orchestra. WJZ—Burns
Brothers, Miners. WGY—Ten Eyck Orchestra. WPCH
—Wayne Brothers and Sis Joan.

6.40—WIP—Benjamin Franklin Orchestra.

6.45—WFI—Base ball scores. WOR—Dorma Lee, con-
tralto. WPG—Organ recital. WEEI—Big Brother
Club.

6.55—WEAF—Base ball scores.

7.00—WIP—Uncle Wip's Roll Call and Birthday List.
Nigro Valenti, violinist, and Vincent Persichetti, pianist.
WFI, WEAF—Voters' Service. "How Party Platforms

Are Made." WCAU—Lucas Harmony Four. WFAN— Hays Orchestra. WJZ—Smalle and Robertson, duets. WIWL—Paulist League Hour. WRNY—"French Humor," Valentine Erskine. WOR—Base ball scores. WPG —Shelburne Concert. WNAC—Dok's Sinfonians.

7.10—WOR—Enginite Boys.

7.15—WLWL—Joseph Martucci, organist. WCAP—Berkeley-Cataret Dinner Music.

7.30—WRAX—International Sunday School Lesson, by Walter S. Smalley. WLIT—Base ball scores. WCAU— Snellenburg Wood-wind Ensemble. WFAN—Robert Fraser, blind Gospel singer. WJZ—Fundamentals of the Law. "The Federal Bill of Rights," John W. Davis. WEAF—Soconyland Sketch. WGBS—Theatre Magazine Period. WOR—Levitow's Orchestra. WRC—Lotus Orchestra.

7.35—WLIT—Arcadia Orchestra.

7.45—WLWL—Opera Favorites. WRNY—Conger's Musical Message. WPG—Playground Highlights.

DANCING TONIGHT

6.00—WJZ.	11.00—WLIT,
6.30—WIP, WCAU.	WCAU, WEAF.
7.35—WLIT.	11.30—WCAU.

CORRECT TIME

6.00—WLIT.	9.00—WJZ.
7.00—WJZ.	11.00—WCAU.
8.00—WCAU.	

WEATHER FORECAST

6.00—WCAU.	7.00—WJZ.

BASE BALL SCORES

6.00—WJZ.	6.55—WEAF.
6.20—WCAU.	7.27—WIP.
6.45—WFI.	7.30—WLIT.

NEW BROADCASTING PERIOD FOR WIP

Beginning tonight station WIP will inaugurate a new broadcasting period, taking the time formerly used by WOO. At 8 the Royal Hawaiian String Quartet will present a program of Hawaiian airs. The WIP instrumental Quartet, at 10, will present the first of a series of musical stories entitled Tone Poems from the World's Musical Centres. Paris will be the city represented tonight.

Sambre Meuse ....Turlet
Un Peu d'Amour ....Silesus
Scenes Pittoresques ....Massenet
Cherie, I Love You.
Jours Passes ....Horne
Prelude de Deluge ....St. Saens
Poupee Valsante.
Frivolette—Entr' Acts ....Baron
Elegie .... Massenet
My Heart at Thy Sweet Voice ....St. Saens

SOUTH AMERICAN PROGRAM

A program dedicated to South America, supposedly being played as their wanderings take them through that country, will be offered by the A. and P. Gypsies tonight at 8.30 over WLIT, WEAF.

Pan Americana ....Herbert
Un Jour de Fete La Havana ....Filippucci
Harp Solo
La Feria (Suite Espagnole) ....LaCombe
Ay-Ay-Ay (Spanish song) ....Freire
Dance Number
Cachuca (Spanish Dance) ....Hadley
Cadiz (Serenade) ....Albeniz
Harp Solo
La Gitanette (Brazilian Dance)
Los Banderillos (Spanish March) ....Valpati

GOLF TALK AND MUSIC

Hookless and sliceless drives will be explained by Johnny Farrell, golfer, tonight at 9 over WCAU, WOR.

Collegiate (Ensemble)
Naila (Orchestra)
Keep Sweeping the Cobwebs Off the Moon (Beaus)
A Kiss in the Dark (Girl)
The Song Is Ended (Beaus)
Every Little Movement (Boy and Girl)
Oldtime Songs: Seeing Nellie Home, Junita, The Old Oaken
        Bucket (Beaus)
Killarney (Boy)
We Love It (Ensemble)

FOLK SONGS AND DANCES AT 9.30

Whirling Dervishes ....Godowsky
                     Orchestra
Gather Ye Rosebuds While Ye May ....Huhn
                   Mixed Quartet
Spanish Dance ....Granados
                     Orchestra
Seguidille, from "Carmen" ....Bizet
                Contralto with Orchestra
Gigue ....Gretry
                     Orchestra
Au Claire de la Lune ....Old French
             Soprano, Male Quartet, Orchestra
The Bartered Bride ....Smetana
                     Orchestra
The Cruickeen Lawn ....Old Irish
                   Male Quartet
My Lagan Love ....Old Ulser
                    Tenor Solo
Slavonic Dance in G Minor ....Dvorak
                     Orchestra
The Lorelei ....German Folk Songs
                   Mixed Quartet
Wooden Shoe Dance ....Kriens
                     Orchestra
Russian Peasants' Festival ....Tschaikowsky
                     Orchestra

ORCHESTRA AND SOLOISTS AT 10.30

Opening Chorus (Band and Ensemble)
Rum, Rum, Jamaica Rum (Male Quartet)
Fast Number (Orchestra)
Songs of the Campfire (Chorus)
Accordion Solo
Drum and Bugle Corps
Pirates' Chorus (Male Quartet)
Finale (Band and Ensemble)

———

PLAY 'FAUST' SELECTION

A selection from Gounod's opera "Faust" will be played by the Riverside Trail Blazers during the Riverside hour at 9 tonight over WJZ. A male quartet will be featured during this program.

Spirit of Progress March .... Riehl
Mary Ann
Band

Mammy's Lullaby
Quartet

Missouri Waltz
March of the Toys .... Herbert
Somewhere a Voice Is Calling .... Tate
Band

You're the First Thing I Think of in the Morning
Quartet

Selection from "Faust" .... Gounod
Spirit of Progress March .... Riehl
Band

———

DIRGE FOR A SOLDIER

In Memory of General Philip Kearney, Killed September 1, 1862.

By George H. Boker

Close his eyes, his work is done!
  What to him is friend or foeman,
Rise of moon, or set of sun,
  Hand of man, or kiss of woman?

Lay him low, lay him low,
In the clover or the snow!
What cares he? he cannot know;
Lay him low!

As man may, he fought his fight,
Proved his truth by his endeavor;
Let him sleep in solemn night,
Sleep for ever and for ever.
Lay him low, lay him low,
In the clover or the snow!
What cares he? he cannot know;
Lay him low!

Fold him in his country's star,
Roll the drum and fire the volley!
What to him are all our wars,
What but death all folly?
Lay him low, lay him low,
In the clover or the snow!
What cares he? he cannot know;
Lay him low!

Leave him to God's watching eye,
Trust him to the Hand that made him.
Mortal love sweeps idly by;
God alone has power to aid him.
Lay him low, lay him low,
In the clover or the snow!
What cares he? he cannot know;
Lay him low!

(This is one of the poems read over radio station WFI, May 29, by Dr. James Hosmer Penniman. George H. Boker (1823-1890), Philadelphia poet and dramatist and U. S. Minister to Turkey and Russia, respectively. He graduated from Princeton and later studied law. His father was a banker. "Poems of War" and "Sonnets" are among his best known volumes. "Francesca" is his best known play.)

MODERN AND OTHER NUMBERS

Some bright compositions by modern music makers will gradually give way to more somnolent selections in this week's program by the Fisk "Time-to-Re-tire" Boys and Orchestra, over WLIT, WEAF at 10.30 tonight.

Beautiful . . . . .Gillespie and Shey
Orchestra

Hush-a-Bye Baby . . . . .Mack and Austin
Vocal Duet

Humoreskimo . . . . .Bryant and Wending
Orchestra

Star of Me . . . . .Rogers
Vocal Duet

I'm Waiting for Ships That Never Come In . . . . .Alman
Salon Orchestra

My Pet . . . . .Ager
Vocal Duet

Nola . . . . .Arndt
Orchestra

Constantinople . . . . .Carlton
Orchestra

Time to Re-tire

SLUMBER MUSIC

Music representative of the best forms of the Eighteenth Century will be played by the Slumber Music string sextet, directed by Ludwig Laurier, at 11 tonight over WJZ.

Overture to "The Messiah" . . . . .Handel
Two Gavottes . . . . .Bach
Pavane and Gagliarde . . . . .Byrd
Minuet . . . . .Rameau
Serenade . . . . .Mozart
   Allegro
   Romanza
   Menuet
   Rondo
Aria . . . . .Tenaglia
Ballet Music . . . . .Gluck

SCHOOLBOY MARKS NEAR COLLEGIANS

Ted Meredith Impressed With Recent Performances— Caveny, Star Jumper, to Enter Princeton

MUNGER GREAT VAULTER

By Ted Meredith
(Holder of world's quarter mile and Olympic 800 meters records)

Little surprise can be shown at the fine performances of the college athletes, if the excellent work of the school boys throughout the country have been followed.

I have been quite interested in following the school boy results this spring, and have seen some of the local meets. Nothing which might be done by these boys in later years would be startling. With added age and experience, many of the boys have bright athletic careers to face.

The college meets rather overshadowed many of the best school boy meets during the past month. However, Moxley, of Columbus, O., High School, ran a quarter mile in 48 2-5 seconds, breaking my mark made at Franklin Field in the Penn interscholastics in 1912; Eliot, of Mercersburg, put the twelve-pound shot over 50 feet, and was just one of several to do this well; Scarlett, of Hun School, Princeton, threw the javelin over 170 feet, and these are only a few of the fine competitions.

Last Friday we had a sample of the improvement of the local private school boys when the Interacademic championships were held at Haverford.

Caveny, of Germantown Academy, high jumped 6 feet 2⅝ inches, making a new mark for that meet. He later tried for the Interscholastic record of 6 feet 3⅝ inches, but failed by a shade.

Caveny is bound for Princeton, and should prove a college champion before he is finished his four years there. In fact, his jump of last Friday will place him in the majority of the intercollegiate championships.

Another meet recorded to fall was the pole vault. George Munger, of Episcopal Academy, vaulted 11 feet 8¼ inches, erasing the mark made in 1925 by Barney Berlinger, Penn Freshman all-round star, when the latter was in Penn Charter.

Berlinger's vault was 11 feet 1¾ inches, and at the time was considered a great performance.

Since that time Berlinger has cleared 13 feet in the vault. This gives us some idea as to what to expect from Munger in later years. Munger never tried to vault until 1925, and was then just past fifteen years of age. I remember his first attempts, and they were certainly not encouraging. That year he did not get much above nine feet.

Haverford School furnished the all-round star of the meet in Bill Watt, who, besides lowering a twenty-four-year-old record for the meet in the quarter mile in doing 52 seconds, won the low hurdles and broad jump, and tied for fourth in the high jump.

This all-round part of the meet I do not like. I think two events are plenty for any school boy to enter, and I would be for discouraging any trophy given for the greatest number of points.

'BING' MILLER TAKES FOURTH PLACE IN AMERICAN LEAGUE BATTING

NATIONAL

	G.	A.B.	R.	H.	P.C.
Hornsby, Bos.	39	139	34	58	.417
Picinch, Cin.	31	101	11	40	.396
Douthit, St. L.	46	200	38	74	.370
Ott, N. Y.	33	129	20	47	.364
Bottomley, St. L. . .	45	176	41	64	.364

Leader a year ago today, Harris, Pittsburgh, .419.

AMERICAN

	G.	A.B.	R.	H.	P.C.
Kress, St. L.	41	141	29	54	.383
Fothergill, Det. . . .	38	124	17	45	.363
Ruth, N. Y.	44	147	49	52	.354
MILLER, ATH. . .	32	104	13	36	.346
Fonseca, Cleve.	36	142	21	49	.345

Leader a year ago today, Gehrig, New York, .416.

Sandlot Scribbles

PENWAY A. C., a fast traveling 18-20-year-old team, wants to arrange games with clubs having grounds in Pennsylvania and New Jersey. Charles Miller, 1101 N. Union st.

———

GIRARD B. C. wants to hear from 14-16-year-old clubs for games at home or away. Lawrence Hefferan, 2536 Ellsworth st.

———

DELPARK A. C., a first class traveling team, would like to book games with clubs in Pennsylvania, New Jersey and Delaware. James McGinley, 3845 N. 10th st.

———

ST. GEORGE'S M. C. wishes games at home with first class teams. Fred Wagner, 2826 E. Venango st.

———

GERMANTOWN B. C., junior team, would like to schedule games with 13-16-year-old clubs. Teams wishing to join base ball league should get in touch with C. T. Arnold, 25 W. Penn st. Phone Germantown 7617.

———

ATHLETIC JUNIORS, a 13-16-year-old team wants games. Mr. Clapp, phone Fox Chase 1991-J.

———

ACE ball team, of North Philadelphia, would like to arrange games with first class teams in Pennsylvania and New Jersey. J. H. Skillam, 2320 N. 13th st.

———

SHAMROCK B. C., a 13-15-year-old club, wants Sunday and twilight games at home or away. James Bradley, 2413 Pine st. Phone Locust 5786.

———

TULPEHOCKEN REDS would like to hear from first class amateur clubs. J. R. Henk, phone Wyoming 2731-W, after 6 P. M.

CUP TEAM READY TO SAIL

Victorious American Tennis Players Go Abroad Saturday

(By Associated Press)

Chicago, June 4.—The long trail which they must travel to recapture the golden fleece of lawn tennis, now stretches to Europe for Captain "Big Bill" Tilden and his American Davis Cup team.

Their last barrier in the West and Far East was brushed aside with ease over the week-end when they met and encountered Japan's team, five matches to nothing on the Chicago Town and Tennis Club's courts. They will sail for Europe Saturday, where they will meet the European zone winner for the right to challenge France, holder of the Davis Cup, emblematic of international tennis supremacy.

The victory over Japan's aces marked the third grand slam in as many tests for Davis Cup play for the Americans. They previously had defeated China and Mexico. Japan entered the American zone finals by conquering Cuba and Canada.

HELEN WILLS WINS FRENCH NET TITLE

American Tennis Champion Easily Defeats Eileen Bennet, England, in Final

COCHET BEATS LACOSTE

(By Associated Press)

Auteuil, France, June 4.—Helen Wills today won her first big tournament of 1928, defeating Eileen Bennett, of England, 6-1, 6-2, in the final for the French tennis championship.

The American champion won the deciding match as she has previous matches in this tournament with consummate ease, dropping only three games, two of which were on her service.

In the entire tournament including the final, she lost but thirteen games and never was forced to extra sets.

14

Henry Cochet won the men's singles championship by defeating his countryman Rene Lacoste, 5-7, 6-3, 6-1, 6-3.

Cochet's victory was something of an upset, as Lacoste, who holds the championship of France and the United States, was a popular favorite before the match.

Cochet, however, had one of his inspired days and played unbeatable tennis after dropping the first set. In the last three sets he kept Lacoste constantly on the run with trap shots and sharply angled returns.

A drizzling rain throughout the morning cleared up about an hour before the match. The weather, however, was heavy and humid and not the slightest breeze relieved the dampness.

Miss Wills started off by winning her service after the game had gone to deuce. Both girls were stroking carefully and using little pace, content to keep the ball in play.

The Californian made it 2-0 in games by capturing Miss Bennett's service with ease. On her next service Miss Wills speeded up her game, adding more power to her strokes. Neither girl had come up to the net as yet. Stroking hard and deep, Miss Wills won her service again and broke through Miss Bennett's, making the score 4-0.

The fifth game was marked by long rallies, both players standing on the baseline and exchanging hard drives to the corners. Helen finally lost her service on a net and an out, giving Miss Bennett her first game of the match. Miss Bennett was not paying particular attention to Helen's backhand, but Miss Wills came back strong in the next two games and ran them off for the score. The point score:

Helen opened the second set by sweeping Miss Bennett's service at love. But the English girl rallied to break Helen's own service with loss of only one point, twice passing the American with severe shots along the side lines.

Continuing her rally in the third game, Miss Bennett attacked resolutely and for a time held the offensive, but she finally lost her service after the score had gone to deuce three times.

Miss Wills then led, two games to one, and from then on the issue was not in doubt, although Miss Bennett rallied again to win her service in the deuced seventh game.

FIRST SET

| Miss Wills | 5 | 4 | 4 | 4 | 3 | 4 | 4—38—6 |
| Miss Bennett | 3 | 2 | 1 | 1 | 5 | 2 | 2—16—1 |

First Set
STROKE ANALYSIS

	A.	P.	N.	O.	D.F.	E.P.	E.
Miss Wills	0	3	3	9	0	3	12
Miss Bennett	0	4	10	12	3	4	25

Second Set
POINT SCORE

									P.	G.
Miss Wills	4	1	7	6	6	4	3	4—35	6
Miss Bennett	0	4	5	4	4	1	5	1—24	2

STROKE ANALYSIS

	A.	P.	N.	O.	D.F.	E.P.	E.
Miss Wills	0	12	10	11	0	12	21
Miss Bennett	0	3	14	7	2	3	23

Meeting his fellow "musketeer," Cochet, in the final for the men's singles, Lacoste got away to a good start by winning the first set, 7-5.

Games went with service until Lacoste and Cochet stood at 5-all, when Lacoste broke through for the set. Lacoste was pegging continually to Cochet's backhand, his deep shots preventing Cochet from coming up to the net. When the latter succeeded in making the game a volleying one, he scored many points on placements.

ILLINOIS TENNIS STARTS

Japanese and Chinese Enter State Title Meet
(By Associated Press)

Chicago, June 4.—Tinged with an international aspect, the annual Illinois State tennis championships were to open today on the River Forest Tennis Club courts.

Heading the largest list of entries in the tournament's history were Tamio Abe, of Japan, and Paul Kong and Gordon Lum, of the Chinese Davis Cup team. Several Western stars also were entered.

WASHINGTON LANDS NEW STAR IN KENNA

Brilliant Young Catcher from Minneapolis Rated Best in Minor Leagues

GRIFFITH GOT HIM CHEAP

BY JOHN B. FOSTER

While the Washington club is languishing in the cellar of the American League, it is nevertheless true it is the most fortunate club in the major leagues as the June campaign gets under way.

Clark Griffith, the Washington owner, at some time must have been a good friend to Mike Kelly, manager of the Minneapolis ball club, because "Griff" has succeeded in luring Kenna, a young catcher, from the team.

Kenna, it should be said without further hesitation, appeared in the early spring to be the best minor league catcher in base ball. He has the smarter requisites that any catcher must have to make the top of his specialty. If he moves on, as he should, with what nature has given him, he will be the best catcher in the American League within two seasons.

Kenna's arm is good, his judgment is fine and he has been well schooled by some one, maybe Mike Kelly, who knows quite a lot about base ball. Kenna has the oldest head on any young catcher—young being used in the sense of major league experience—who has been obtained by a big league club since Muddy Ruel began to show what he had in him. If Kenna proves to be another Ruel, what a fortunate owner Griffith is —proceeding from one good catcher to another.

Kenna batted .340 for Minneapolis in 1927. That should make him easily a .300 batter in major league base ball. He was on the heels of a group of batters, some of whom had been in the major leagues. Joe Hauser batted .353 last year for Kansas City. Hauser had been a major leaguer with the Athletics, while Kenna never has been. That is why Kenna's showing as a batter is particularly impressive.

But getting back to the skill of the young man as a catcher, there is no doubt that the Washington team has made a ten strike if Kenna has not developed any physical defect. Any club in either major league could have used this ball player.

STAGE GOSSIP

"Is your understudy a true friend, do you think?"
"Well, she's always ready to take my part."

RAIN HALTS TENNIS

Sears Cup Tryouts and Girls' Championships Tomorrow

The Sears Cup tryouts and the opening of the Philadelphia and district girls' tennis championships, both scheduled for today at the Cricket Club, St. Martins, were postponed until tomorrow because of the rain.

Singles in the girls' championship tourney will begin at St. Martins at two o'clock tomorrow. Doubles will start on Wednesday.

Miss Virginia Hilleary, winner of the championship in 1925 and '26 and runner-up to Miss Anne Page, of Merion, last year for the title, is playing in the girls' tourney for the final time. Miss Page is no longer eligible for the juniors' event.

The draw:

SECOND ROUND (Bye in First Round)

K. Wiener, Germantown, vs. Margaret Ullom, Germantown.
Josephine Doughton vs. Anne Parry, Germantown.
Katharine Griddel vs. winner Collier-Penrose match.

FIRST ROUND

Margaret Collier, Cricket Club, vs. B. Penrose, Cricket Club.

D. E. Parry, Germantown, vs. Bodine Moon, Cricket Club.

Frances Le Boutillier vs. Margaret Mattson, Germantown.

Virginia Hilleary, Cricket Club, vs. Charlotte Humphrey, Cricket Club. Peggy Fassit, Cricket Club, vs. E. Meyers.

Dorothy Bullitt, Cricket Club, vs. Anne Hammett, Cricket Club.

Nona Martin, Cricket Club, vs. Betty Tausig, Cricket Club.

SECOND ROUND (Bye in First Round)

Rose Hofkin, Woodford, vs. Frances Sadtler, Cricket Club. Christine Hamilton, Cricket Club, vs. Helen Kirk.

SHADOWS AND SUCCESS

Success seems to be like one's shadow, says a commentator in Farm and Fireside. Chase it and it flees away.

SHIFT CREWS FOR 'NAVY DAY' RACES

Bachelors, Pennacs and Undine Make Changes— Senior Four Contest Will Feature Regatta

HOOVER TRIES DOUBLES

With less than two weeks remaining before the Navy Day Regatta on the Schuylkill, June 16, numerous shifts in crews have been made by Bachelors Barge Club, Penn Athletic Club and Undine Barge Club.

The outstanding race in the regatta will be senior fours. The Bachelors four is credited with three races this year, but the Pennsylvania Barge crew has not shown its power because it failed to start in two races in the Henley. The contest between these crews on Navy Day will be a fight to the finish and the winner will be the foremost Olympic prospect.

Charles Karle and Harold Wilson, who formerly rowed together, will stroke the rival crews. The Penn Barge shell will contain Bayer, Healis, Miller and Karle. The Bachelors have Wheeler, Hensell, Callahan and Wilson.

Charles Karle

The seating of the Penn Barge four has not been changed since Healis entered the crew three weeks ago. The Bachelors have shifted around several times and Coach Hartman has tried out each man at stroke. The Bachelor four now is a smooth working machine.

Coach Sam Hunter has confidence in his four. He asserts there is no significance in the fact they were late getting to the starting line and missed two races in the Henley and he declares they will have plenty of speed on June 16. Karle and Miller, the "supermen," also will race in pair-oared shells.

———

Twenty-nine races are listed for the Navy Day Regatta. Some oarsmen think this is too many and a few are likely to be eliminated because of lack of entries.

———

Harold Wilson

The Bachelors Barge Club have fourteen prospective entries and lead the list. Their crews will be: Junior, eight, junior four gig, senior four, senior eight, senior single and $\frac{1}{4}$-mile dash, senior and junior doubles, senior squad, senior 150-pound single, association single, intermediate single, intermediate double and junior single gig. Bachelors have won nine races out of ten starts in two regattas this year.

Walter M. Hoover has started to row senior doubles with Charles "Sparky" Coulston. They have been on the water only a few times, but if they get going well they will enter the Navy Day races. Hoover also continues to train for singles and again will oppose Ken Myers who beat him in the Henley.

———

Ken Myers is sculling better than any time in his career and his friends have confidence he will represent the United States in single sculls at Amsterdam. This week he will race with W. E. Garrett Gilmore and Emanuel McGreel to determine who will represent the Bachelors in the dash. Myers will enter singles while Gilmore and McGreel will race in doubles.

———

Bachelor oarsmen will be permitted to race only twice on Navy Day. Coach Hartman contends more than three races in one day may injure the oarsman.

———

Penn Athletic Club has disbanded its senior eight, following its defeat in the Henley by the Bachelors. No other senior eight may be entered on Navy Day.

———

Bud Johnson, powerful and handsome stroke, is trying the pair-oared shell with Lew Johnson. Both are good sweeps but they may find they are starting too late for Karle and Miller.

———

Costello and McIlvaine are rowing senior doubles. Coach Juvenal has Al Vogt at singles and Algernon Fitzpatrick for the dash. There will be a junior eight squad, four-oared gig, single and several other crews which are in the process of formation. ———

"Babe" McNichol again will stroke West Catholic High in the interscholastic race. An effort is being made to find a stroke seat for McNichol in a Pennac crew, rowing the same day. ———

Sid Jelinek, former Penn varsity oarsman, has returned to the Bachelors. Cornog, who rowed in the Red and Blue victorious 150-pound eight, also is back. Welsford, Gerhardt,

Gilmore, Jelinek and Wilson, now in the Bachelor squad, are former Olympic oarsmen.

———

Tom Loefler, former Vesper oarsman, has joined the Bachelors and is stroking the light four containing Cornog, Welsford and Dinsmore. Switzer has switched from the heavy four to association singles. Dinsmore is training for 150-pound singles, Galbraith is in intermediate singles and the same sculler is with Lyford in doubles. Stoll has the work boat and Mancuso may stroke the junior eight, which will contain several Germantown Academy oarsmen.

———

Coach Sam Hunter finds that his launch is too slow for Penn Barge crews or the crews are too fast for the boat. John Schmitt and Paul McDowell are rowing pair-oared without coxswain and Dave Grubb and Tony Smith have the junior double. Jim Boyd will be the entrant in intermediate singles and the junior squad consists of Rhoades, Marick, Heiderer and Hone, bow. ———

The Penn Barge light four contains Monahan, bow; Grubb, Cassidy and McKay, stroke. The junior eight seats Jimmy Ismay, bow; Smith, Byrd, Ruelius, Waltrick, Mendenhall, Scheel, Olsen, stroke, and Fischle, cox. The stern four will be entered in the junior gig race.

———

The Clark twins are being counted upon by Coach Graef to win the lightweight double race for Undine Barge Club. The junior eight, which has not been definitely picked, seats North, Leonard, Wood, McFeeters, Gowan, Kink, Glick, Sweizer, stroke, and Choat, cox. A half dozen junior scullers will race to decide who will be entered in junior singles, junior gig and junior doubles.

———

YELLE NEW DES MOINES PILOT
(By Associated Press)

Des Moines, Ia., June 4.—Archie Yelle, veteran catcher, was appointed acting manager of the Des Moines Western League base ball team today, following the resignation of L. J. (Danny) Boone, infielder. Yelle played with the Detroit Tigers from 1917 to 1919, and since has been with the San Francisco and Portland clubs in the Pacific Coast League.

BOXER HAS FRACTURED SKULL
(By Associated Press)

Allentown, Pa., June 4.—Johnny Leonard, local junior light-weight boxer, is in the Allentown Hospital here with a fracture of the skull, the result of a knockout at the hands of Bobby Brady in the eleventh round of a bout in Jersey City two weeks ago.

P. M. C. SURPRISES ARMY IN POLO GAME

Cadets, Viewed by Secretary Hughes and Commander Byrd, Easily Defeat West Point 9–2

THEIR PONIES 'STOOD UP'

By Earl Eby

The one-sided victory of the Pennsylvania Military College polo team over the United States Military Academy at Chester on Saturday undoubtedly spread considerable consternation among the various teams which will compete in the outdoor intercollegiate polo championships at Rye, N. Y., June 16. Gaining momentum as the game grew older, the Chester Cadets trounced the West Pointers, 9 to 2.

Colonel Frank Hyatt's charges startled the Eastern polo fans several months ago by clinching the indoor intercollegiate championship. But when the outdoor season rolled around Colonel Hyatt and other P. M. C. officials were rather reluctant to venture an opinion on the chances of the Cadets in the outdoor game.

The question of mounts resided in the minds of the P. M. C. devotees. The cadets would be handicapped at Rye, they thought, when they bumped up against the fast, well-trained ponies the Princeton and Yale teams would ride on the field. Then there was the superb horsemanship of West Point also with which to contend.

But the contest Saturday relieved the minds of those who hold the Pennsylvania Military College close to their hearts— the P. M. C. riders outplayed the Army poloists in every department of the game. The good ponies were divided. That is, an Army man rode a good pony one chukker and in another, a P. M. C. man would get it. Of course, the Chester cadets were more familiar with the mounts, but that advantage did not amount to a 9 to 2 score.

In one chukker, Chick Bower, who was playing No. 3 for the Cadets, had a mount who deliberately sat down on two occasions.

Shortly after the outdoor season started P. M. C. was beaten badly by Princeton. It was right after that game that Colonel Hyatt regarded the Cadets' chances in the forthcoming intercollegiates as rather slim. But after that contest the Cadets took a turn for the better and began to win games. They reached the top of their form Saturday, which if they can hold, will make them the most formidable entry in the college tournament.

The game Saturday was colorful in itself, but it was made more colorful by the presence of Secretary Charles E. Hughes and Commander Richard E. Byrd, who sat in a box and watched the Chester players. Secretary Hughes remarked in his talk that P. M. C. deserved praise in being able to cope with a team of a much larger institution.

Chick Bower was the star as far as the Cadets were concerned. He drove the white ball through the posts four times. Danny Jones, No. 4, was always dangerous. Danny scored two goals and might have chalked up two more had he not been hitting so hard. Jones is a slashing player. Once he is right he is a dangerous man with a mallet.

The other two players, Whitehurst, No. 1, and Schaffhauser, No. 2, each tallied once, while one of the ponies kindly kicked in the ninth goal for the Cadets. It must have been a great consolation to Colonel Hyatt to know that his ponies were working for him, too.

'WATCH GERMANY' GLANCY'S WARNING ABOUT OLYMPIC SWIMMING MEET

Champion Optimistic Over America's Chances, But Expects Teutons to be 'Big Surprise'—Picks Japs as Keen Rivals

"Watch Germany."

That's Harry Glancy's warning and prediction about the swimming competition in the forthcoming Olympic games to be held in Amsterdam this summer.

Glancy, who is making his home in Philadelphia, will wear the colors of the Penn Athletic Club at the Olympic swimming trials in Detroit next week. He was a member of the American world champion relay swimming team that toured the Orient last year and competed in the Pan-Pacific games in Tokio.

A broad-shouldered, powerful young man, said by experts to be one of the finest crawl stroke swimmers in the country, Glancy is optimistic about America's chances in the Olympic, but expects Germany to be the big surprise.

———

"Germany has been training athletes of all kinds since the war, and this will be the first chance for them to show how good they are," he said. "Very few of their stars are known to America except one or two runners, but I know they are training some crack swimmers and great divers.

———

COMPETITION IN SPRINT RACES

"In sprint races America will be given plenty of competition, but there will not be any real contenders for first place. In water polo France or Belgium should win, but here, again, the Germans may spring a big surprise.

"The best race should be the 100-metre free style. It will bring into competition Johnny Weismuller, Walter Laufer, George Kojac, of Rutgers; Paul Sampson, of the University of Michigan; Katso Takashi, of Japan; Paul Jones, of Australia, and Troila, of Sweden. Weismuller should win, but Takashi has shown remarkable speed. It wouldn't surprise me if the Jap pushed Weismuller to a new world record.

"At the Pan-Pacific games in Tokio last October Takashi beat Laufer by a yard. Takashi has the greatest finish sprint I have ever seen. He cuts through the water with a powerful crawl and when he is within twenty yards of the finish summons up a reserve power that is astonishing. In the last Olympics, while hardly more than a novice, Takashi finished fourth, but he has improved so much that Weismuller is going to have tough going to pull away from him.

"Paul Jones has been credited with some excellent time in Australia, but he has never taken part in international competition. He may show up great in the Olympics, but I don't figure him for a winner. America should take first, third and fourth places. Laufer has been doing some fine swimming in Chicago, but he is not good enough to beat Takashi.

"America will be seriously handicapped in the 400-metre free style, as Johnny Weismuller will not compete in this event, it is said. He will be saved for the relay races and water polo, because of his speed and agility in the water.

"Arne Borg, of Sweden, will be the class of this event. But in this race again there will be lots of competition for the other four places. Albert Zorilla, of the Argentine, who has been swimming for the New York A. C., but who will compete as a member of the Argentine team, has been swimming around world record time. 'Buster' Crabbe, of Honolulu, will be another leader, and 'Boy' Charlton, of Australia, has to be counted in.

"I may place in this race; in fact, if I get going right at the trials and can keep in good shape until the race, I may be able to fight for Borg's first place. I have defeated Takashi and made the fourth fastest quarter mile ever recorded. I think if I could make the same speed at the Olympic that I did against Takashi, I can beat Borg. Takashi pushed me to the record, and if the race is close enough, I think I can summon up more reserve power than these other fellows can and beat them."

1,500 METERS BETWEEN FOUR MEN

"The 1,500 meters is between four men, Arne Borg, Charlton, Crabbe and a newcomer, Ray Ruddy, the son of old Joe Ruddy of the New York A. C. In 1924 Charlton beat Borg, but since then Borg has beaten Charlton's time, and Crabbe has come to within five seconds of Borg's time.

"Crabbe may be the big surprise in this race. He is not counted on as a winner, but he is the youngest entrant and has the best stroke. He, too, is a strong finisher, and may prove to be the deciding factor in the race.

"There will be no foreign competition in the 100-meter back stroke unless Bliss, of Belgium, springs a surprise. I look for Kojac, Laufer, George Young, of Georgia Tech.; George Fissler, of the New York A. C., and maybe Paul Wyatt, of Uniontown, to be the main contenders. Laufer is the indoor champion and Kojac is the outdoor champion.

"The conditions of the race seem to favor Kojac, but if Wyatt can get in shape in time he will be a foremost contender. Wyatt was injured in a motor accident in his tome town a few months ago. He was the national champion in 1926, and was second in the 1924 Olympics in Paris. Bliss was third in the same race, and there are several Japanese who have shown great promise in the back stroke. But I don't think any of them are near Wyatt's class for speed or Kojac's class for endurance.

—————

"The divers will have the same tough opponent this year they had in 1924—Eve, of Australia. Then the Finns are always keen contenders for diving honors. Pinkston, of the American team, was a winner in the 1920 Olympics at Antwerp, but he has fallen back greatly, and can hardly be counted on as a serious contender. The fancy diving should go to Pete Des Jardins, of Miami, Fla., with 'Dutch' Smith and 'Mickey' Riley, of the Los Angeles A. C., right up with him.

—————

RINGLER SPLENDID DIVER

"Eve, I am told, may not compete this year, but he has given no notice of the fact himself, so I think it's just as well to realize that there is tough competition, and be ready for it.

"Herman Ringler, of the Penn A. C., the eighteen-year-old phenom, may show some tricks that the big-timers haven't seen yet. He has a marvelous style and is as graceful as the swan he imitates in his diving. The tryouts for the divers will be in San Francisco and Herman thinks he can make the team. I am sure of it.

"The best race of the meet will be the 800-meter relay. Our team in the Pacific of Weismuller, Laufer, Kojac and myself made the new world record of 2.20 1-5. But I think we are going to have serious work making the team this year. Sampson is showing great form and Albert Swartz, of Northwestern University, is another tough swimmer to beat. Some of the Argentine fellows are swimming 200 meters in 2.20 and 2.25 and this is exceptionally good time.

"America's foremost rival will be the crack Japanese aggregation. Swimming anchor will probably be Takashi with Arai, Nado and Sato as the first three men. They are remarkable swimmers and Arai has marvelous form. I feel certain these fellows have improved greatly since the Pan-Pacific games and may give us a tough battle. I swam against Arai and he made me hang up a new record for the relay lap.

"Sweden will bid for third place, with Australia and Germany as the others. I mention Germany, at the end, but I really don't know what they will do. It may be that they will fight with us for first place. They have a diver named Mund who won the European championship in 1926 and who came to Honolulu in 1927 to compete, but he twisted his back while practising and could not take part, but I am told he is the greatest diver in Europe.

———

"The water polo team to represent the United States may be the winner of the Chicago A. A. and Illinois A. C. playoff. Weismuller's Illinois A. C. team was playing against Chicago and walked out of the tank on a referee's decision, but at the time Chicago was leading by one point. Heretofore, the teams have been selected from among the foremost water polo players of the country but this method is not successful. The National Swimming Committee has suggested that these two teams play off the match again and the winner be sent to the Olympics. That's probably the only way we could get a good enough team to make any serious bid for the international honors."

GLANCY WITH 1924 TEAM

Glancy is twenty-three, and is in the oil business. He was graduated from Mercersburg Academy and attended the University of Cincinnati Law School. He was runner up to Crabbe in the one-mile swim and to Weismuller in the quarter and half-mile events. He was captain of the American swimming team in the Orient and was a member of the winning relay team in the 1924 Olympics.

While touring the Orient, Glancy married Irma Mae Lucas, of Covington, Ky., who was one of the outstanding women members of the team. She was the first white woman to compete in Japan and won several of the spring races for women.

APPROPRIATE

"Can you suggest a suitable course for a golf dinner?"
"Something with about eighteen holes? Try Swiss cheese."

POSTPONE BOXING SHOW

Elks' Ball Park Opening Halted by Rain—Put off to Tomorrow

The opening outdoor boxing show of the season, scheduled at the Elks' ball park, 48th and Spruce sts., tonight, was called off at noon today by Promoter Al Nash.

The program of five bouts will be held tomorrow evening, weather permitting.

Henri de Wenker, of France, and Joey Hadfield, of Conshohocken, principals in the ten-round windup, and the other eight boxers on the card, will be weighed officially at 2 P. M. tomorrow at the Arcadia gym. The other scheduled bouts are: Jean Mengeot, France, vs. Eddie Dempsey, South Philly, ten rounds;

Joe Bashara, Norfolk, Va., vs. Battling Willard, Lancaster, ten rounds; Tommy Gleason vs. Joe Parker, four rounds, and Erwin Baus vs. Jimmy De Marco, four rounds.

Thirty-six rounds of boxing are booked for the Broadway A. C. Thursday, with Al Gordon and Young Jack Gallagher as the principals of the cast of ten glovesters. They meet in the eight-round headliner. Harry Kid Wallace meets Teddy Martin and Eddie Reed tackles Joe (Kid) Firpo in other eight-rounders.

Two six-rounders open the show, as follows: Paulie Walker vs. Bobby Wallace and Herb Brandow vs. Joe Britt.

NAME COMMITTEES FOR COBB'S CREEK

Chairman Selects Men Who Will Handle Detail of Public Links Golf Championship

CORSON INSPECTS LINKS

By J. E. Ford

With the selection of the committees by the chairman last week, preparations for the national public links golf championship at Cobb's Creek beginning July 31 entered the later stages of completion.

Charles Todd, the tournament committee chairman, has named the longest list of assistants. It includes C. Emerson Brown, Harry Krug, Charles McGregor, John Haire, Frank Boyd, Cecil Culver, Dr. Benjamin Benedict, Howard Coughlin, Jack Stoeckle and Dick Egan.

The registration committee of which Horace Cannon is chairman is composed of F. A. Francis, William R. Russell and D. F. McLarty. Earl Shaw, who heads the transportation body, has named Frank N. Barnett, John P. Rudissil and William N. Hirsh as assistants. These men, with the addition of D. P. Polk, have been selected by I. Goldberg for the entertainment body.

Alfred E. Hand, chairman of the caddy and green bodies, will undertake the entire duties of these committees himself.

Conditioning of the Cobb's Creek links for the championship is progressing steadily. Alan Corson, chief engineer of the Park Commission, recently made an inspection tour of the course with A. H. Smith and J. Franklin Meehan, two of the original designers of the links, and E. D. Mendell, general chairman of the tournament. The purpose of the inspection was to decide upon certain improvements, particularly the locating of grass tees that will be used during the championship.

---

2 LANSDOWNE BOYS ON DISTRICT TEAM

Haseltine and Loughlin Logical Players to Represent Middle States in Tennis Tourney

PENN CHARTER JR. CHAMPS

INTERSCHOLASTIC LEAGUE

SCHOOL	Points Won	Points Lost
Lansdowne High School	44	10
Penn Charter School	49	16
Germantown High School	40	15
Central High School	35	15
Camden High School	35	15
Lower Merion High School	35	20
Simon Gratz School	31	34
Overbrook High School	29	21
West Catholic High School	25	39
West Philadelphia High School ..	22	23
Germantown Academy	18	37
Frankford High School	13	47
Northeast High School	5	45
Catholic High School	3	47

JUNIOR INTERACADEMIC LEAGUE

SCHOOL	Points Won	Points Lost
Penn Charter School	15	4
Germantown Academy	11	7
Episcopal Academy	3	9
Haverford School	2	10

———

By Dr. Clinton A. Strong

Chairman of Jr. Tennis, Middle States Tennis Association, President of Philadelphia Interscholastic Tennis League.

Though a number of matches were played in the Interscholastic Tennis League last week, nevertheless it will take most of this week to clean up and settle the final standing.

Penn Charter won the Junior Interacademic championship last Saturday for the thirteenth consecutive year, when in a postponed match, Dixon Spangler, Penn Charter, gave Rotan Sargent, Haverford, winner of the recent boy's tournament, his first defeat of the season, 3-6, 6-4, 6-2.

The singles championships for the cups offered by the Harvard Alumni of Philadelphia to players in the Interacademic League, have been determined. William Condon, Penn Charter, won the Senior cup, meeting the stiffest opposition in the finals where he defeated Jack Pillard, of Episcopal, 6-1, 6-4, 17-19,

Fred Storck, of Penn Charter, won the Junior cup, eliminat-7-5.

ing William Tilden, 3d, Germantown Academy, in the semi-finals, 6-4, 3-6, 6-3 and defeating Dixon Spangler, Penn Charter, in the finals, 4-6, 6-1, 6-4.

Early in the week William Haseltine, Lansdowne, defeated Fred Roll, Abington, for the Middle States Junior title, 4-6, 6-2, 6-3, 6-0, and Rotan Sargent, Haverford, and Clothier Jones, Episcopal, won the boys' doubles championship from Spangler, Penn Charter, and Tilden, Germantown Academy, 6-3, 1-6, 6-3.

The tryouts for the Middle States Junior team to play the Juniors of the Eastern and New England Associations at New Haven, Conn., June 8th and 9th, have been in progress during the past two weeks.

The following were the most promising candidates in the competition: Bertram Claster, Harrisburg Academy, junior champion of the Harrisburg district; William Haseltine, Lansdowne High, Middle States junior champion; Elliott Loughlin, Lansdowne High, junior champion last year; Fred Roll, Abington High, finalist in Middle States tournament this year; Franklin Kready, Franklin and Marshall Academy, National Boys' doubles champion; William Condon, Penn Charter, finalist Middle States tournament last year; Joseph Case, Lansdowne, junior doubles champion two years; Harry Joslyn, Wilmington High School; Frank O'Neill and Paul Langner, of the Penn Fresh team, and Paul Wells, captain of Germantown High. William O'Loughlin, Jr., champion of the Pittsburgh district, was invited to enter the competition but as yet has not accepted.

Tomorrow Kready and Condon will play, and on Wednesday, Loughlin and Case will play Haseltine and Condon in doubles. If O'Loughlin does not enter the competition and since Roll will remain to participate in the graduating exercises of his class, the logical make-up of the team seems to be Claster, Haseltine, Loughlin, Kready, Condon, Case.

MRS. KIND RETAINS TITLE

Beats Marjorie Bissinger in Final of Philmont Tennis Tourney

Mrs. Philip Kind, captain of the Philmont Country Club women's tennis team, retained the singles championship of the club when she defeated Marjorie Bissinger, 3-6, 8-6, 8-6, yesterday.

Mrs. Kind is sailing for Europe Friday. She expects to play in tournaments abroad.

RAIN HALTS PHILLIES

Game With St. Louis at Baker Bowl Today Is Postponed

This afternoon's scheduled game between the Phillies and the St. Louis Cardinals was called off shortly before noon today because of rain.

The game will be played as part of a double header tomorrow, the Phils' management announced.

RACING RESULTS
At Belmont Park, N. Y.

FIRST RACE—The Jamesport claiming, 3-year-olds up, mile:

	Straight.	Place.	Show
1—Effie, 101 (P. Goodwin)	8-1	4-1	2-1
2—Friedjof Nansen, 114 (J. Bollero)...		5-1	5-2
3—King Jimmy, 119 (K. Force)	...	...	6-1

Time—1.40 1-5.

Temeraire Manchu, Blockhead, Mosque, Black Bart, Lanyard, Harass, Captain Martin, Supersede, Valentino, Larock, Fire Wacth, Stiff Shirt also ran.

WEEK-END SPORTS RESULTS

SATURDAY
BASE BALL
WESTERN CONFERENCE
Ohio State 6, Michigan 1.

OTHER COLLEGE GAMES
Columbia 14, Penn 3.
Rutgers 18, Swarthmore 6.
Fordham 9, Georgetown 0.
Amherst 2, Wesleyan 1.
Penn State 8, Bucknell 6.
Susquehanna 7, Drexel 4.
Yale 8, Princeton 3.
Holy Cross 6, Harvard 3.
Army 9, Navy 6.
Dartmouth 5, New Hampshire 2.
Lebanon Valley 9, Mt. St. Mary's 6.

HIGH SCHOOL
Rutgers Prep. 13, Montclaire Academy 4.
Central Eve. 11, P. I. D. 6.
National Farm 6, Palmer School 1
Wenonah 10, Pennington 3.
Perkiomen 6, Wyoming Seminary 5.
Point Pleasant 12, Barnegat 2.
Red Bank 19, Alumni 7.
Atlantic City 5, Holy Spirit 4.
Hopewell Jr. 9, Clayton Jr. 2.
Trenton Normal 7, New Brunswick Normal 1.

Blair 6, Peddie 3.
Manlius 19, Oswego Nor. 7.

INDEPENDENT MONTGOMERY COUNTY LEAGUE
Ambler 9, Pottstown 5.
Lansdale 20, Norristown 3.
Perkasie 10, Souderton 6.

INTERBORO LEAGUE
Tully Memorial 11, Folcroft 5.
Glenolden 4, Westinghouse 1.
Darby A. C. 19, Prospect Park 6.
Ridley Park 9, Collingdale 0 (forfeit).

MAIN LINE LEAGUE
Berwyn 6, Ardmore 5.

BURLINGTON CO. LEAGUE
Medford 2, Riverside 0.
Delanco 10, Moorestown 2.
R. D. Wood 3, Vincentown 0.
Burlington 5, Palmyra 0.

PERKIOMEN LEAGUE
Graterford 12, Trooper 11 (11 innings)
Schwenkville 3, Collegeville 1.
Skippack 9, Oaks 3.

NORTH PHILA. CATHOLIC LEAGUE
Assisi 16, Immaculate 7.

PHILA. SUBURBAN LEAGUE

N. E. Shrine 7, Hatboro 3.
Glenside 14, Ft. Washington 5.
Benner 14, Jenkintown 8.

NORTH PHILA. CHURCH LEAGUE

Bethany Baptist 23, Disstonia 0.
St. Philip's 11, Burholme Baptist 3.

BUX-MONT LEAGUE

Jenkintown Moose 11, Willow Grove 7.
Horsham 7, Bridge Valley 2.
New Britain 10, Hatboro 4.

N. E. SUBURBAN LEAGUE

Sheridan C. C. 9, Evergreen 4.
Lawndale 11, Cresentville 9.

PHILA. INDUSTRIAL LEAGUE

Leeds & Northrup 11, Middleshape 5.
Proctor & Schwartz 16, Jefferies & Manz 4.

DELCO CATHOLIC LEAGUE

St. Joseph's 6, Media 5.
C. T. A. 6, Resurrection 5.
Immaculate 16, Laurentius 10.
St. Rose 8, Shamrock 2.

NORTH PENN LEAGUE

North Wales 12, Telford 6.
Hatfield 13, Lansdale 5.
Chalfont 11, Ambler 5.

YORK COUNTY LEAGUE

West York 4, York Haven 3 (12 innings).
North York 12, New Holland 10.
Wrightsville 16, Spring Grove 7.
Girard 7, Mount Wolf 3.

SOUTHERN YORK COUNTY LEAGUE

Stewartstown 16, New Freedom 5.
Glen-Rock 18, Shrewsbury 9.
Loganville 7, Albermarle 6.

GERMANTOWN SUBURBAN LEAGUE

Germantown Artisans 7, Wyndmoor 5.
Conshohocken 4, Mount Airy 3.
Biggans Pros. 7, Lighthouse 3.

OTHER GAMES

Kingsessing 4, Buist Park 3.
Harrowgate 15, Lincoln Giants 2.
Mortimer 14, Eureka Artisans 2.
Elks 7, Kensington Congregational 0.
Roxborough 11, Golden Leaf 8.
Triangle 12, Blue Anchor 2.
McKee's Stars 3, Tacony Pros. 2.
Powell Pros. 6, Chew A. A. 2.
Lancaster 5, Atlantic City Police 0.
Welcome C. C. 18, Westwood 4
Drexel A. A., 17, American A. C. 2.
Camden 11, Lancaster 1.
Corley C. C. 13, Reading Pros. 4.
Cuban Stars 10, Hilldale 9.
Wentz-Olney 14, Dunkirk 5.
Darby Heights 16, Delwyn 5.
Penn A. C. 9, Narberth 8.
State Hospital 8, Aquinas C. C. 3.
Rowan A. C. 7, Chestnut Hill 3.
Northeast Pros. 10, Belfield 6.
Camden P. C. 24, Columbia A. C. 6.
Holmesburg 17, Kaywood C. C. 4.
Chester Fifth Ward 7, Mitchell A. A. 6.
Jeffrey A. C. 2, Chester Eighth Ward 0.
Edison 15, Lebanon Red Sox, 13.
Hershey 9, Myerstown 2.
Christiania 7, Rothsville 3.
Woodstown 4, Camden City Catholic 3.
Shannon A. A. 2, Sacred Heart 1.
Lincoln Giants 12, Kensington Congregational 6 (second game).
Victrix 4, Mount Joy 2.
St. George's M. C. 19, Naborhood 4.
Coatesville 11, Frankford Caseys 5.
Tioga 11, Roslyn 7.
Cliveden Imps. 15, Northeast Pros. 3.
W. Manayunk S. C. 6, Germantown B. C. 5 (11 innings).

TRACK

CENTRAL INTERCOLLEGIATES

Marquette 56, Michigan State 53.

OTHER MEET

Army $84\frac{1}{2}$, Navy $41\frac{1}{2}$.

NORRISTOWN INTERSCHOLASTICS

Suburban

Ridley Park $32\frac{1}{2}$, Lower Merion $29\frac{3}{4}$, Media 18, West Chester $16\frac{1}{2}$, Upper Darby $11\frac{1}{4}$, Abington 16, Norristown $16\frac{1}{2}$, Haverford 10, Swarthmore 9, Glen-Nor 3, Cheltenham $2\frac{1}{2}$

OPEN EVENTS

Germantown 43, Bethlehem 43, Frankford 53½, Lancaster 17½, Coatesville 15½, West Philadelphia 11½, Catholic 8, Du Pont 4, Pitman 3⅔, Lansdale ⅓.

MIDDLE STATES CATHOLIC HIGH SCHOOL CHAMPIONSHIPS

West Catholic 110, North Catholic 34, St. Joseph's 33, La Salle 16, Holy Spirit 1.

SCHUYLKILL COUNTY INTERSCHOLASTICS

Tamaqua 37½, Pottsville 29, Coaldale 23, Minersville 9, Mahanoy City 8½, Shenandoah 6.

CHICAGO INTERSCHOLASTICS

Fort Collins, Col. 56, Froebel High, Gary, Ind. 38, Libbey High, Toledo 26, Tilden Tech, Chicago 26, Blackwell, Oklahoma 22, Cass High, Detroit, 20, Baton Rouge, La. 20.

NEW JERSEY STATE PREP. CHAMPIONSHIPS

Peddie 58½, Lawrenceville 29, St. Benedict's 22.

DELAWARE COUNTY GIRLS' MEET

Haverford High 31, Upper Darby 18½, Lansdowne 11, Radnor 11, Ridley Park 4, Media 1½.

LACROSSE

Army 14, Navy 4.
Swarthmore 9, Lacrosse Club 3.
Peekskill Military Academy 2, Brooklyn Manual Training 1.

POLO

MORRELL CUP PLAY

Phila. Country Club 10, Freebooters 8.
Bryn Mawr 14, Magpies 11.

OTHER GAMES

P. M. C. 9, Army 2.   Yale 5, Harvard 4.

TENNIS

MIDDLE STATES LEAGUE

Division A

University Courts 9, West Jersey 0.

Division B

Idle Hour 6, Greenpoint 3.
Glenside 8, Penn A. C. B. 1.

Division C

Norwood 9, Swarthmore 0.
Phila. and Reading 8, Glenside 1.
Brookline Square 6, University Courts 3.
Greenpoint 6, West Chester 3.

Division D

Frankford 5, Girard Estate 3.
University Courts D. 7, Elberon 2.
Penn Mutual 7, Pharmacists 2.
Phila. & Reading B. 6, Greenpoint C. 3.

INTERCLUB CHAMPIONSHIPS

First Division

Cynwyd 6, Overbrook 0.
Belfield 4, Germantown C. C. 2.
Merion 5, Phila. Cricket Club 1.
Belfield 6, Overbrook 0.
Phila. Cricket Club 6, Germantown C. C. 0.
Cynwyd 3, Merion 3.

Second Division

Germantown C. C. 4, Belfield 2.
Merion 5, Belfield 1.

HIGH SCHOOL MATCHES

Peddie Institute 4, Battin High 1.
Germantown High 4, Girard College 1.
Easton High 5, Bethlehem High 1.
Lansdowne High 3, Central High 2.
Simon Gratz High 4, Catholic High 1.
William Penn High 5, John Harris High 1.
Blair Academy 4, Montclair High 1.

GOLF

Woodbury C. C. 28¾, Oak Valley 2.

SOCCER

EXHIBITION GAMES

Glasgow Rangers 4, Bkln. Wanderers 0.
New Bedford 3, Boston 2.

TRAPSHOOTING

LANSDALE GUN CLUB SHOOT WINNERS

Class A—Keyser, Beaver 73. Class B—
P. A. Jones, Englert, 68. Class C—
Harry Metzger, Isaac Becker. Class
D—Oscar Wilde, Howard Rader.

SUNDAY
BASE BALL

DELCO CATHOLIC LEAGUE

Laurentius 17, C. T. A. 6.
St. Joseph's 18, St. Rose 12.
Shamrock 5, Resurrection 3.

NORTH PHILA. CATHOLIC LEAGUE

St. Benedict's 10, Immaculate 8.
Kirlin 11, Holy Rosary 6.

MONTGOMERY COUNTY LEAGUE

Ambler 9, Norristown 2.
Lansdale 6, Perkasie 3.
Pottstown 6, Souderton 4.

DELAWARE RIVER LEAGUE

Marcus Hook 7, Essington 4.
Aberfoyle 3, Fifth Ward 2.

OTHER GAMES

Gtn. Artisans 7, Benner A. A. 5.
Pleasant Hill 4, Tacony A. A. 3.
St. Barnabas C. C. 7, Kayoula C. C. 0.
Chew A. A. 14, Denmar 7.
Roxborough 6, St. John C. C. 4.
Clearview 14, Northeast Shrine 0.
Bacharach Giants 5, Hilldale 2.
Olympic 8, Golden Leaf 7.
Clementon 8, Northampton 7.
Allentown A. A. 7, Fullerton 4.
Aquinas C. C. 5, St. Callistius 4.
Temperance 12, Amicus 5.
Columbia C. C. 7, St. Charles C. C. 5.
Coplay 12, Macungie 11.
Catasauqua 3, Emaus 2.
Darby A. C. 3, Twentieth Ward 1.
Ephrata 6, Bridesburg 3.
Atlantic City Orioles 18, Somers Pt. 4.

Palmerton 4, Slatington 2.
Maple Shade 11, Collingswood 10.
Tuckerton 6, Lindwood 0.
Eighth Ward, Lancaster 5, Philadelphia
    Tigers 4.
Pennsgrove 3, Millville 1.
Corley 6, Reading Pros. 3.
Edison 11, Rothville 3.
West Lebanon 2, Victrix 0.
Pennsgrove 8, Vineland 2.
Farmers 4, Camden 2 (first game).
Farmers 8, Camden 7 (second game).
Rosemont 7, Sacred Heart 4.
Quaker City 4, Crescentville 1.
Coatesville 5, Merrill Pros. 2.
Phoenixville 4, St. Stanislaus 2.
Moose 12, Darby Heights 4.
Elmer 11, Pleasantville 2.
LaMott 11, Dunkirk 7.
Bushwicks 7, Philadelphia Pros. 4.
Silver Lake 6, Watsontown 5.
Triangle 14, Blue Anchor 9.
Riverton 9, Philco 1.
Twenty-ninth Ward 3, Wyndmoor 0.
Merchantville 9, Browns Mills 4 (first
    game).
Browns Mills 5, Merchantville 1 (sec-
    ond game).
Hayward 4, Philadelphia Elks 3.
Kingsessing 4, Elmtown 1.
Kaywood 5, Holmesburg 4.
Assumption 9, Spring Mills 4.
Wharton C. C. 11, Hizer A. C. 3.
Jolly Rovers 6, Rangers 4.
Cayuga F. C. 10, Comet A. C. 5.

TENNIS

INTERCLUB CHAMPIONSHIPS

Cynwyd 5, Belfield 1.
Merion 5, Germantown 1.
Phila. Cricket Club 6, Overbrook 0.
Cynwyd 6, Germantown |Cricket Club
    0.
Merion 6, Overbrook 0.
Belfield 4, Phila. Cricket Club 2.

SOCCOR

EXHIBITION GAME

Fall River 0, Glasgow Rangers 0.

POLO

Sands Point 11, Meadow Point 7.

CLOSE-UPS ON THE SPORT SCREEN
BY LYNN C. DOYLE

TAKING THE AIR

The open season for trans-oceanic flying is on.
Several planes and an airship already have landed in impromptu manner.

Islanders and camel chauffeurs who never saw a gas buggy before are kept busy ducking propellers now.

If this keeps up the enterprising pilot won't bother to buy a plane at all. He'll just start with a can of gasoline confident that in due time he will find a stranded plane.

Like the Scotchman who told his caddy to find a ball and they'd start.

Seven men roaming about in Alaska, and six tables of bridge on the Italia. And this is vacation time, too.

These airmen are a flighty lot. You can't expect such temperamental boys to chart icebergs all summer without taking some time out.

And who could pick a niftier spot to rest the eyes than in some South Sea isle? Smart chaps, these sky pilots.

SOCKING A LEGEND

Another tradition of base ball busted.
Jimmy Foxx turned the trick without a rabbit's foot.

Any ball player will tell you that a home run that goes foul takes the luck out of a bat. The victim is expected to strike out as a matter of sacred routine.

Playing the White Sox yesterday Jimmy lammed one into the stands that was foul by a horsefeather.

Then he double-crossed tradition. Instead of fanning he belted another ball up in the same stands where not even a White Sox rooter could call it foul.

It isn't often a ball player has to hit eight bases to get four.

———

If Jimmy can continue to play encore performances of home runs like that, they'd better keep him on third base.

———

After a week of marathon dancing the Arena management has decided to stage some more fights.

That's one way of helping the boxing game.

No matter how terrible the fight card is it can't be any worse than the dancing.

Cash customers who have been watching a slow clinch for a week aren't so likely to throw chairs when a couple of preliminary fighters start dancing.

———

As a means of acclimating the fight fan to sour bouts this Marathon dancing stunt has its points.

———

ROSE MARCUS TENNIS VICTOR

———

Rose Marcus is the new champion of the Woodford Courts Girls' Tennis Club.

Miss Marcus sprang a surprise in the club tourney at Strawberry Mansion yesterday when she defeated Rose Hofkin, defending titleholder, 5-7, 6-3, 6-4.

Miss Hofkin is the champion of the Girls' High School and holder of the women's municipal singles title.

THE WEEK'S SCORING

NATIONAL LEAGUE

	Sa.	Su.	M.	T.	W.	T.	F.	T's.
Cincinnati	20	..	..	..	..	..	..	20
Pittsburgh	6	9	..	..	..	..	..	15
Chicago	10	5	..	..	..	..	..	15
New York	4	10	..	..	..	..	..	14
St. Louis	13	..	..	..	..	..	..	13
Brooklyn	6	7	..	..	..	..	..	13
PHILLIES	12	..	..	..	..	..	..	12
Boston	12	..	..	..	..	..	..	12

AMERICAN LEAGUE

	Sa.	Su.	M.	T.	W.	T.	F.	T's.
New York	5	7	..	..	..	..	..	12
Cleveland	6	3	..	..	..	..	..	9
ATHLETICS	3	5	..	..	..	..	..	8
Chicago	2	6	..	..	..	..	..	8
St. Louis	5	..	..	..	..	..	..	5
Detroit	2	2	..	..	..	..	..	4
Boston	0	4	..	..	..	..	..	4
Washington	2	..	..	..	..	..	..	2

INTERNATIONAL LEAGUE

	Sa.	Su.	M.	T.	W.	T.	F.	T's.
Baltimore	5	23	..	..	..	..	..	28
Toronto	15	3	..	..	..	..	..	18
Reading	10	6	..	..	..	..	..	16
Rochester	12	4	..	..	..	..	..	16
Newark	2	11	..	..	..	..	..	13
Montreal	3	6	..	..	..	..	..	9
Buffalo	1	5	..	..	..	..	..	6
Jersey City	1	4	..	..	..	..	..	5

EARNSHAW, MACK'S NEW PITCHER, FAILS IN BIG LEAGUE DEBUT

Chicago Ends A's Winning Streak Despite Foxx's Homer With Two On in 9th Inning—Jimmy Likes to Play Third Base

BY JOHN J. NOLAN

Chicago, June 4.—Next to the whirlwind New York Yankees, the Athletics find the now lowly White Sox the hardest team in the American League to squelch. And the Sox are an especially tough proposition to conquer on their home grounds.

Four times the runners-up to Yanks and the tail-enders have clashed this season and the count stands even at two victories each and every game has been a bitter struggle. Once the A's were victors 2-0, and again 3-2, while the White Sox won in Philadelphia, 6-5 and repeated by the same score before a 20,000 crowd in Comisky Park yesterday.

Alphonse Thomas, the masterful right hander, who curved the A's into submission at Shibe Park was the winner yesterday. Although the Athletics caused their opponents some anxious moments in the ninth when Thomas was routed, Ted Lyons, the ace of the staff, was called in to save the day.

De luxe pitching by Lefty Grove, the strike-out king, has saved the Macks on two occasions. Lefty has an impressive record of allowing the Sox only five hits and two runs in eighteen innings against them and he has fanned twenty-two batters, eleven in each game, to increase his season's strike-out total to sixty-six.

Grove's marvelous chucking and the keen duels the Sox and A's wage are the talk of the league. Here is the Yank's leading opponent, the class of seven other teams in the circuit who can ruthlessly sweep aside most of their rivals, unable to trample over the tail-enders.

None of the base ball sages with the Athletics can account for this phenomenon. They blame it on the White Sox pitching, which has always been hard for the A's to fathom.

Faber, Thomas and Lyons, three of the leading right handers in base ball, can perform feats of legerdemain when they step on the mound against the A's, and one of the Athletics' chuckers is capable of twirling equally as smooth a game.

EARNSHAW MAKES DEBUT

George Earnshaw, erstwhile Swarthmore College athlete, made his major league debut yesterday, but retired after five innings because of lack of control.

This six-foot three right-hander, with the powerful overhand pitching sweep, joined the Athletics last Monday in a trade which sent Bill Shores and Jing Johnson to Baltimore.

Earnshaw was slated to pitch against Boston last Thursday, but the game was rained out. Connie decided to give him a chance yesterday, but Earnshaw was over-anxious and he had spells of wildness which proved costly and ended the A's winning spurt of four straight.

Two out in the ninth inning, with the score 6 to 2 against them, the Athletics uncorked a rally that showed they are passing out gamely these days. Mickey Cochrane started it with a two-bagger to centre field. Then Joe Hauser walked, and rosy-cheeked Jimmy Foxx stepped to the plate. Foxx cracked Thomas' first pitch into the left field stands, but the drive was foul by several feet.

The next pitch was sent soaring into the right field pavilion. This time the ball was foul by inches. Under all the rules of base ball it was Foxx's cue to strike out on the next pitch.

Instead, as Thomas attempted to slip a fast one over the inside corner, Foxx whacked a terrific liner into the lower deck of the left field stands, three runs scoring and young Jimmy registering his fifth circuit slam of the season.

Up came Captain Eddie Collins, pinch-hitting for Hassler, and the former White Sox manager slapped a single. The fans howled in protest and Thomas was hastily removed, while

Ted Lyons came on the scene and forced Orwoll to tap to the pitcher's box for the final out.

Although removed from the box, Earnshaw acted like a big leaguer during his brief regime. He displayed an assortment of curves and blinding speed, almost as paralyzing as the cannon ball pitches of another former Oriole, Lefty Grove. The Sox nicked his curves for four runs, three in the third and one in the fourth. And they added a run each off relief pitchers, Ed Rommel, who pitched two innings and Ossie Orwoll, who twirled the ninth.

Aside from the defeat, the big feature was Jimmy Foxx playing third base. Sammy Hale pulled up with an injured shoulder and Jimmy Dykes replaced him on third.

Foxx entered the game as a pinch-hitter for Dykes in the seventh round and the chunky catcher played a sparkling game at what was considered a new position for him.

But as Jimmy explains—"I always wanted to be a third baseman. In fact, I got my start with Easton, Md., in '24 as a third sacker. One day our catcher got hurt and Frank Baker made me do the receiving. Then two weeks later the A's bought me as a catcher and, with the exception of some outfielding at Providence, I've been a catcher ever since.

"I don't believe I ever enjoyed anything more in base ball than getting a chance to play third base. I was so happy, maybe that's why I socked that home run. I was certainly feeling good."

BLOOMINGTON GETS DANEY

Chief Arthur Lee Whitehorn, otherwise known as Chief Daney, the picturesque Choctaw Indian pitcher, has been sent  by the A's to Bloomington of the Three-Eye League. Daney will report to his new team in Danville tomorrow.

There are reports another of Connie's young pitchers is to be sent to the minors for seasoning and it is probable that Bloomington will also be the team selected.

Daney, who was discovered by Ira Thomas on a scouting trip in Colorado last summer, is a graduate of Haskell Indian Institute. Thomas saw him pitch against Concordia, Kansas, and although the Indian was beaten, he signed him up immediately.

The deal was completed at a conference with Grover B. Helm, president and owner of the Bloomington team. Mr. Helm is a winter resident at the Athletics' spring training quarters, Fort Myers, Florida, and through watching the team's practice took an intense interest in base ball and decided to buy a minor league franchise.

"Connie Mack sent us Johnny Lyons, of Germantown," said Mr. Helm, "and this youngster has already won four and lost two games for us. He's the best right hander in the league, bar none, and he is sure to be back in the majors next season.

"We also have Jeff Emerson, a catcher from Vincentown, N. J., and the battery of Lyons and Emerson is about the most formidable in our league, a speedy class B circuit.

"We are in third place now and I figure Daney and Lyons are the boys to pitch us to a pennant. Lyons, in particular, is one of the most promising young pitchers I have ever seen."

PENN-NAVY CREWS ARRIVE ON HUDSON

Callow Expects Little from Red and Blue Oarsmen in Poughkeepsie Regatta

WON'T PICK A WINNER

Poughkeepsie, N. Y., June 4.—Rusty Callow, University of Pennsylvania rowing coach, has that nonchalance of manner which keeps him young while at the same time any normal being, weighted down with the cares of turning out a winning crew from the more or less meager material which comes to his hands at Pennsylvania would grow old and gray before his time.

Fred Spuhn, Callow's assistant, is a case in point. Spuhn, one of the most likeable fellows that ever handled the coaching reins over a Poughkeepsie entrant, became gray from worry in the two years that he guided Penn's destinies alone before Callow could disengage himself from his contract to take hold of the Quakers.

But although Callow has been running things at the college boathouse on the Schuylkill for the last year, he is as happy and carefree as he was when his Washington crews were making a clean sweep of everything from the Oakland estuary to the Broad Hudson at Poughkeepsie.

Callow and Spuhn arrived in town last night as the vanguard of the Pennsylvania squad, and Callow, without mincing words, made the flat assertion he expected little in the way of honors for his crews and that all he wanted the boys to do was to make a showing that would make them feel that their year's work had not been in vain.

"Our varsity has improved a great deal," said Rusty, "but I'm afraid it hasn't improved enough to be at the top. The freshmen, too, are coming along nicely and I'm well pleased with their recent work. The juniors are a problem and we just hope for the best. But seriously we haven't the material in these crews to get very far. At best all Spuhn and I have been able to do this season is to lay a foundation and try to build up the rowing spirit at the University again.

"Give me a chance to see some of the other crews before asking me who will win, but from what I have heard this California crew is tremendously big and powerful and Washington, too, has another good crew. Everybody knows pretty well what the Eastern crews have done and I'm no better guesser just now than anybody else. The records of the early season races speak for themselves."

The Pennsylvania and Navy squads arrived at Highland within a few hours of each other and were beaten to quarters by Columbia by only a single day. In the past Columbia has enjoyed a week or more of solitary practice on the Hudson before any other crews put in their appearance but Dick Glendon, of the Navy, discovered the tremendous advantage that accrued from a long training period on the Hudson when he was assisting his son, Dick, Jr., at Columbia last year, and luckily got the Navy's permission to bring the Middies here early this year.

Callow, too, wanted to get in a long training siege on the course, which explains the presence of two of Columbia's rivals on the river almost a full week before they would have normally put in an appearance.

MAJOR LEAGUE STANDINGS
NATIONAL

	Won	Lost	Percentage	Cincinnati	New York	St. Louis	Chicago	Brooklyn	Pittsburgh	Boston	PHILLIES
Cincinnati	32	17	.653	..	2	8	7	1	6	5	3
New York	25	16	.610	2	..	3	1	8	2	4	5
St. Louis	27	19	.587	3	1	..	5	2	7	3	6
Chicago	27	21	.563	4	4	4	..	3	6	3	3
Brooklyn	23	21	.523	2	3	2	0	..	3	6	7
Pittsburgh	20	25	.444	4	1	1	7	2	..	3	2
Boston	16	25	.390	1	2	1	1	3	1	..	7
PHILLIES ...	7	33	.175	1	3	0	0	2	0	1	..

AMERICAN

	Won	Lost	Percentage	New York	ATHLETICS	Cleveland	St. Louis	Boston	Detroit	Chicago	Washington
New York	36	8	.818	..	7	2	2	7	6	4	8
ATHLETICS .	26	15	.634	3	..	3	3	7	3	2	5
Cleveland	24	22	.522	1	2	..	5	3	6	4	3
St. Louis	22	23	.489	0	0	6	..	0	5	8	3
Boston	16	23	.410	2	1	2	3	..	2	2	4
Detroit	19	28	.404	0	0	6	4	1	..	6	2
Chicago	17	28	.378	0	2	3	4	1	5	..	2
Washington ...	14	27	.314	2	3	0	2	4	1	2	..

16

YESTERDAY'S RESULTS

NATIONAL LEAGUE—New York, 10, Chicago, 5; Pittsburgh, 9, Brooklyn, 7 (14 innings). Other clubs not scheduled.

AMERICAN LEAGUE—Chicago, 6, Athletics, 5; Boston, 4, Cleveland, 3; New York, 7, Detroit, 2; Washington-St. Louis, rain.

SATURDAY'S RESULTS

NATIONAL LEAGUE—St. Louis, 13, Phillies, 12; Cincinnati, 20, Boston, 12; Brooklyn, 6, New York, 4; Chicago, 10, Pittsburgh, 6.

AMERICAN LEAGUE—Athletics, 3, Chicago, 2; Cleveland, 6, Boston, 0; St. Louis, 5, Washington, 2; New York, 5, Detroit, 2 (ten innings).

TODAY'S SCHEDULE

NATIONAL LEAGUE—St. Louis at Philadelphia; Pittsburgh at Brooklyn; Cincinnati at Boston; Chicago at New York.

American League—Athletics at Chicago; Washington at St. Louis; New York at Detroit; Boston at Cleveland.

MINOR LEAGUE STANDINGS

INTERNATIONAL

	W.	L.	PCT.		W.	L.	PCT.
Toronto ..	26	18	.591	Rochester .	20	20	.500
Montreal ..	19	16	.543	Reading ..	18	20	.474
Buffalo ...	20	19	.513	Baltimore ..	20	25	.444
Newark ...	23	22	.511	Jer. City ..	18	24	.429

AMERICAN ASSOCIATION

	W.	L.	PCT.		W.	L.	PCT.
St. Paul ..	30	20	.600	Toledo	26	21	.553
Kan. City .	28	21	.571	Min'polis ..	27	22	.551
Milwaukee .	28	22	.560	Louisville ..	15	32	.319
Indian'lis ..	26	21	.533	Columbus ..	15	36	.294

SOUTHERN ASSOCIATION

	W.	L.	PCT.		W.	L.	PCT.
Birm'ham .	35	18	.660	Nashville ..	26	25	.510
Memphis ..	29	20	.592	Lit. Rock .	20	30	.400
N. Orleans	26	22	.542	Ch'nooga ..	21	32	.396
Mobile	27	24	.529	Atlanta ...	19	32	.373

EASTERN

	W.	L.	PCT.		W.	L.	PCT.
N. Haven .	25	12	.676	Pittsfield ..	19	21	.475
Provi'nce ..	20	16	.556	Springfi'ld .	16	21	.432
Hartford ..	20	16	.556	Waterb'y .	16	21	.432
Bridgep't ..	19	17	.528	Albany ...	14	25	.359

NEW YORK-PENNSYLVANIA

	W.	L.	PCT.		W.	L.	PCT.
Bingh'ton .	20	12	.625	W.-Barre .	17	17	.500
W'msport .	20	13	.606	York	14	20	.412
Harrisb'g .	19	13	.594	Syra'cuse ..	13	19	.406
Scranton ..	17	16	.515	Elmira	12	22	.353

BLUE RIDGE

	W.	L.	PCT.		W.	L.	PCT.
Hanover ..	14	4	.778	Martinsb'g	10	9	.526
Hagersto'n	12	7	.632	Chambers'g	5	13	.278
Frederick .	10	8	.556	Waynesboro	4	14	.222

EASTERN SHORE

	W.	L.	PCT.		W.	L.	PCT.
Salisbury .	1	0	1.000	Cambridge	0	1	.000
Northam'n	1	0	1.000	Parksley .	0	1	.000
Easton ...	1	0	1.000	Crisfield ..	0	1	.000

YESTERDAY'S RESULTS

INTERNATIONAL LEAGUE—Reading, 6, Jersey City, 4; Baltimore, 18, Newark, 10 (first game); Baltimore, 5, Newark, 1 (second game); Montreal, 6, Buffalo, 5; Rochester, 4, Toronto, 3.

AMERICAN ASSOCIATION—St. Paul, 2, Louisville, 1, (first game, 11 innings); St. Paul, 7, Louisville, 3 (second game); Columbus, 9, Milwaukee, 8 (first game); Columbus, 7, Milwaukee, 6 (second game, 12 innings); Toledo, 8, Kansas

City, 7 (13 innings); Minneapolis, 4, Indianapolis, 3 (first game); Minneapolis, 3, Indianapolis, 0 (second game).

SOUTHERN ASSOCIATION—Mobile, 1, Little Rock, 0; Birmingham, 6, Chattanooga, 4 (first game); Birmingham, 2, Chattanooga, 3 (second game); Atlanta at Nashville, post-poned, rain; New Orleans at Memphis, double-header, post-poned, rain.

EASTERN—Providence, 4, Waterbury, 1; New Haven, 7, Bridgeport, 4; Hartford, 9, Pittsfield, 7 (first game); Pitts-field, 7, Hartford, 5 (second game); Albany, 13; Spring-field, 6 (first game); Albany, 6, Springfield, 3 (second game).

NEW YORK-PENNSYLVANIA—York, 1, Harrisburg, 0; Syracuse, 11, Scranton, 1; Binghamton, 6, Wilkes-Barre, 4; Elmira, 4, Williamsport, 3.

PHILS COME OUT OF HITTING SLUMP

Slam Eighteen Hits of Assorted Sizes, But Still They Manage to Lose

THREE PINCH HOME RUNS

BY HARRY ROBERT

The 5,000 fans up at Baker Bowl Saturday felt like the Phillies had been away and had come home. What did it mat-ter if they lost, since few expected them to win? And what if it was their eighth straight defeat? They looked natural again, furnishing two hours and a half of wild-eyed base ball, the kind you used to see at the Phillies' Park.

They used to go up there for old-time slugging, and they haven't seen much of it this season. Not by the Phillies. For the past few years the Phils banged the ball around the park at a great old rate, and gave the other team all kinds of heart failure. They were usually licked in the end, but they were dangerous to the finish, because they packed a punch. Even if they were usually licked, the crowd had a good time watching them wallop the ball and sending some of the best pitchers reeling off the mound.

This season, until Saturday, the Phils had been hitting like pygmies, averaging about five safeties a day. That sort of stuff didn't drag out but mighty few. The fact that the pitching has been a little better made no difference, for so weak was the punch, the Phils have won only seven games all season.

The Phils said some day they would start hitting so hard the other team might never get them out. And Saturday was the day. The St. Louis Cardinals finally did manage to wash them up, but it took six pitchers to do it, and after putting up two apparently invincible leads, they just squeezed out the victory by 13 to 12.

The Phils spattered eighteen hits off the six pitchers. Two of them were homers, one was a triple and four were doubles. It really did look as if the Cards would never stop them, and they didn't until the Phils had the tying and winning runs on base in the ninth.

The Cards had four home runs, of which two went to Jim Bottomley. Wattie Holm hit one, a pinch homer with the bases full, and Roettger hit the other. Cy Williams and Johnny Schulte, both pinch-hitting, drove the boundary wallops for the Phils.

The Phils leveled a five-run lead by the Cards in the middle of the game, and later, when the Redbirds hung up another advantage of four runs, the Phils got back into the game sufficiently to make the finish thrilling enough to set the fans whooping it up for a win.

For the Phils the hitting of Leach, Hurst and Southern was, encouraging. They've all been in a slump, with the whole team, but Leach Saturday paddled three singles and a triple, Hurst two doubles and a single and Southern three singles.

What ruined the game for the Phils was Sweetland's failure in a relief role. With the Phils two runs ahead, Sweetland relieved Ring with two on and none out in the eighth. He pitched to just five men. He got one out, hit one with a pitched ball and the other three hit home runs.

"If that wasn't the place for a left-hander to go in, I never saw one," said Shotton. "The first two men up, both right-hand batters, got on against my right-hand pitcher, Ring.

The next four men in a row, High, Toporcer, Bottomley and Harper, were all left-hand hitters. The trouble was Sweetland was wild and pitched right in the alley for each hitter. And Holm, who hit for Toporcer, was a pinch-hitter."

WENTZ-OLNEY NINE GETS LEFTY NOLAN

Veteran First Baseman Will Join Charlie Ziehler's Base Ball Club Tomorrow

EDDIE GALLAGHER LOST

BY RAYMOND A. HILL

Lefty Nolan, veteran first baseman, has been signed to play with the Wentz-Olney base ball team. Nolan will make his first appearance under Charlie Ziehler's banner tomorrow night against the Cuban Stars.

One of the best first sackers on the semi-pro lots, Nolan twice had major league trials. Last year he was one of the mainstays of the Kensington team. Only yesterday he helped George Brand's 8th Ward Club take a 5-4 engagement from the Philadelphia Tigers up in Lancaster.

While Ziehler is glad to get hold of Nolan, he is mourning the fact that Eddie Gallagher decided to quit base ball, temporarily at least. The clever little shortstop decided he could not devote as much time as he would like to the game.

This means that Lukens, a regular outfielder, will be tried at shortstop. Lukens can hit the ball and has a wonderful throwing arm. If he fields up to expectations, perhaps Gallagher's loss will be somewhat compensated.

Wentz-Olney also has secured Kearney, third baseman of the Dunkirk Club. Although Dunkirk lost to LaMott uptown yesterday, Kearney delivered three solid smashes that helped in the West Philadelphia team's scoring.

Maybe you'd like to know that—

Eddie Gerner, one of the sweetest left-hand hitters in semi-pro ranks, says Dudley, the new Cuban pitcher of the Philadelphia Tigers, is the best man he's ever battled against.

Lou Schaub has been trying to get Jake Munch to go back with the Camden Club.

Jim Blake forgot to report to Harrowgate last Saturday, leaving Manager Munch worried whether the former West Catholic star has quit the team without notice.

Febby Moore, who hit in about fifty straight ball games last season, did not find his 1928 batting eye until he faced Hilldale last Friday night.

Pud McHenry, West Catholic High coach, is playing with Hayward C. C.

Joe Meiman finally has succeeded in establishing his priority rights to the name Chester, under which his club travels.

Harry Willsman is playing a better game at third than ever before for Corley.

When George Carr left the Lincoln Giants he took the only first baseman's glove with him. Consequently, Rojo has been playing the bag for three days with a catcher's mitt.

MAJOR LEAGUE LEADERS

(By Associated Press)
(Including Games of June 3.)

NATIONAL

Batting—Hornsby, Boston, .417.

Runs—Bottomley, St. Louis, 41.

Runs batted in—Frisch, St. Louis; Wilkins, Chicago; Bissonette, Brooklyn, and Bottomley, St. Louis, 36.

Hits—Douthit, St. Louis, 74.

Doubles—Hornsby, Boston, 16.

Triples—Walker, Cincinnati, 7.

Homers—Wilson, Chicago; Bissonnette, Brooklyn; Bottomley, St. Louis, 9.

Stolen bases—Frisch, St. Louis, 12.

Pitching—Clark, Brooklyn, won 6, lost 1, .857.

AMERICAN

Batting—Kress, St. Louis, .383.

Runs—Ruth, New York, 49.

Runs batted in—Ruth, New York, 49.

Hits—Manush, St. Louis, 61.

Doubles—Speaker, Athletics, 19.

Triples—Rice, Washington, 7.

Homers—Ruth, New York, 19.

Stolen bases—Barrett, Chicago; Sweeney, Detroit, 8.

Pitching—Pipgras, New York, won 9, lost 1.

BAD SPILL MARKS SPRINGBROOK SHOW

Eugene Walton Thrown Against Hurdle When Mount Refuses to Take Jump

ALOE'S 'PAT' CHAMPION

Eugene Walton, Willow Grove horseman, was recovering at the Springbrook Farms Riding Club today after a breathtaking spill which electrified spectators at the club's second annual horse show.

Walton's mishap was the only serious spill of the show yesterday afternoon, when hundreds of horse lovers gathered in the picturesque natural green amphitheatre of the club's grounds on the Terwood road, one mile east of Willow Grove.

"Gene," who lives at the clubhouse and was riding for several members, was up on "General," a beautiful but somewhat erratic jumper recently sold by Edward L. Aloe, chairman of the horse show committee. Walton was about to take what would have been his last jump of the day when "General" refused the leap so abruptly that the rider was thrown against the solid wooden hurdle, his head hitting a corner.

Walton lay unconscious, blood streaming from a long scalp gash, as a group of judges and exhibitors ran from the infield and, wading a ditch, lifted him into an automobile. He was taken to the Abington Memorial Hospital, where he recovered consciousness and doctors permitted him to return home after an X-ray showed his injuries were not serious.

AT THE SPRINGBROOK FARMS HORSE SHOW

Eleanor C. and Elizabeth M. Mathiew are shown watching the jumping events at the horse show of the Springbrook Farms Riding Club yesterday.

Sylvan Hirsch making a jump on "Pat," owned by Edward L. Aloe.

Walton had given "General" a perfect ride in the last event, the championship class for hunters, but it was not good enough to beat Mr. Aloe's "Pat," the outstanding jumper of the day, and winner of two other blue ribbons beside the championship honors, ridden by Sylvan Hirsch, another member of the committee.

Nine-year-old Betty Cortright, sister of Peggy, famous on many a horse-show oval for her horsemanship and the mounts she exhibits, began emulating her sister's success when her "Seaham Terry" cantered off with the honors in the children's pony and saddle horses class.

The only other spill of the day came in the first event, when Cecil Billger, son of George W. Elkins' groom, was thrown from Mr. Elkins' "Pete" on the second jump, narrowly missing the falling horse as the rails were scattered, but remounting and putting "Pete" perfectly over the other jumps. The other members of the committee were Elias Wolf, Nathan Snellenburg and Richard I. Baum. The judges were Harry Baxter for hunters and George Null and Joseph Moos for the saddle events.

The summaries:

Green hunters class—Won by Edward L. Aloe's "Pat," with Sylvan Hirsch riding; second, Mrs. S. K. Mulford, Jr.'s "Kentucky Lee," with Ralph Schwartz up; third, J. Kugelmann's "High Over," with Mr. Kugelmann up.

Saddle horses, open—Won by Miss Stella Elkins, riding her "Bob;" second, George W. Elkins' "Kona," with Cecil Billger up; third, Miss P. Carpenter's "Dark Flower," with Miss Betty Bray riding.

Qualified hunters—Won by Edward L. Aloe's "Pat," with Sylvan Hirsch riding; second, Nathan J. Snellenburg's "Silver Prince," Mr. Snellenburg up; third, Howard Wolf's "Up and Over," Charles Krier up.

Saddle horses and ponies ridden by children not over eighteen—Won by Miss Betty Cortright's "Seaham Terry," with George Boyle, Jr., riding; second, Miss Betty Bray's "Question Mark," with Miss Bray up; third, Miss Betty Mathieu's "Ginger," ridden by herself.

Touch and Out Stake—Won by Howard A. Wolf's "Up and Over," Charles Krier up; second, John A. Roatsch's "General," Gene Walton up; third, Miss Elinor Loebe's "Subway Rose," William Loeb up.

Ladies' saddle horses, open—Won by Louise Worthington, riding her "Coronette"; second, Miss Stella Elkins' "Bob," Miss Elkins up; third, Miss P. Carpenter's "Dark Flower," Miss Betty Bray up.

Pony jumpers, 14.2 hands and under—Won by George W. Elkins' "Puddles," Francis Billger up; second, Donald Snellenburg's "Going Up," ridden by owner; third, John A. Roatsch's "Bitta Pep," Miss Amy Kooker up.

Championship hunters, open to first and second prize winners in previous hunting classes—Won by Edward L. Aloe's "Pat," Sylvan Hirsch up; second, Mrs. S. K. Mulford's "Kentucky Lee," William Krimmel up; third, Nathan J. Snellenburg's "Silver Prince," ridden by Mr. Snellenburg.

TODAY'S RACING SELECTIONS

(By Associated Press)

The following selections are made by the Louisville, Ky., Times:

AT FAIRMOUNT

1—Coverlet, Cleo, Royal Cause.
2—The Doctor, Uncommon Gold, Sporting Blues.
3—Alex Woodliffe, Rundark, Kitty Cat.
4—Golden Wanderer, Rodrigo, Happy Bob.
5—Prisoner, Polygamia, Sister Ship.
6—Kiyi, Erla Lee, Gaffney.
7—Junior's Nurse, Fire Dog, The Tailor.
Best—Prisoner.

AT THORNCLIFFE

1—No selections.
2—Tetra Glass, Encamp, Exultant.
3—Showery, Highland Fling, Rea.
4—Beau of the West, Taurus, Perlapides.
5—Patricia J., Silver Song, Charles H.
6—Remedy, Sun Kin, Seth's Hope.
7—Dixie Smith, Maxie, Sun Rajah.
Best—Patricia J.

AT BELMONT

1—Mosque, Black Bart, King Jimmy.
2—Atlantis, Stupendous, Bravery.
3—Algernon, Vito, Knapsack.
4—Sandy, Indian Scout, False Pride.
5—Holiday, Hiawatha, Blue Heron.
6—Royal Stranger, Peter Simple, Ironside.
Best—Sandy.

AT ARLINGTON PARK

1—Dr. Maxon, Talladega, Ball Gee.
2—George Groom, Myrtle Belle, The Badger.
3—Jack Horgan, True Bay, Know Me Gnome.
4—Alto, Judea, Yam Toy.
5—Billy Culbertson, Blackwood, Tiger Flower.
6—Chicago, Flat Iron, Sankari.
7—Mally Jane, Arno, Mino.
8—Xtra, Resourceful, Iscara.
Best—Chicago.

CONSENSUS SELECTIONS

AT BELMONT PARK

1—Blockhead, Mosque, Effe.
2—Atlantis, Lisa, Stupendous.
3—Knapsack, Bystander, Algernon.
4—Sandy, Candy Hog, False Pride.
5—Holiday, Blue Heron, Bargello.
6—Ironsides, Royal Stranger, Gerard
Best—Knapsack.

AT THORNCLIFFE

1—Pinwheel, Irish Sphere, Rose Spot.
2—Santa Sweep, Lannie, Lady Herbert.
3—Showery, Highland Fling, Charming Spot.
4—Nealon Kay, Beau of the West, Duchess.
5—Rockady, Charles H., Clearance.
6—Remedy, Hesper, Sun King.
7—Dixie Smith, Maxie, Casting.
Best—Remedy.

AT FAIRMOUNT

1—Cleo, Royal Cause, Coverlet.
2—The Doctor, Uncommon Gold, Sporting Blues.
3—Alex Woodliffe, One Way, Intense.
4—Rodrigo, Sweepstakes, Alborak.
5—Sistership, Polygamia, Broadside.
6—Dr. Larrabee, Kiyi, Praise.
7—Junior's Nurse, Fire Dog, Ponimoi.
Best—Alex Woodliffe.

AT ARLINGTON PARK

1—Dr. Maxon, Wildrake, Talladega.
2—Elfkin, Cloud Idolizer, George Groom.
3—Jack Horgan, Treasurer, True Boy.
4—Alto, Judea, French Lane.
5—Blackwood, Participate, Rurik.
6—Sankari, Chicago, Crystal Pennant.
7—Mally Jane, Mino, Arno.
8—Isoard, Resourceful, Jasonette.
Best—Sankari.

---

24 PHILA. WOMEN IN EASTERN GOLF

Hurd, Vanderbeck, Stetson, Barlow and Fox Head Contingent in Opening Day of Play

GRISCOM CUP FOLLOWS

Montclair, N. J., June 4.—Twenty-four women golfers from Philadelphia clubs were in the field of 108 entered in the twenty-first annual Eastern championship, which started today over the number two and number three courses of the Montclair Golf Club.

The Philadelphia entry included Mrs. Dorothy Campbell Hurd, Mrs. Clarence H. Vanderbeck and Mrs. G. Henry Stetson, all former national champions; Mrs. Ronald H. Barlow, who has held the Eastern title five times, and Mrs. Caleb F. Fox.

Miss Helen Payson, the Canadian champion, led the New England entry, and Miss Maureen Orcutt, who recently won the Metropolitan championship for the third straight year, headed the New Yorkers.

Mrs. Hurd was a close second and Miss Orcutt was third last year when the Eastern was won by Miss Glenna Collett. Miss Collett decided not to defend her title. She is still abroad, where she went to play in the British championship.

BORELL, HITTING .605, WILL JOIN A'S SOON

Graduation of Muhlenberg's Star Athlete Delayed Until Fall—Pitcher Spotts Attracts Scouts

BENFER'S NINE UNBEATEN

BY ROSS E. KAUFFMAN

Hitting above the .600 mark, Nick Borell (changed at his own request from Borelli), star of the undefeated Muhlenberg College base ball team, will round out his collegiate career this week-end against Lehigh and Lafayette.

Borell will then be ready to join the Athletics when they return from their present western trip. The Grantwood, N. J., all-around athlete plans to visit his home about June 15 and from there will go over to New York to report to Connie Mack when the series opens with the Yankees, four days later.

Although a senior, Borell is not in the graduate list of ninety-three students at Muhlenberg College. He needs sev-

eral more units of work before he is eligible to receive his
diploma but plans to make up the deficiency in summer school
by putting in the time now and then.   He will graduate in
October.   The hard-hitting infielder and line bucking half-
back was a bit careless in his classroom duties during his freshman and sophomore terms but the last two years has been a
first class student.

Borell has been at bat thirty-eight times in the nine games
this season and hammered out twenty-three hits for an average

Nick Borell

of .605.   Of these he made one home run, six
three baggers and five doubles.

In Muhlenberg's season of success with
consecutive victories over Haverford, Lehigh, Gettysburg, Temple, Crescent A. C.,
F. and A. M., Penn A. C., Ursinus and
Lafayette, pitcher Frank Spotts of Barring-
ton, N. J., has stood out prominently.   He
won his fourth straight when he blanked
Lafayette last week, 3 to 0.

Spotts, standing 6 feet, 2 inches and
weighing 210 pounds, has attracted the attention of big league scouts.   Ira Thomas,
of the Athletics, saw him beat Ursinus and

commented on his ability.   Coach Harry (Haps) Benfer considers he has a coming catcher in Joee Evans, although the lad
started the season at shortstop.   When catcher Jack Smith
suffered a dislocated vertebra, Benfer was up against it and
decided to swing Evans, the foot ball end, back of the plate.
That move brought Borell in from the outfield.

Connie Mack had intimated to Coach Benfer that he wanted
Borell to be groomed for the outfield, but the infielders were
scarce at the Allentown institution and once again Nick found
himself in the infield.   He played third base most of last
season.

———

Notre Dame's infield that faces Villanova in the Main Line
stadium tomorrow is composed of four veterans.   They are:
John Colerick, of Newark, at first base; Captain Joe Sullivan,
second base; Leo Schrall, of Cresson, Pa., shortstop, and
Johnny Niemiec, third base.

Sullivan is a son of Billy Sullivan, former White Sox star catcher, who handled the curves of Ed Walsh for many years.

Ed, Jr., and Bob, sons of pitcher Walsh, are also with the touring "Irish" nine.

———

Alfred Smith Forsyth, of St. Davids, captain and star sprint swimmer of the Columbia University team, claims he lost two pounds during a philosophy examination.

The Main Line athlete went in to the philosophical room at 12.50 P. M. weighing 183 pounds and three hours later when he put down his fountain pen, was weighed on the same scales and recorded 181.

———

7% MONEY HITS STOCKS, PRICES FELL 2 to 10 POINTS

Radio Tumbled 24 and a Few Specialties 8 to 10 in Last Half Hour

At 7 per cent. rate for call money, the highest in seven years, cast its shadow over the New York stock market this afternoon. Forthwith the whole market began to turn downward at a rapid pace with losses of 1 to 10 accompanying the selling wave. Radio was the greatest sufferer, tumbling more than 24 points after 2.30 o'clock. The money rate started at 6, went to 6½ around noon then hit its maximum within thirty minutes of the close. Banks called $15,000,000 brokers loans. Thereafter large institutions reporting growing scarcity of funds available for speculative purposes. Stocks, which had been in the forefront of the recent advance underwent the most severe losses. Curtis Airplane sank 10 and General Motors 9. Heaviest pressure was seen near the close.

Announcement was made of 2,000,000 gold for export to Italy. On heels of this, Chicago sent out a report of possibility of the Federal Reserve Bank rate in that city going to 5 per cent. It was this bank that gave the first sign the Federal Reserve authorities meant to employ stern measures in regulating rates.

The volume of trading was of large proportions becoming

17

so great that the tape fell more than 25 minutes behind in the final half hour. The market had not acted right all morning, according to the street's judgment. There were precipitate declines in International Telephone and Radio due to denial that negotiations were pending for the sale of Radio Corporation's communication business. Prior to this more than 20 stocks went to the best of the year with the coppers most conspicuous, but all succumbed at the end.

Influenced by continued high rates for call and time money and talk of a further increase in the Federal Reserve Bank rediscount rate, the bond market pursued a variable drift. Some went forward; others lost ground. Mining and smelting issues turned strong. Anglo Chilean 7s were at the top of the year, in spite of the unfavorable showing made in the last report. High grade corporation issues were weaker. At 94, Northern Pacific first 4s were off 4 from the year's top. Duquesne Light 4½ went to par against 104 a few weeks ago. Texas Pacific first 5s at 109½ compared with 115 when the market was at its highest point.

Eight out of ten Stock Exchange houses said they had not seen any curtailment of public interest in stocks as a result of the high rate of money. A higher rate than 6 per cent. for demand loans has not been quoted in seven years prior to the past week. What the future rate will be, largely rests with the stock market's behavior. One well known Wall Street operator was quoted as saying brokers' loans at New York could go to ten billion dollars without harming the market. The total now is less than half that amount. This view as to expansion is at variance with that of the Federal Reserve Board.

The summer is usually a period of cheap money due to slack commercial requirements. Ease was experienced in the memorable market upswings of 1919 and 1906 and even the high rates of the spring of five years ago did not hold through the summer. The difference between that year and the present is, that 1923 was a liquidating period. The present high charge has brought average prices for bonds to the year's minimum. The recession is not likely to go far as the wealth of the country is unprecedented and too many investors are awaiting an opportunity to reinvest.

PHILADELPHIA MARKET

*New Top for Lit Bros. and Manufacturers Casualty—U. G. I.
Down*

Three new high records were scored on the Philadelphia market today. One was in Lit Brothers; the other in Manufacturers Casualty and the third, Lehigh Power. Following these came a point advance in Consolidated Traction of New Jersey, but recognized leaders turned reactionary. Blauners, Inc., one of the newly listed stocks, had a setback of 1½. There was an absence of incentive in the more popular shares. Lehigh Navigation got up almost a point then wavered. Selling of U. G. I. by a trader forced it down more than 2. Utilities were quiet but a block of 800 Northeastern Power was taken at 28½, and Lehigh Power crossed 44½. Regarding the latter, it was said all but 2 per cent. had been deposited in exchange for National Power & Light. Near the close a block of 1,000 U. G. I. sold at 145. A similar lot of Lehigh Navigation was taken at 149. Following the downward trend in Wall Street in the final hour, inroads upon prices were made in the market. Moderate selling came into Stanley Company forcing it down fractionally but Mohawk Hudson went forward on buying reported to have been for New York account. One house took 1,000 Lit Bros., 700 of this was at 27½. Pennsylvania Railroad, which was expected to go forward with passing of the rights, eased fractionally.

With Wall Street laying emphasis on possibility of a technical reaction and with call money holding at 6 per cent. there was a disposition to move with greater caution. This found expression in the smallest turnover in the local markets in weeks. United Light and Power A slipped more than a point, and Louis Mark Shoe preferred sold equal to the low. American Stores yielded.

Large shipments of gold to Europe in the next four weeks were predicted by bankers here today. They figured 10% of the U. S. holdings had been taken in six months and could not see how Europe's rehabilitation needs could be met without the supply in this country being tapped. It made no difference, in their judgment, whether England, Holland or some other country was called on to meet demands from France, the United States, they said, would have to supply the yellow metal.

This, in bankers' judgment, pointed to continuance of firm money rates during June. They thought commercial borrowers would have to pay the penalty in the form of 5% charge for loans. It is a question of supply diminishing and rates stiffening to meet this situation, bankers asserted. Last week's ratio of reserve of all Federal Banks dropped to 68.9, the lowest of the year.

There is no scarcity of money and banks are being criticised for marking up rates. Merchants or stock brokers can get ample accommodation. The banks deny the higher charges are aimed at restricting speculation on the stock market. Brokers, nevertheless, exacted 6% on nearly all marginal accounts for May. Thus far there is no evidence the higher rate is checking public interest in stocks.

PEAK FOR BANK LOANS

Loans of Philadelphia banks and trust companies leaped today $3,376,000 to a new peak at $1,141,134,000. A year ago today they were $987,201,000. At the same time deposits gained $21,708,000 to $1,078,869,000. This compared with $951,336,000 in the same week in 1927.

WEST CHESTER BANK'S NEW DIRECTORS

West Chester, Pa., June 4.—Announcement was made today that the stockholders of the Farmers Mechanics Company, of West Chester, have elected three new directors. R. Parke Regester, Dr. Norman W. Cameron, and P. H. Corcoran were chosen.

NEW YORK STOCKS

Extensive trading in stocks caused the ticker to fall 15 to 20 minutes behind at the close. Following prices are those received up to 3 o'clock. Closing prices will appear in a later edition.

Div. in $	Sat. Clos.	High.	Low.	3.00
Abitibi P&P (4)..	67½	68⅜	67	68⅛
Abitibi pf (6).....	102	102	102	102
Abrah & Straus..	107½	107	103	103
Adams Exp (6)..	338½	340	338	340
Advan Rumely..	41⅞	46½	41½	41½
Advan Rumely p.	60¾	63¾	59½	59½
Ahumada Lead..	4⅝	4¾	4½	4½
Air Reduction (2)	70¼	70	68⅜	68⅞
Ajax Rubber....	9⅜	9⅜	9⅛	9¼
Alaska Juneau...	3¾	3⅞	3¾	3¾
Albany PWrP (2)	28½	28⅞	28⅛	28⅞
Al Chem&Dye (6)	173	175	167½	167½
Allis-Chal (6)....	123	123	123	123
Amal Leather....	13⅞	13⅝	13⅜	13⅜
Amal Leather pf.	86½	86	86	86
Amerada Cor (2).	34⅛	34¼	33¾	34
Am Ag Chem....	21⅞	21⅞	21	21
Am Ag Chem pf.	70⅛	71½	69	69
Am Bk Note (†3)	130½	130⅛	130	130
AmBkNotepf(3)*	63⅛	63	63	63
Am Beet Sug....	18⅞	19⅛	18⅞	19
Am Beet Sug pf..	59	60	59½	59½
Am-Bosch.......	40	41	38	38
Am Br Sho (1.60)	44⅞	45¼	44	44
Am Brown Bov..	22	23⅞	21	21¼
Am Brown B pf*.	59¾	58¾	58¼	58¾
Am Can (2).....	91⅞	93⅝	89¼	89¼
Am Can pf (7)...	144	143½	143½	143½
Am Car Fdy (6).	101¼	103	102	102¼
Am Chain pf (7).	103½	105	105	105
Am Chicle (3)...	86½	87	85½	85½
Am Drug (.80)...	14	14½	13¾	13⅞
Am Enc'stic (2.40)	68	68	68	68
Am Express (6)..	195	204	194	198
Am & For Pow..	37	38	35	35
Am For P 2d pf..	92¾	92	92	92
Am Hide & Lea..	12⅞	12⅞	12⅞	12⅞
Am Home Pr (3).	80	80⅞	78	78
Am Ice (†2½)....	40	40⅞	39½	39½
Am Inter Corp (2)	119⅜	119¾	111⅝	111⅝
Am LaF&Foam'e.	6¾	6⅞	6½	6⅝
Am LaF&Foa pf.	68	68	68	68
Am Linseed Oil..	103⅛	109⅜	103	103½
Am LinseedO p(7)	110½	112⅜	110¾	112⅜
Am Loco (8)....	106¼	106½	106	106
Am Mach F (†2½)	156⅛	158	158	158
Am Metal (3)...	48¼	51	48½	49⅝
Am Piano p (7)*.	67⅜	67	65⅛	66¼
Am Pow&Lt (n1)	87½	87⅞	85	85
Am P&L pf (6)..	107	107	106⅞	106⅞
Am Radiator (5).	144	144⅞	142	143
Am Ry Express (6)	123	129½	126	129½
Am Republics...	77¾	77⅞	73⅝	73⅝
Am S Raz (†4½)..	68	68⅜	66¼	67
Am Seating (3)..	40⅜	40¾	40½	40¾
Am Ship & Com.	6	6	5⅞	6
Am Shipbldg (8)*	103	105	103	105
Am Smelt (8)....	201½	201½	197	198
Am Smelt pf (7).	135⅝	134½	134	134
Am Snuff (12)...	169	167½	167½	167½

Div. in $	Sat. Clos.	High.	Low.	3.00
Am Steel Fdy (3).	60⅜	61¼	60⅜	60⅜
Am StlFdy pf (7)*	113	113	113	113
Am Sugar.......	74¼	75¼	73½	73¾
Am Sugar pf (7).	110½	110½	110½	110½
Am Sumatra Tob	54⅞	54	54	54
Am Tel & Tel (9).	189	189	186⅛	186⅛
Am Tel & Tel rts.	14⅛	14¼	13⅝	13⅝
Am Tobac (8)...	160	160⅛	160	160
Am Tobac B (8).	162½	161¼	161¼	161¼
Am Type F (8)..	118	117⅞	116¾	117⅞
Am Wat Wks (c1)	64	64	63	63
A W Wks 1 pf (6)	104¼	105	105	105
Am Woolen.....	21⅝	21⅞	21⅞	21⅞
Am Woolen pf...	52½	52½	52¼	52¼
Am Writ Pap ct..	13¾	14	13¾	13¾
Am Zinc........	28⅞	29⅞	28	28
Am Zinc pf......	89⅞	90	89¼	89¼
Anaconda (3)....	74	74⅞	72¼	72¼
Archer Dani (3)..	77½	78½	75⅞	75⅞
Arm Del pf (7)...	94½	95½	94½	95
Armour Ill A....	18	20	18½	18½
Armour Ill B....	11¾	12¾	11¾	11¾
Armour Ill pf (7).	88½	90½	88½	90
Arnold Consta...	46¼	45½	44	45
Artloom (3).....	39⅝	40	40	40
Art MetConst(1½)	31¼	31½	31½	31½
Asso Dry G (2½).	44⅜	44½	43¾	44
Asso Dr G 1st (6)	103½	104	103	104
Asso Oil (2)*....	43½	43⅝	43½	43½
Atchison (10)....	192⅛	191⅛	191	191
Atchison pf (5)..	106¼	106⅜	106¼	106¼
Atlan C L (†10)..	184	182¾	182½	182¾
Atlan G & W I..	58½	59¾	56	56½
Atla G&W I pf(3)	55½	56¼	54	54
Atlan Ref Co (4).	130½	130½	126¼	126¼
Atlas Pow pf (6)*	110½	108½	108½	108½
Atlas Tack......	16¼	15¾	15¼	15¼
Austin Nichols...	7¾	7⅞	7⅝	7¾
Austin Nich pf...	34	33⅛	33⅛	33⅛
Autosales.......	15¾	15⅞	15	15¾
Balt. & Ohio (6).	113¾	114¼	112¾	112¾
Balt&Ohio pf (4)	80½	80¾	80½	80½
Bangor & Ar (3½)	71⅛	71¼	71	71
Bang & Ar pf (7)*	112¼	111¼	111¼	111¼
Bk of Com (18)*.	750	770	751	751
Bk of Man C (16)*	910	913	895	895
Barnet Leather..	32	31¾	31¼	31¼
Barnsdall A.....	23⅛	23⅝	23¼	23¼
Bayuk Cigars....	116	119	119	119
Beacon Oil......	17¾	17⅝	16½	16½
Beechnut (†3)...	80	79¼	79	79
Belding Hem (2).	18½	18½	18½	18⅛
BelNR prpf(4.12)	90	90¼	90¼	90¼
Best Co (3).....	68⅞	69¾	68	68
Bethlehem Stl...	62¼	62⅞	60⅝	60⅝
Bethle Stl pf (7).	121	121¾	121½	121¾
Blumenthal pf*..	95	96	95	95
Bon Ami (4).....	76⅞	76⅞	75⅞	75⅞
Booth Fish......	6½	7½	6⅞	7
Booth Fish 1 pf..	46¼	47⅜	46	47⅜

Div. in $	Sat. Clos.	High.	Low.	3.00
Borden Co (6)...	170	170	167¼	167¼
Boston & Maine.	80¼	80	80	80
Briggs Mfg......	42	42⅞	38½	38½
Brit Emp Stl....	6⅞	6⅞	6½	6½
Brit Emp 2d pf..	9⅜	9¼	9	9¼
BrockwayMTr(3)	54⅞	55	54⅞	55
BrkwyMTr pf(7)	116	116½	116	116
Brk Ed El (8)....	252¾	254	249	249
Brk Manhat (4).	65⅞	65¾	64½	64½
Brk Manh pf (6).	90½	91⅝	91	91
Brk Un Gas (5)..	148¾	149½	149½	149½
Brunswick Blk (3)	46⅞	47¼	44⅛	44⅛
Brunswick Ter...	38¼	42¾	38⅜	38⅜
Bucyrus ErieC(1)	44½	44⅞	42½	42½
BucyrusCv pf(2½)	50	50⅞	47¾	47¾
Burns Bros pf(7)*	108½	108	108	108
Burns Bros B....	42	43⅜	40	40
Bur Add M (†4).	159	158¾	158¾	158¾
BushTBldg p(7)*.	118¼	118	118	118
Bush Ter (g2)...	57½	57¼	57	57
Bush Term D(7)*	111¾	113	111¾	113
Butte Cop & Z..	9½	9½	8⅝	9
Butte Sup (2)...	15⅜	15⅛	14	14
Butterick........	58	58	55	55
Byers A M......	104	107½	103½	103½
By-Pr Coke (†2¾)	76	75¼	75	75½
Cal Packing (4)..	74⅝	74⅞	74¼	74¼
Cal Petrol (1)....	31	32	32	32
Cal Lead & Z....	4⅜	4⅜	4	4
Calu&Arizona (6)	105¾	106⅛	102½	102½
Calu & Hecla (2).	24¾	24⅞	24	24
Canada Dry (3)..	79½	80⅞	77½	77½
Canada South(3)*	64¾	64⅜	64¼	64¼
Can Pac (10)....	213¼	213¾	210	210
Case Thresh (6)..	327	334	319	320
Case Thre pf (7).	132	132	132	132
Cent Alloy (2)...	37⅞	38⅛	36¼	36¼
Cent R R (†12)..	350	337	337	337
Cen Rig Mills...	14½	14	14	14
Cerro de Pas (4).	76½	77⅜	75	75
Cert-Teed (4)....	50⅛	50¼	48⅝	49
Certo-Corp (†4)..	76	76	75	75
Chandler Clev...	11	11	9⅝	9⅝
Chand Clev pf...	19⅞	20½	18½	18½
Ches Cor p(3)...	74	74¼	73½	73½
Ches & Ohio (10)	195¼	195½	194	194
Chi & Alton.....	11½	11¼	11¼	11¼
Chi & Alton pf...	16⅛	16⅞	16	16
Chi Gt West....	12½	13¾	12⅜	12⅜
Chi Gt W pf.....	26⅞	27⅞	26¼	26¼
Chi M St P&Pac.	35⅛	36	34¾	34¾
Chi M St P&P pf	46¼	46¾	45⅛	45⅛
Chi & Nthw (4)..	86¼	87	85½	85½
Chi Pneu T (6)..	128	131	130	130
Chi R I & Pac (6)	118	117⅝	115¾	115¾
Chi R I & P pf (6)	104½	104⅞	104	104
Chi R I & P pf (7)	109	108½	108	108
ChickashaCoil (3)	49	49½	49	49½
Childs (2.40).....	48	49	47¼	47¼
Chile Cop (2½)...	44¾	45⅜	43¼	43½
Christie B (1.20).	95	90	90	90
Chrysler (3).....	83⅞	85⅜	80⅛	80⅝
City Stores B (b5)	94⅞	97½	96⅞	96⅞
Cluett Peab (5)..	92¾	92¾	92¾	92¾
Coca-Cola (6)....	170	170¾	168	168
Collins & Aik....	75⅜	76⅜	74¼	74¼
Coll & Aik p (7).	98¼	97⅜	97⅜	97⅜
Colorado Fuel...	76¼	75	72½	72½
Colo So 1st p (4)*	83¾	84	83½	84
Colum Carb (4)..	90	90	90	90
Colum Gas (5)...	113⅛	114⅞	112⅛	112⅛
Colum Gas pf (6)	107⅞	108½	108⅜	108½
Com'weal P (†3).	83⅝	84¼	83¼	83¼

Div. in $	Sat. Clos.	High.	Low.	3.00
Com Inv Tr (3.60)	71	70¼	69	69
Com Credit (1)..	33	33	32¾	32¾
ComCre1st p(6½)*	93	94¾	92⅞	94½
Com Solv (8).....	170	170	166¾	166¾
Conde Nast (2)..	65	64¾	64	64
Congoleum......	27¾	28¼	26⅝	26⅝
Cong Cigar (†4½).	74½	75¾	74	74¼
Cons Cigar (7)...	95¼	98¾	93	93⅞
Consol Cig pf (6½)	99⅞	100⅛	100	100⅛
Consol Dis......	1⅞	2⅛	1⅞	2⅛
Consol Gas (5)...	157	157⅜	154¼	154¼
Con Gas pf (5)..	102	102½	101⅞	102½
Con R Cub pf (6)	87¼	87¼	85¼	85½
Cons Textile.....	4	4⅛	4	4
Contain C A(1.20)	34¾	34½	33	33
Contain'rC B(.60)	17¼	17⅜	16⅞	16⅞
Cont Baking A..	32½	33	32½	32½
Cont Baking B..	5½	5⅝	5½	5½
Cont Bak pf (8).	82½	83	82¾	82¾
Cont'l Can (5)...	108½	109¾	107	107
Cont Ins (2).....	90⅛	89⅞	89	89
Cont Motor (.80).	13½	13¾	13¼	13¼
Corn Ex Bk (20)*	725	725	725	725
Corn Prod (†3)...	77½	77½	76¼	76¼
Corn Prod pf (7).	143¾	145¼	145¼	145¼
Coty Inc (g5)....	174	175	173¾	174
Crucible Stl (6)..	85⅞	86	85½	85½
Crucible Stl pf (7)	121	120½	120½	120½
Cuba Cane pf....	28	28½	28½	28½
Cuba Co.........	28¾	28⅞	27	27
Cuba R R pf (6)*	91	94	94	94
Cuban Am Su (1)	23	23	22½	22½
Cudahy Pkg (4)..	67¼	68¾	66⅝	66⅝
Curtiss Aero (1)..	130	131⅛	118⅝	119⅞
CutlerHamM(3½)	58⅞x	58⅞	58	58
Cuyam Fruit....	52½	53½	53½	53½
Davison Chem...	51⅜	52¾	49⅛	49⅛
Debenh Sec (2.18)	47⅞	47⅛	46¾	46¾
Deere Co pf (7)*.	126	126	125½	125½
Del & Hud (9)....	209	208⅛	204	204
Del L & W (†7)..	142	141½	141½	141½
Den & Rio Gr pf.	61⅞	62	61	61
Det Edison (8)..	209	209¾	209½	209½
Devoe A (†2.80).	54	54¼	54	54¼
Diam'd Mat (†9)*	151	152⅝	152⅝	152⅝
Dodge Bros A...	16¾	17⅞	16⅛	16
Dodge B pf (7)..	80⅜	80½	77½	77½
Dome Mine (1)..	9¼	9½	9½	9½
Drug Inc (4)....	98¼	98½	97	97
Dul S Sh & Atl..	4⅛	4⅛	4	4
Dul S S & Atl pf.	7	8	8	8
Dunhill (4)......	66	65⅝	65	65
DuP de N (†13½)	398	405½	392	392
DuPont (6).....	118¾	119	119	119
Eastman (†8)....	182⅛	182¼	179	179½
Eaton A & S (2).	41	41¾	39	39
Eisenlohr pf (7)*.	90	90	90	90
EitingSchild (2½)	40	40¼	39	39
Ele Auto Lt (6)..	205	204¾	200¾	200¾
Elec Boat.......	16⅜	17¼	15½	15½
Elec P & Lt (1)..	41¼	41⅞	40	40
El P & L pf (7)..	110	109¾	109½	109¾
El Storage B (5).	83	83	80⅝	81¼
Emer Brant A...	14½	15½	14⅜	14½
Emer Brant B...	9	9	9	9
Endicott (5).....	81⅞	82	81¾	81¾
Eng Pub Serv...	42¾	43¼	42¾	42⅞
Eng Pub Ser pf(7)	110¾	110¾	110¾	110¾
Equit Off Bld (8)	139¼	136	136	136
Equitable T (12)*	585	588	575	579
Erie...........	56¾	56⅞	55½	55½
Erie 1st pf......	55¼	55½	54⅝	54⅝
Fairbanks Co....	4	3⅞	3⅞	3⅞

Div. in $	Sat. Clos.	High.	Low.	3.00
Fairbanks Co p*.	9⅝	10	10	10
Fairb'ks Mor (3).	43	43	42¼	42¼
Fed L & T (h1.40)	54⅞	55	54⅞	55
Fed Lt & T pf (6)*	106⅞	106½	106½	106½
Fed M & S pf (7)	98	98½	98½	98½
Fed Motor (f.80).	23¾	24⅞	23½	23½
Fid Ph Fire.....	91	91¼	89	89
Fifth Av Bu(.64)*	15	13½	13	13½
First N Str (1½)..	36⅞	36¾	35	35
Fisk R & T.....	15	15	14⅞	14⅞
Fisk R & T 1st (7)	89½	89⅜	88	88
Fleischmann (3)..	72⅝	72⅝	71½	71½
Foundation......	49½	49½	49½	49½
Fox Film A (4)..	90½	90⅞	88	88
Freep Tex (†5½)..	65½	67½	65½	65½
Gab Snubb......	18½	19⅜	18⅞	18⅞
Gardner Mot....	14¾	15½	14¼	14¼
Gen Am Tan (4).	76	75¾	75	75
Gen Asp........	87¼	87⅞	84⅝	84⅝
General Cable...	30	29	28	28
Gen Cable A (4).	76	76¾	75	75
Gen Cigar (4)...	67	67⅜	66⅝	66⅝
Gen Elec (†5)....	162½	162¼	155¼	155¼
Gen Motors (†7).	200	201⅞	189¾	190¼
Gen Mot pf (7)..	126	126⅛	126	126
Gen Out A (4)....	55¼	55	55	55
Gen Out A ct (2).	41½	42⅜	41⅛	41½
Gen Ry Sig (5)..	96	98	94⅝	94⅝
Gen Refrac (3)..	56	57	56¼	57
Gillette Saf R (5)	106¼	107¼	105	105
Gimbel Bro.....	55¼	56½	51	51¼
Gimbel Bro pf (7)	98⅜	98⅞	98½	98½
Glidden Co......	25¾	26	25¾	26
Glidden pr pf (7)*	103⅜	101	101	101
Gold Dust (3)...	99⅞	102	94½	94½
Goodrich (4)....	85½	85¾	82¾	82¾
Goodyear T.....	53¾	53¾	52½	52⅝
Goodyr 1st pf (7)	96	96	96	96
Goth Hos (‡2½)..	87	86⅛	86⅛	86⅛
Goth Hos n (‡2½)	86	86⅛	86⅛	86⅛
Granby Min (1).	56⅛	56⅜	54⅛	54⅛
Graham-Paige M.	37⅛	38	35¼	35¼
Gt North pf (5)..	102⅞	102	102	102
GreatNor pf ct(5)	100¾	100⅞	100⅞	100⅞
Gt North Ore (1½)	22⅛	22⅛	21⅞	21⅞
GtWest Sug(2.80)	36⅝	36⅞	36½	36½
Greene C Cop (4)	125⅜	126⅞	120½	121
Guanta Sugar....	8½	8½	7¾	8½
Gulf Mobile.....	56	56	55	55
Gulf Mob pf (6).	105½	107⅛	107⅛	107⅛
Hack'ns'kW (1½)*	25	24⅞	24⅞	24⅞
Hacken W p (1¾)*	24⅞	27½	27½	27½
Hartman B (1.20)	20⅜	20½	20¼	20¼
Havana Elec....	17⅝	17⅜	16	16
Hershey Choc...	61¾	61⅝	58	58
Hershey pf (4)...	80	80⅛	79⅞	80
Hollander (2½)...	32⅞	33	33	33
Homestk M (†7).	73	73	73	73
Household (†4)...	72⅛	72⅛	70½	70½
Houston Oil.....	150⅞	150¾	144	144
Howe Soun (4)..	61½	62⅜	60¼	60¼
Hud & Man (2½).	63⅞	63½	61½	61½
Hudson Mot (5).	92	92⅜	87⅛	88
Hupp Mot (f1.40)	65	64½	60	60⅛
Ill Central (7)...	144⅝	144⅞	144	144
Ind Oil & Gas (1)	27½	27½	26¾	26¾
Indian Mot (1½).	55	56	55	55
Indian Ref......	18¾	18⅞	18⅝	18⅞
Indian Ref ct....	17½	18⅛	17½	17¾
Indian Ref pf....	132½	132¾	132¾	132¾
Inger-Rand (†5).	94	94⅞	94⅞	94⅞
Inland Stl (p†6¼).	58	58	57	57
Insp Copper.....	25¼	25¼	23½	23⅞

Div. in $	Sat. Clos.	High.	Low.	3.00
Interboro Rap T.	42	42	40	40
Intercont Rub (1)	12¾	13	12⅝	12⅝
Inter Agr.......	19½	19⅝	18⅛	18⅛
Inter Agr pr pf..	78½	78	78	78
Int Bus Mach (5)	125½	126½	125	125
Int Cement (4)..	72	72	71¼	71¼
Int Combus (2)..	62¼	65½	62½	62½
Inter Harv (j6)..	286⅛	290	282	282
Inter Harv pf (7)	144	143½	143½	143½
IntMatch pf(3.20)	113½	114¼	109¾	109¾
Inter Mer Mar..	6	6	5⅝	5⅞
Inter Mer Mar pf	41¼	41⅜	39½	39½
Inter Nickel (2)..	101½	102¼	96	96
Inter Paper (2.40)	77⅝	79¾	76⅜	76⅜
Inter Paper p (7).	107	107	107	107
Inter Salt*......	57	57	57	57
Inter Tel&Tel (6)	196	195	187½	187½
Island Cr Coal (4)	57	56½	56½	56½
Jewel Tea (4)....	111½	111	107⅞	108
Johns-Manv (3)..	123⅜	123⅜	120½	120½
Jones Bros ct....	31½	31	31	31
Jordan Mot.....	13⅞	13¼	13⅛	13⅛
K'nCP&L1pB(6)*	112	113	112	113
Kan City Sou...	55⅛	†53¾	53	53½
Kan C Sou pf (4)	73¾	75	75	75
Kans C Sou rts..	..	1¾	1⅛	1⅛
Kayser & Co (5).	71¾	72¼	71½	71½
Keith Albee Orp.	23	24	22⅝	22⅝
Keith Albee pf (7)	87	87¾	87½	87¾
Kelvinator Corp.	19⅝	19⅞	19	19
Kelly-Spg.......	21⅞	21¾	21⅛	21⅛
Kelly-Spg 6 pf...	67½	70½	70	70½
Kelly-Spg 8 pf...	77	78	75	78
Kelsey Wh (2)...	35⅞	35⅞	35	35
Kennecott Cop(5)	94½	94½	89⅜	89⅜
Kinney G R p(8)*	94½	94⅛	94⅛	94⅛
Kraft Che (g1½)..	72½	73	71¼	71¼
Kresge SS (†1.60)	74¾	75¼	74	74
Kresge D S......	24	23	21⅞	23
Kress & Co (1)..	107½	108½	108½	108½
KrogerGr&B (cl)	98¾	98¾	95⅛	95⅛
Lacle Gas pf (5)*	108	102	102	102
Lago O & T.....	35	35	35	35
Lambert Co (†5½)	112⅞	114⅝	112	112
Lee Rub & T....	21	21	20¾	20¾
Lehigh Val (3½)..	110	109⅛	108	108
Leh Port Cem Co.	52	52	51¾	52
Leh Pt Cem pf (7)	110½	110⅝	110⅝	110⅝
Lehn & Fink (3).	48¼	48¼	47½	47½
Life Savers (1.60)	32¾	32⅞	32⅞	32⅞
Lig & Myers (†5).	100¼	98	97	97
Lig&Myers B (†5)	95⅞	95¼	95¼	95¼
Lima Loco (4)...	58¼	59¼	59¼	59¼
Liq Carbon (3.60)	72¼	75	72½	75
Loews Inc (†3)...	73¼	74	73⅛	73⅛
Loft Inc........	6⅝	6¾	6⅝	6⅝
LooseWil B (1.60)	52⅜	53⅜	52	52
Lorillard........	29¼	29⅝	29	29
Lorillard pf (7)..	98⅛	99	98½	98½
Louisiana Oil....	17½	17⅞	16½	16½
LouGas&El A(1¾)	39¼	40	37¼	37¼
Ludlum Stl (2)..	64⅛	65¼	62	62
McAnd&Fo (2.60)	51⅛	52½	51¼	51¼
McCall Corp (3)..	70⅛	70	70	70
McCrory St A(2)*	99	99	95	98⅞
McCrory St B (2)	105	107⅝	106	107
Mack Truck (6).	96¾	97⅛	94⅝	94⅝
Mackay Co pf (4)	78	77½	77½	77½
McKee Tim P (4)	68¼	68¼	67½	67½
Madi Sq Gar (1½)	30⅞	31⅜	30¼	30¼
Magma Cop (3)..	56	56¾	54⅝	54⅝
Mallinson.......	22	22⅛	22	22
Man Elec Sup (5)	62½	64¼	61⅜	61⅜

Div. in $	Sat. Clos.	High.	Low.	3.00
Man El M Gr(d5)	50½	50	49½	50
Man Shirt (2)...	39½	39¼	38⅝	38⅝
Maracaibo Oil...	19¾	19⅝	19	19
Mkt St Ry pr pf.	47¼	47½	47½	47½
Marland Oil.....	38½	39⅜	38½	38½
Marlin Rock(†2¼)	64⅝	63¾	62½	62½
Martin Parry C..	24¾	25⅝	22⅛	22⅛
Math Alk (6)....	129¼	128⅞	128	128
May Dept Str (4)	80¾	81	79⅝	79⅝
Maytag.........	21½	21⅝	21½	21⅝
Maytag pf war..	50	50	50	50
Maytag 1 pf (6)..	101	101	101	101
MetGolP pf(1.89)	26⅞	26¾	26¾	26¾
Mex Seab Oil....	33½	34¼	31⅜	31⅜
Mexican Seab rts	⅞	⅞	¾	¾
Miami Cop (1½).	21¾	22	21⅝	21⅝
Mid-Con Pet....	30¾	30¾	30¼	30¼
Middle Sta Oil...	5⅝	5⅞	5½	5½
Middle Sta O cts.	3⅞	4	4	4
Midland S pf(†12)	226	228	226	225
Min & St Louis..	3⅛	3¼	3⅛	3⅛
Mo Kan & Tex..	34⅞	35¼	34½	34½
Mo K & T pfA(7)	104⅞	104⅞	104⅞	104⅞
Misso Pacific....	66⅞	69⅝	65	65
Misso Pacific pf..	120¾	121⅝	119	119
Montg Ward (†5)	155¼	154¼	147¾	148½
Moon Motor....	10⅝	11¼	10	10
Mo Lod C M (.50)	3¼	3½	3¼	3½
Motor Met A....	17⅞	17½	17½	17½
Mot Whl Cor (2)	39¼	39¾	38	38
Mullins Mfg Cor.	83¼	83½	83	83
Mun'wear (3)....	57¼	57½	57½	57½
Murray Corp....	56½	56⅞	53¼	53¼
Nash Motor (†6).	93⅛	93½	91	91
Nat Acme Sta...	16⅝	17	16½	16½
Nat Bell Hess...	82	84⅞	84	84⅛
Nat Bell H p (7).	108	109½	109	109½
Nat Biscuit (6)..	171	172¼	170	170
Nat Cash R A (3)	65	65¾	62⅝	62⅝
Nat Dairy (3)...	84⅛	85⅜	82⅞	82⅞
Nat Dept Stores.	26⅝	29	27	29
Nat Distill......	39¾	42½	40¼	40¼
Nat Distill pf....	57	58½	58¼	58½
Nat En & Sta....	31	32⅜	30½	30½
Nat Lead (5)....	126	127	127	127
Nat Park Bk (24)*	930	918	918	918
Nat Pow & Lit (1)	35½	35¾	33¼	33¼
Nat Radiator (3).	24	25	24	24
Nat Rad pf (7)..	82½	82½	82½	82½
Nat R Mex 1st p.	6	6½	6½	6½
Nat Mex 2 pf....	4¼	4¼	3⅞	3⅞
Nat Supply (†6).	91	90½	90	90
Nat Surety (10)*.	337¼	345¾	344	344
Nev Consol (1½).	25	25¼	24	24
N Y Air Brake(3)	45¼	45	45	45
N Y Central (8).	184	184½	180⅛	180¼
N Y C & St L (6)	138	137¼	134	134
N Y Dock......	55¾	55¾	55	55
NY & Harlem(5)*	295	300	295	295
NY Lack&W (5)*	110¾	112¼	112¼	112¼
NY NH & H (1).	61½	61¼	60¾	60¾
N Y Ont & West.	33	34	32⅜	32½
N Y Railways pf.	7⅜	10	9¾	9¾
N Y State Ry....	18	17⅞	17	17⅞
Niagara F p (1¾)	28	27⅞	27⅞	27⅞
Norf&West (†10)	188½	188¼	188¼	188¼
North Am (b10).	75⅝	76⅜	75⅛	75⅛
North Am pf (3).	55⅜	55⅜	55¼	55⅜
Nor Pacific (5)..	101½	101⅛	100	100
Nor Pac cts (5)..	99⅛	99	98	98
Norwalk T & R..	4	4	4	4
Nunnally (.50)...	10½	10¼	10¼	10¼
Oil Well Sup (2).	27⅛	27⅞	27⅛	27½

Div. in $	Sat. Clos.	High.	Low.	3.00
OilWellSup p(7)*	103½	104⅞	103½	104⅞
Omnibus Corp...	12¾	13¼	12⅞	13
Omnib C pf (8)..	98	99	99	99
Oppenh-Col (f4).	71¼	71¾	71¾	71¾
Otis Elev (†7)...	202	202	198	198
Otis Steel.......	24⅜	24¾	22⅝	22⅝
Outlet-pf (7)*....	114	114½	114½	114½
Owens Bot (c†4).	84½	84½	84½	84½
Pac G & Elec (2)	50	50⅛	49	49
Pac T & T (7)*..	157¾	158	158	158
Pacific Oil.......	1⅜	1½	1⅜	1⅜
Packard (3).....	79½	80⅜	76	76
Pan-A-Pet......	47½	47½	47½	47½
Pan-A-Pet B....	48¾	49⅜	48¼	48¼
Pan A W P B...	23½	23⅞	23½	23½
Panhandle......	17⅞	18	17¼	17¼
Par Fa Lask (j8).	131	131	127¼	128
Park & Til (‡3)..	82	81½	80	80
Park Utah (.80)..	14¼	14½	13¼	13¼
Pathe Exchange..	7⅛	7⅛	6½	6½
Pathe Ex A.....	19½	20⅛	18½	18½
Patino M (2.92)..	35	35⅞	35	35
Peerless Mot....	23⅜	23	22¼	22¼
Penick & Ford...	31¾	32	31	31
Penn Dix (2)....	30	30	28¾	28¾
Penna R R (3½)..	66¼	66½	65½	65½
Pere Marq pf (5)	96½	98	98	98
Phila Co. 6 pf (3)	54⅜	54⅛	54⅛	54⅛
P & R Cl & I....	32	32⅝	31¾	31¾
Phillip Morris (1)	23	23	21½	21½
Phillip Pet (1½)..	40	40⅝	39¾	39⅞
Pierce Arrow....	17	17	16	16
Pierce Arrow pf..	53¾	54	50	50
Pierce Oil Cor...	3	3⅛	3	3
Pierce Petrol....	4¾	4⅝	4½	4½
Pills Flour (1.60).	39⅜	40⅞	40	40
Pittsburgh Coal..	46¼	46½	45½	45½
Pitts Ter Coal...	30¾	31⅝	31	31½
Pitts Ter C pf*..	76¼	77	77	77
Porto Ric Tob B.	31⅞	31	31	31
Postum Co (5)...	134	134⅞	130¾	131¼
Prod & Ref.....	23	22	22	22
P S El & G p (6).	107⅝	107¼	107¼	107¼
Public Ser N J (2)	60	60	57½	57½
P Ser N J p (6).	114	114½	114	114
P Ser N J pf (8).	149½	150	150	150
Pullman new (4).	89¼	90½	88¼	88¼
Pure Oil (.50)....	23¼	23¾	23¼	23¼
Pure Oil pf (8)*..	113	114	114	114
Purity Bak (3)..	84	84⅝	84	84⅜
Purity Bak pf (6)	111	111	110⅝	111
Radio Corp.....	223	223½	198½	202
Reading (4).....	111⅜	110	108½	108½
Rdg 1st pf (2)...	43½	43¾	43¾	43¾
Real Silk pf (7)*.	92½	92½	92½	92½
Rem Rand......	34⅜	34⅞	32¼	32¼
Rem Ran 1st p(7)	98	98	98	98
ReoMotCar(†1)..	32	33¾	31¼	31¼
Rep Iron & St (4)	60	60	59	59
Rep I & St pf (7)	107	106¾	106¾	106¾
Reynolds Spr....	14½	14⅞	13⅜	13½
Rey Tob B (5)..	132½	132½	132¼	132¼
Richfld O (s1)...	50⅜	52½	50½	50½
Rossia Ins (6)...	206¾	209	208	208
Roy Dut (a1.343)	52⅜	52¾	52	52
St Jos Lead (†3).	47	47⅜	46	46
St L & S F (†8).	117½	117½	117¼	117¼
StLSF pf 1 pd (6)	100⅜	100¼	100	100
St L So Westn..	90½	91¼	89¼	89¼
St L So W pf (5).	91½	92	92	92
Savage Arms (4).	83	83	82½	82½
Schulte (j3½)....	63½	63⅞	61½	61½
Schulte pf (8)*..	123	124	124	124

Div. in $	Sat. Clos.	High.	Low.	3.00
Seaboard A L....	18	18¼	18¼	18¼
Seagrave (e1.20).	12¾	13	13	13
Sears-Roeb (2½)..	110¼	110¾	105¾	105⅞
Seneca Cop......	3⅝	3⅝	3½	3½
Shattuck Co (2)..	118	123¾	117½	122¼
Shell Un O (1.40)	28	28¼	27¾	27¾
Shubert T (5)...	62	62¾	62⅛	62¼
Simms Pet......	22¼	22⅜	22	22⅛
Simmons Co (3)..	65½	65¼	64¼	64½
Simmons Co rts..	1⅜	1½	1¼	1¼
Sinclair.........	26½	26⅞	26	26
Skelly Oil (2)....	32	31⅞	30½	30½
Snider Pack.....	19⅜	19¾	18¾	18¾
So Port Sug(†2½)	46⅜	47⅞	46⅛	46⅛
So Cal Edison (2)	50¾	50¾	49⅝	49⅞
So Daries A.....	55¾	56⅛	50	50
So Daries B.....	23¾	23½	22⅛	22⅛
South Pacific (6).	125½	126	124¼	124¼
Southern Ry (8).	159⅞	159⅞	158	158
South Ry pf (5)..	100¾	100⅞	100¾	100⅞
SouRM&O ct (4)*	132	132⅞	132	132⅞
Spalding pf (7)*..	115	115	115	115
Spear & Co*.....	16	16¾	16¾	16¾
Spicer Mfg Co...	39	39⅝	37⅞	37⅞
Spicer Mfgpf(8)*	113	112¼	112¼	112¼
Stan Com Tob (1)	34	31½	31½	31½
Stand G & El (3½)	70¼	70½	69¼	69¼
Stand C & E p (4)	70½	71½	71½	71½
Stand Milling (5).	123¼	123½	118⅛	118½
Stand Mill p (6)*.	108	180	108	108
Stand O Cal (2½).	59⅛	59½	58⅜	58⅜
Stan O NJ (†1½)	46⅛	46¼	45⅛	45⅛
Sta O NY (1.60).	36½	37⅛	36	36
Stand Plate G...	4½	5¼	4½	5
Stand Plate p*...	17	20	16⅞	19⅞
StanSanMf (1.68)	39⅜	39¾	39⅛	39½
Stewart War (6).	93¾	93⅞	91½	91½
Strom Carb (2)..	72	74¾	72	72
Studebaker (5)...	78½	78⅞	75½	75½
Submarine......	4½	4⅝	4⅜	4⅜
Superior Oil.....	7¾	8¼	7¾	7¾
Sweets Co.......	17¾	17⅞	16⅜	16¾
Symington A....	16⅝	16⅝	16⅝	16⅝
Telautogr'ph (.80)	20⅞	21	20½	21
Tenn Cop (.50)..	15¼	15¾	15¼	15¼
Texas Co (3)....	63½	64¾	63½	63½
Texas Gulf (4)...	70½	71¾	69⅞	69⅞
Texas Pac (5)...	147	146½	144	144
Tex Pac C & O..	14¾	15½	14⅝	14⅝
Tex Pac Land T.	27⅝	27¾	26¼	26¼
Thatcher Mfg....	38⅜	37⅝	37	37
The Fair (2.40)..	40	40½	39⅜	39½
Third Ave.......	40	39	39	39
Thomp J R (3.60)	64⅝	71¾	66½	68
Tide Wat O (.80)	25	25⅛	25	25⅛
Tide W O new...	17⅞	18	17½	17½
Tide Wat O p (5)	92¼	91¾	91¾	91¾
Tide W pf nw (6)	87	88	88	88
Timken Roll (†5)	128¾	129¼	124¼	125
Tob Prod (r)....	110⅛	111⅜	110¼	110½
Transcon Oil....	8¾	8⅝	8⅜	8⅜
Trico Prod (2½)..	39½	40	38½	38½
Und Ell Fisher (4)	72½	73½	72	72
Union Carb (6)..	153¾	154½	150	150
Union O Calif (2)	52⅝	52½	51	51
Union Pac (10)..	200¾	200½	199¾	199¾
Union Pac pf (4).	85	85	85	85
Union Tank C (5)	122½	122½	122½	122½
United Bisc (1.60)	37½	37	37	37
United Cig (c.80)	29¾	29⅞	29¾	29⅞
United Cig pf (6)	109⅞	109⅛	109	109
Unit Fruit (†5½).	137⅜	138½	137	137
United Paperb...	22½	22½	22½	22½

Div. in $	Sat. Clos.	High.	Low.	3.00
U S C Pipe (10)..	270	272	267¾	267¾
U S Distributing.	16½	16¾	16¼	16¼
U S Hoff Ma (4).	52½	52½	52⅛	52½
U S IndAlcohol(5)	112⅜	113	112	112
U S Leather Co..	45½	46⅜	45	45
U S Leather A...	65¼	66	64	64
U S Lea pr pf (7).	108	108¼	108	108
U S Realty (4)...	86½	86½	84½	84½
U S Rubber.....	43½	42⅝	42	42
U S Rub 1st pf...	77½	77¼	77	77
U S Sme & M (3½)	50	52	50	50
U S Sm&M pf(3½)	54½	54	53⅞	54
U S Steel (7)....	145¼	145¾	142	142⅞
U S Steel pf (7)..	142½	142⅝	142½	142½
U S Tob 1 pf (7)*.	137	138	138	138
Uni Pic 1st p (8)*	96½	96½	96½	96½
Univ Pipe&R (2)	23	24⅜	23	23½
Uti P & L A (e2)	43½	44½	40⅛	40⅛
Vanad Steel (†4).	84½	84½	80½	80½
Vicks Chem (4)..	70⅛	70½	70	70
Victor (4).......	99¾	99¼	94⅝	94⅝
Vic Prior pf (7)..	108½	107	107	107
Va-Car Chem...	15¼	15¾	15⅜	15⅝
Va-Car Che 6 pf.	51¾	52	52	52
Va-Car Ch p (7).	96⅜	95⅜	95⅜	95⅜
Vivaudou.......	17⅛	17¼	17⅛	17⅛
Vulcan Detinn (*)	31½	31½	31½	31½
Wabash.........	89½	90	89	89
Wabash pf A (5).	101	101	101	101
Waldorf Sys (1½)	23	23	22⅞	23
Walworth (1.20).	16⅞	x16½	16½	16½
Ward Bak A (8)*	104¼	106¼	105	106¼
Ward Bak B....	22⅝	23⅜	22¾	22¾
Ward Bak pf (7).	93	93⅛	93⅛	93⅛
War Picture A...	40⅜	43¾	40¼	40¼
Warner Quin (2).	37½	39¾	37⅞	37⅞
Warren Bro (4)..	188	185	182	182
Warren Fdy & P.	21	21	21	21
Wells Fargo.....	2¾	2⅞	2⅞	2⅞
WestDairyP A(4)	66	69⅝	67	69⅜
WestDairy Pr B.	38⅝	38⅞	37⅝	37⅝
WestPennE p(6)*	103	103	102⅞	103
W Penn E pf (7)*	112¼	114	112⅛	114
WestPennP p(6)*	109¾	112	110½	112
WestPennP p(7)*	115	115⅜	115¼	115¼
West Maryland..	48⅝	50	47½	47½
West Union (8)..	150	148½	145	145
Westing A B (2).	49	49	48¼	48¼
Westing M (4)...	105¾	106	102	102¼
Weston Elec In..	19⅛	22	19¼	21
West Elec I A (2)	34	35	32½	34¼
White Motor (1).	41	41⅞	39¼	39½
WhiteRock ct (2)	42¼	43½	42⅝	43¼
White Sew Mach.	41¾	42½	40⅝	40⅝
WhiteSewM pf(4)	53½	53¾	53½	53¾
Willys-Overland..	26	26⅞	25⅞	25⅞
Willys-Over pf (7)	101¼	101¼	101	101
Wilson Co.......	14⅞	15	15	15
Wilson Co A.....	32¼	32¾	32⅜	32⅜
Wilson Co pf....	70⅞	71½	71	71
Woolworth (5)...	191⅛	192¾	189	189
Worth Pump....	36⅛	36⅞	34	34
Wrights Aero (2).	180½	182	171½	171½
Wright Aero rts..	15½	15⅞	13¾	14
Wrigley Jr (†3½).	72	71¼	71	71
Yale & T Mfg(†5)	74	74⅞	74⅛	74⅛
Yellow T & C...	36⅝	38½	36½	36⅝
Youngstown (5)..	88	88	88	88

x Ex-dividend today. † Ex-rights.

Dividend rates as given in the above table are the annual cash payments based on the latest quarterly or half-yearly declarations.

* Unit of trading less than 100 shares. † Partly extra. ‡ Plus 4% in stock. § Plus $3 in preferred stock. ¶ Plus 1-25 in stock. a Paid this year—no regular rate. b Payable in stock. c Plus 5% in stock. d Payable when earned. e Payable in cash or stock. f Plus 10% in stock. g Plus 6% in stock. h Plus 1-100 of a share in stock quarterly. j Plus 2% in stock. k Plus 1-120 a share quarterly in stock. m Plus 3% in stock. n Plus 1-150 share in stock. p Plus 1½% in stock. r Payable 1-10 share quarterly in United Cigar Stores common stock. s Plus 1% in stock.

Sales of Active Stocks to 3.00 P. M.

Advance Rumley 18,000, Advance Rumley pfd 4,600, Ajax Rubber 400, Al Chem & D 14,200, Am Can 14,000, Am Drug 34,600, Am Linseed 27,700, Amer Metal 9,200, Am Radiator 200, Am Smelt 5,600, Am Sugar 800, Am Tel & Tel 1,800, Anaconda 51,200, Armour Co of Ill 74,100, Armour Co of Ill B 68,200, Atchison 900, Atl Coast Line 100, B & O 1,000, Barnsdall A 500, Beth Steel 3,800, C & O 500, Ches Corp 200, Chicago & Alton pf 1,000, Chi Gt West pf 2,300, Chi R I & Pac 300, Chi M & St P 3,400, Chi M & St. P pf 1,000, Chi & Ntwst 300, Chile 5,300, Chrysler Mot 40,600, Col Gas 2,100, Congoleum 4,600, Con Cigar 14,000, Con Gas 8,200, Cons Textile 2,900, Cont'l Bak A 1,400, Cont'l Bak B 1,000, Cont'l Can 3,500, Cont'l Motors 2,400, Corn Product Ref 1,000, Crucible 400, Davison Chem 1,000, Dodge Bros A 3,600, Dodge Bros pf 18,000, duPont 2,600, Elec Pow & Light 3,400, Erie 800, Fisk R & T 700, Fleischmann Co 2,000, Freeport Tex 5,000, Gabriel Snubber A 1,200, Gen Asp 1,200, Gen Elec 7,600, Gen Ry Signal 14,500, Gen Motors 95,000.

Glidden Co 1,200, Goodrich 2,200, Greene Cop 6,00, Hartman B 400, Houston Oil 1,200, Huldson M 24,000, Hupp Motor 43,300, Inter Com 96,400, Inter Nickel 32,100, Inter Paper 12,500, Inter Rapid T 200, Inter Tel & Te 3,400, Jordan Mot 600, Kelly-Spg Tr 400, Ken Copper, 4,800, Kresge S S 700, Lago Oil & Trans 100, Liq Carbon 2,700, Loews 2,700, Lorillard (P) Co 400, Louis Oil 12,700, Mack Truck 5,100, Marland 2,200, Mex Seabd 15,800, M K & T 2,600, Mo Pac 19,100, Mo Pac pf 2,800, Montg Ward 10,600, Nash Motor 6,400, Nat Dairy 10,100, Nat Dist Products 2,500, Nat Pow & Lt 14,400, Nev Consol 8,000, N. Y. Central 3,000, N Y Ont & W 2,200, N Y N H & H 1,600, Norf & West 600, North Am 3,000, Otis Steel 4,800, Patino Mines 3,400, Park Utah 18,200, Packard Motor 23,600, Pan-A Pet B 400, Pan-A Pet W B 400, P R R 1,000, Phillip Pet 2,600, Pierce Arrow 1,700, Pittsburgh Coal 400, Pierce Petrol 1,100, Postum Co 13,500.

Producers & Refin 500, Public Ser N J 5,900, Pure Oil 1,200, Radio Corp 40,500, Reading 600, Remington Rand 11,000, Schulte Ret Stores 3,400, Sears Roeb 21,000, Shell Un 3,400, Simmons Co 1,000, Sinclair 5,000, Skelly Oil 500, South Cal Edison 2,000, South Dairies "A" 4,500, South Dairies "B" 1,300, Stand Gas & Elec 2,000, Standard Oil of New York 6,500, S O of Cal 2,800, S O of N J 5,500, Spicer Man 2,500, Stew Warner 1,800, Studebaker 21,500, Texas Co 16,500, Texas Gulm 8,100, Texas Pac 500, Tex Pac L T 3,200, Timken 800, Tob Prod 1,200, Transcon Oil 1,900; Union Carb & Carb 7,000, Union Pac 600, United Distrib 500, U S Ind Alco 200, U S Leather A 1,500, U S Realty 400, U S Rubber 3,000, U S Steel 21,100, Universal P & R 3,000, Util Pow & Light 2,500, Vanadium Corp 1,200, V. Vivaudou 1,000, Victor Talk Mach 11,400, Wab 1,800, Wabash pf A 1,000, Warner Bros A 8,400, West Md 2,000, Westinghouse 4,500, White Motor 600, Willys-Overland 42,200, White Sewing Machine 2,400, Woolworth 1,500, Yel T & C 16,100.

PHILADELPHIA STOCKS

Sales.		Last prev.	High.	Low.	3.00
40	Alliance Ins	84¾	85	85	85
200	Almar St...	14	14	14	14
1200	Am Stores..	72	72	70⅞	70⅞
100	Am St Sec A	11¼	11¼	11¼	11¼
45	Am T & T.	189⅛	189¼	187½	187½
1200	Am T&T rts	14⅛	14¼	14	14
38	Bell Tel of Pa pf....	117	117½	117⅛	117½
290	Blauners...	60	58½	58½	58½
500	Cam Fire..	34⅛	34½	34	34
45	Cns Tr NJ.	59	60	59	59
130	Cramp S&E	3⅜	3¼	3	3
400	Elec P & Lt	41¼	41¼	40⅛	40⅛
800	Fire Asso..	77¼	77⅜	76¾	76¾
600	Fire As rts.	2¼	2⅜	2⅜	2⅜
100	Gen G&Elct	17	17	17	17
100	Hudson Mot	92	88⅝	88⅝	88⅝
100	Ins Co NA.	98	97	97	97
100	Lake S Cor.	6¾	6¾	6¾	6¾
5700	Leh Nav...	150	150⅞	148⅛	148⅛
600	LehPow Sec	41¾	44¾	43⅛	43⅛
3600	Lit Bros...	27⅜	28⅜	27½	28¼
100	L Mark Sh.	7¾	6¾	6¾	6¾
10	L Mark pf.	84	70	70	70
1700	Mfg Cas...	60	65½	60	65
1000	Moh & Hud	44⅝	45	44	44
2700	Nat P & Lt	35½	35⅝	34	34
75	North Amer	75⅞	75⅞	75½	75⅞
800	Nthe'st Pow	28¼	28½	28½	28½
100	P R T pf...	50¼	50¼	50¼	50¼
1700	Penna.....	66¼	66¼	65½	65½
110	Pa Salt....	99	99½	99	99
10	PhDaiPr pf	94	93	93	93
58	Phila Co pf.	48½	48	48	48
100	Phila Elec..	73	72⅞	72⅞	72⅞
200	Ph El P rcts	28¼	28⅜	28¼	28⅜
100	Phila Trac.	62½	63	63	63
10	Ph&W Ry.	10⅞	10½	10½	10½
300	Pub Ser NJ.	60	59½	58¼	58¼
50	Reliance Ins	31¾	31¾	31¾	31¾
18	Scot P pf..	113½	113½	113⅜	113⅜
500	Shreveport.	32	32	31½	31¾

Sales.	Last prev.	High.	Low.	3.00
2700 Stanley Co.	35¼	35	34½	34½
1800 Servel ct...	15	15¼	14¾	14¾
700 Shrev P L..	32	32	31½	31½
2600 Stanley Co.	35¼	35	34½	34⅝
100 Tono Bel..	1 1/16	1	1	1
400 Tono Min..	4⅛	4⅛	4⅛	4⅛

Sales.	Last prev.	High.	Low.	3.00
6200 U G I.....	147¼	147	144½	144½
100 U S Dai A..	60	60½	60½	60½
400 Un Lt&P A.	24½	23⅜	23⅜	23⅜
800 Un Trac...	45½	45⅝	45½	45½
900 Vic Talk M	100½	98⅝	97	97

TODAY'S BOND SALES

	3.00		3.00
$1000 Elec & Peo ctfs 4s............	64	500 Phila Elec 5½s 1953..........	107¼
1000 Phila Co 5s new............	99⅜	2000 Phila Elec Pow 5½s 1972.....	105⅞

ELECTRIC AUTO-LITE INST. DIVD.

New York, June 4.—Electric Auto-Lite Co. declared an initial quarterly dividend of $1 a share on the new common stock, placing it on a $4 annual basis. The old common paid $6 annually and was exchanged one share for 2 3-5 shares of new. A dividend of 58 1-3 cents a share for June was declared on the preferred. The merger with U. S. L. Battery has been completed.

—New lows were made on the New York Bond market today, U. S. Treasury 4¼s, 4s, 4¾s and 3⅜s.

NEW YORK CURB

Sales.	High.	Low.	2.30
300 Acetol Prod A...	25	24⅝	24⅝
100 Adams Mills.....	28½	28½	28½
100 Ala Gt South....	171	171	171
400 Alb P Bar A pfd.	21⅛	21	21⅛
100 Allied Pack......	1⅜	1⅜	1⅜
200 Allison Dr A....	17⅝	17½	17½
1000 Alpha Port Cem.	47	46¼	46¼
300 Alum Co Am....	187¾	185	185
4600 Am&For Pow war	18⅞	18⅛	18½
400 Am Arch Co....	51⅜	50½	51⅜
400 Am Br Bov El F.	13	12½	12½
100 Am Colortype...	30¾	30¾	30¾
100 Am Cyanamid B.	47⅝	47⅝	47⅝
2000 Am Dept Stores..	24¾	23⅞	24
700 Am Gas & El....	172¼	172	172¼
400 Am Hawaiian S S.	20⅞	20⅞	20⅞
2700 Am Rayon Prod.	23⅜	23	23⅛
1200 Am Roll Mill....	101¼	100¼	101
2800 Am Sol & Chem..	27½	26½	26½
200 Am S & C p pfd..	36¾	36¾	36¾
2200 Am States Sec A.	12	11⅝	12
500 Am States Sec B.	15¾	15½	15½
2600 Am States Sec war	4⅞	4⅝	4⅞
1100 Am Superp A....	43	42⅜	42⅜
200 Am Superp B.....	44¾	43¼	44¾
200 Am Super 1 pfd..	103¼	103¼	103¼

Sales.	High.	Low.	2.30
200 Anchor P Fence..	15	14	15
8900 Anglo Chil Nitra.	51	47½	48
400 Asso D & P......	31¼	31	31¼
500 Asso Gas & El...	48	48	48
200 Atlas Plywood...	90½	90½	90½
100 Atlas Port Cem..	43	43	43
400 Auburn Auto Co.	137¼	136	136
100 Axton Fisher A..	49½	49½	49½
300 Bahia Corp......	14⅝	14⅛	14⅛
300 Bahia Corp pfd..	19¾	19½	19½
700 Bancitaly Co....	215	213⅛	214⅜
200 Barker Bros.....	35¼	35¼	35¼
100 Beld Hall Elec...	1¾	1¾	1¾
100 Bliss E W........	20½	20½	20½
100 Blum S..........	34¼	34¼	34¼
700 Bohn Al & Br....	84	83½	83½
100 Brill Corp A.....	28	28	28
700 Brillo Mfg......	26½	25	26½
200 Brillo Mfg A.....	27¾	27½	27½
300 Brist Myers w...	72½	72⅛	72½
500 Brit-Celanese Ltd	27⅛	26½	27⅛
1100 Bklyn City R R..	7¼	7⅜	7⅛
400 Buf Niag & E P.	44⅛	44½	44½
500 Buf Niag & E P A	41½	41	41
200 Buf N & E P pfd.	26⅞	26¾	26⅞
400 Burns Bros rts...	9⅝	9½	9½

Sales.		High.	Low.	2.30
900	Butler Bros	27⅞	26½	26½
21700	Can Marconi W	7⅞	7⅝	7⅞
800	Carnation Milk	58	57½	57½
300	Case Plow	4⅜	4¼	4⅜
2400	Cavanagh Dobb	43½	42¾	42¾
200	Cavan Dobb pf	112	112	112
300	Celan Cor Am	84⅜	83⅝	83⅝
700	Cent Pipe Cor	10½	10½	10½
100	Cent Pub S A	26½	26½	26½
200	C G Sp & Bp	8⅞	8⅞	8⅞
300	Check Cab Mfg	28	28	28
100	Cit S P & L 6% pf	101¼	101¼	101¼
700	City Ice & Fuel	54¾	53½	54¾
300	Club Alum Uten	34⅛	34	34
13000	Col Graph	77⅜	74⅛	74⅛
100	Commonwlth Ed	186½	185	185
200	Commonw P pf	104	103¾	104
1500	Consol Dairy P	50	49	49½
800	Consol Film	16⅞	16½	16¾
1400	Cons Film PT pf	26¼	26	26
2300	Consol Laund	17¾	16¾	16¾
300	Cons Ret Strs	32⅛	32	32
100	Copel Prod A	15⅛	15⅛	15⅛
400	Courtaulds Ltd	24⅛	24	24⅛
100	Curtis Pub pf	117⅞	117⅞	117⅞
400	Curtiss Aero Exp	32⅞	32	32
500	Davega Inc	36¾	35¾	36¾
100	Davenport Hos	17	17	17
50	Deere & Co	400	399¾	400
4800	De For R C xtc	13½	12¾	13⅜
4300	De F R C vtc dep	13⅜	12½	13⅜
100	Det Motorbus	15¼	15¼	15¼
3500	Doehler Die C C	44½	42¼	43¼
600	Dubilier C & R	4⅜	4¼	4⅜
18900	Durant Motor	15½	13⅜	15
900	E States Pow B	26⅛	26	26⅛
1900	El Bond & Sh Cor	115¼	110	110
100	El B & Sh Co pf	110¼	110¼	110¼
2100	El Invest Inc	76	72⅛	73½
100	El R Securi Co	29	29	29
300	Em Pow Cor	37½	37⅛	37½
100	Evans E S A	89⅞	89⅞	89⅞
1000	Evans E S B	90	89	89
400	Fageol Motor Co	6¼	6⅛	6⅛
900	Fansteel Prod	15	15	15
300	Fedders Mfg A	47⅜	47	47
200	Fed Metal ctf	17½	17½	17½
500	Federal Water A	39½	39⅛	39½
400	Fiat deb rts	6	5⅞	5⅞
300	Fire An Phila	76⅛	76	76
125	Firestone Tire	175¼	175	175
200	Florsh Shoe A	51⅝	51⅛	51⅛
200	Florsh Shoe pf	101	101	101
25	Ford Mot Co Can	589	589	589
200	Forhan Co A	28	28	28
300	Foundation For A	18¾	18	18
10300	Fox Theatres A	31	30⅛	30⅛
400	Frk H H Mfg Co	16⅜	16⅜	16⅜
1100	Freed Eisem R C	6⅜	6	6
200	French Line B	68	67½	67½
5700	Freshman Chas	9¼	8¾	8¾
1400	Fulton Sylphon	38	37⅞	38
100	Gen Am Inv	70¼	70¼	70¼
19000	Gen Bak	14½	13½	13⅞
1700	Gen Bak pfd n	81⅞	80½	80½
200	Gen Bronze	50	50	50
1600	Gen Elec reg	9¼	8¾	8¾
9500	Gen Ice Cream	76⅜	72½	75⅛
1900	Gen Laund Ma	33	32¾	33
700	Gobel A	124¼	123	123
500	Gnd 5-10-25c St n	71⅞	70¼	71⅞
900	Hart Parr	61⅞	60	60
3000	Happin C St A	7⅛	6¾	6¾
100	Hazeltine Corp	15	15	15

Sales.		High.	Low.	2.30
200	Hires Ch A	24⅞	24⅞	24⅞
200	Holland Furn	41	41	41
2100	Hygrade Food	45	44	44¼
2600	Ind Ray Cor A	23⅝	23	23
100	Insur Co N A	97	97	97
600	Insur Secur	30⅞	30½	30½
200	Int Cig Mach Co	93½	92½	93½
2800	Intern Util B	18⅜	17	17
100	Interst Dep Strs	50½	50½	50½
800	Joske Bros vtc	42¾	42	42
200	Kemsley Millb	19¼	19¼	19¼
100	Lane Bryant	40½	40½	40½
1300	Lefcourt Real	33	31	33
100	Lefcou Real pfd	41½	41½	41½
3100	Leh Coal & Nav	151¾	149¾	150
1200	Leh Pow	44½	42½	44½
100	Leh Val C cfs	31	31	31
75	Leh Val C Sales	58½	58½	58½
600	Libby McN & L	12	12	12
1000	Lit Bros	27½	27⅛	27⅛
100	Loews deb rts	20	20	20
100	Ludwig Baum pfd	101	101	101
100	Marc Wire Lon	15½	15½	15½
600	Marion Stm Shov	91⅞	89⅞	91⅞
75	Maryl Casual	181¼	181	181
11300	Mavis Bottling	20¼	19¾	20¼
400	May Drug Str	24⅞	24½	24⅞
100	May Hosiery pfd	44	44	44
50	Melv Shoe	19¼	19¼	19¼
50	Mengel Box	125	125	125
200	Mercantile St C	149⅞	149¾	149⅞
7500	Mesabi Iron	3⅞	3¼	3¼
400	Metro Chain Strs	62⅞	62¾	62⅞
100	Met 5 & 50c St A	8	8	8
100	Met 5 & 50c S pfd	80⅝	80⅝	80⅝
100	Mid West Util	154	154	154
3300	Mohawk Hd Pow	45⅜	44¾	44¾
500	Mohawk Hd war	18½	18¼	18¼
1500	Mohawk Val	68	67	67
300	Monsanto Chem	60½	59½	60½
300	Motor Prod	95	94	94
500	Municipal Serv	20¾	20½	20½
100	Nanheim Phar	28½	28½	28½
600	Nat El Pow A	36⅞	36⅞	36⅞
500	Nat Food Prod	13⅞	13½	13½
500	Nat Leather	4¾	4¾	4¾
100	Nat Mfg & Stores	38⅞	38⅞	38⅞
300	Nat Pub Ser A	27⅝	27⅝	27⅝
1000	Nat Theatre Sup	13¼	12¾	12¾
400	Nat Trade Jour	34⅝	34⅛	34⅛
200	Nebel Oscar	25	24⅞	25
500	Nelson H	32½	32	32
100	Neve Drug	29½	29½	29½
300	Neve Drug A	39⅞	39⅞	39⅞
25	N Y Tel Co pfd	113¾	113¾	113¾
1400	Nichols & Shep	73	67½	69⅛
600	Nichol&Shep war	53	48	50½
1100	Niles Bem Pnd	73	68⅛	70
300	Noma Elec	23	22⅞	23
200	North Amer Cem	10⅞	10⅞	10⅞
100	North Am Utility	9¾	9¾	9¾
100	Nor Am Ut 1 pfd	95	95	95
5400	North Pow	29	28	28
800	North O Pow C	30	29½	29¾
300	Nor Sta P C A	145	144	144½
50	Ohio Bel T 7 pfd	112	112	112
100	Parke Davis Co	47⅛	47⅛	47⅛
300	Pend D Groc A	55	54¼	54¼
100	Pend D Groc B	50	50	50
275	Penney A pfd	103¾	103⅝	103¾
200	Penn Ohio Ed	42½	42	42
50	Penn O Ed p pfd	106¾	106¾	106¾
200	Penn Ohio Ed war	21½	21½	21½
100	Penn Ohio Sec	17	17	17

Sales.		High.	Low.	2.30
100	Penn Wt P C....	86⅛	86⅛	86⅛
200	Peop Drug Store.	62⅞	61⅜	61⅜
150	Perfection Stove.	119	119	119
75	Phelp Dodge Cor.	137¾	137	137
200	Philip Morris....	5¾	5¾	5¾
300	Pie Bak Am A...	34⅛	33½	33½
1500	Piggly Wiggly...	29½	28½	28½
300	Pines Wint F C A.	116	115	115
50	Pittsb & Lake E..	160¼	160¼	160¼
25	Pitts Pl Glass....	223	223	223
300	Pyrene Mfg.....	8	8	8
800	Rainbow Lumin.	32⅞	32	32
25	Real Assn Bklyn.	327	327	327
500	Repetti Candy...	1 3/16	1⅛	1 3/16
25	Richman Bros...	286	286	286
100	Rich R con pfd...	37	37	37
500	Ruberoid........	114	113¼	114
25	Safe C H & Lt...	156¼	156¼	156¼
6500	Safe-T-Stat......	52	48¼	49
25	Safeway Stores...	510	510	510
1200	St Regis Paper...	88¾	86¼	86¼
112	Sanitary Grocery.	331	330	330
200	Schulte Real Est.	27⅜	27	27⅜
300	Schulte United...	19½	19¼	19¼
300	Seeman Bros....	54⅜	54¼	54⅜
1800	Serv El n vtc....	15¼	15	15⅛
1100	Seton Leather...	31	31	31
1200	Silica Gel vtc....	24¾	23½	23¾
350	Smith Co AO....	120	119	120
200	Southeast P & L n	56⅞	56⅞	56⅞
100	Southe P&L p pfd	90	90	90
1200	Southe P & L war	21¾	20¾	21⅛
1500	South Asbestos..	32	30⅞	31
100	Sou C E B pfd...	27	27	27
300	South Coast.....	24	24	24
200	Sou Col Pow A...	25½	25½	25½
100	South Ice & U A.	25⅜	25⅜	25⅜
1200	South Ice & U B.	27⅞	27	27
1000	Spald A G & Bro.	155	155	155
4400	Spanish & Gen reg	5⅝	5⅜	5½
1800	Sparks Withing..	97	95½	96
2200	Spiegel May Stern	63¾	60¼	63
200	Stand Pow & Lt..	57⅞	57	57
200	Stern Bros B vtc.	16	16	16
500	Stinnes Hugo....	13⅞	13⅝	13⅞
100	Strocok Co......	42½	42½	42½
100	Stutz Mot.......	16¾	16¾	16¾
1500	Swift Intl.......	30¼	29½	29½
200	Swift Intl S 15 D.	29¾	29¾	29¾
200	Swift & Co......	135¾	135⅛	135½
300	Thomps Prod A..	38½	38	38
600	Timken Det Axle.	16¾	16¼	16¾
400	Tishman Realty.	44¼	43⅛	44¼
500	Todd Ship.......	58½	57⅜	58
3800	TransconAirTrsp.	30	28⅞	28⅞
2800	Trans Lux Pict..	4¼	3¾	4¼
1400	Triplex Safe Glass	66½	66	66
9000	TubizeArt S B vtc	594½	581	581
1500	Tung Sol Lamp..	13⅜	12⅞	13¼
1100	Tung Sol L A....	23	22½	22⅞
800	Uni Biscuit A....	59	59	59
400	Uni Biscuit B....	16⅛	16⅛	16⅛
4900	Uni Elec & Bd rts.	2⅝	2½	2½
600	Uni El Coal vtc..	55⅞	55	55½
2600	Uni G Imp C....	148	145	145½
3300	Uni Lt & P A....	24¼	23⅝	23⅞
200	Uni Pft Shar.....	9½	9½	9½
100	U S Dairy A.....	60	60	60
100	U S For & Sec pfd	98½	98½	98½
900	U S Freight.....	82½	80	81¼
30000	U S Gypsum.....	94⅞	90⅛	94⅞
5000	U S Gypsum pfd.	125	125	125
100	U S L Battery B.	11	11	11
300	Util P & L vtc B.	31½	31¼	31¼

Sales.		High.	Low.	2.30
900	Util Shar........	16¼	15⅝	15⅝
100	Waitt & Bond A.	27⅛	27⅛	27⅛
500	Walgreen.......	43⅞	43⅝	43⅝
1500	Warner Bros Pic.	36	34	34⅝
300	Watson J W.....	9	9	9
70	Wesson O & S vtc	84¾	84	84
100	West Auto Sup A	59½	59½	59½
100	Wheatsworth....	52	52	52
8500	Wire Wheel Corp.	36	34	34⅝
100	Woodworth Inc..	38⅛	38⅛	38⅛
100	Worth Inc A.....	20⅛	20⅛	20⅛
10	Young S & W pfd	42¼	42¼	42¼
2600	Zonite..........	41¾	39¾	41

MINING STOCKS

1000	AmConM&M Ltd	4c.	4c.	4c.
1100	Ariz Globe C....	6c.	5c.	5c.
500	Carnegie Metals.	24	24	24
1200	Cent Am Mines..	4⅛	4	4⅛
200	Chief Cons Min..	4⅛	4⅛	4⅛
24600	Comstock T & D.	53c.	45c.	45c.
2700	Cons Cop Mines.	13⅞	13¼	13¼
3000	Cortez Silver....	28c.	27c.	28c.
300	Cresson Gold....	1 11/16	1 11/16	1 11/16
100	Dolores Esper....	1¼	1¼	1¼
700	Eng Gold M Ltd.	4¾	4½	4¾
1000	Falcon Lead Min.	14c.	14c.	14c.
8000	Flor Goldfld M..	23c.	20c.	23c.
1300	Golden Center M	12⅞	12½	12½
300	Hecla Min......	15⅝	15⅝	15⅝
300	Hollinger........	14⅞	14½	14⅞
3700	Hud Bay M & S..	18¼	18	18
3300	Iron Cap Copper.	7¼	6¼	6¾
800	Mason Val......	1½	1⅜	1½
600	New Cornelia....	29¾	29⅝	29⅝
7300	Newmont Mining	185¾	182	182
75	N J Zinc........	225	225	225
400	Nipissing.......	4⅜	4⅛	4⅛
19300	Noranda........	31½	29¾	30⅜
1500	Ohio Cop........	85c.	83	83
1000	Parm Por M Ltd.	35c.	35	35
300	Premier Gold M.	2⅜	2¼	2¼
3000	Shattuck Denn..	20⅛	19	19
300	So Am Gold & P.	3½	3⅜	3⅜
100	Tech Hughes....	10⅜	10⅜	10⅜
1000	Tonopah Ext....	14c.	14	14
100	Uni East Min....	85c.	85	85
3300	Uni Verde Est...	21½	19⅛	20
100	Uni Zinc Smelt...	80c.	80	80
200	Unity Gold......	1 3/16	1⅛	1 3/16
200	Utah Apex......	4½	4½	4½
200	Walker Mines...	1¼	1⅛	1¼
1800	Wenden Cop....	1½	1 1/16	1½
200	Yukon Gold.....	52c.	52	52

INDEPENDENT OIL STOCKS

2700	Am Con Oilflds..	1⅛	1 1/16	1⅛
1700	Am Marcaibo Co.	6	5¾	5¾
400	Ark Nat Gas....	9¾	9¾	9¾
100	Barnsd deb rts...	5¼	5¼	5¼
4000	Carib Synd......	23¼	21⅝	22½
100	Cities Serv n.....	71	70⅜	70⅜
100	Cit Serv pf......	103	103	103
200	Cit Serv B......	35¼	35¼	35¼
16500	Colombia Synd..	2 1/16	1⅞	1⅞
4600	Creole Synd.....	15	14⅝	14¾
4500	Crown Cent Pet..	3¼	2⅞	2⅞
900	Darby Pet......	27	26½	27
300	Emp G & F 7 pf.	103⅞	103⅞	103⅞
100	Emp G & F 8 pf.	113	113	113
1400	Gibson Oil Cor...	1⅜	1¼	1⅜
200	Gulf Oil Pa......	135½	134	135½
600	Houston Gulf Gas	19	18⅝	18⅝

Sales.		High.	Low.	2.30
400	Intercontl Pet...	1⅝	1⅝	1⅝
200	Leonard Oil.....	7⅞	7⅞	7⅞
200	Lion Oil.........	31⅝	31½	31½
1200	Lone Star G Del.	54¾	54⅛	54½
1700	Magdal Synd....	1½	1⅜	1⅜
5300	Mex Oil.........	67c	61	64
1400	Mount Gulf.....	89c	89	89
2900	Mount Prod.....	24	23⅞	23⅞
100	New Bradford O.	27¾	27¾	27¾
1000	Northwest Oil...	10c	10	10
600	Nor Cent Tex Oil.	13¼	12¾	12¾
100	Pandem Oil.....	3	3	3
4400	Pantepec Oil.....	12¾	12⅛	12¾
500	Reiter-Foster Oil.	8⅛	7⅞	7⅞
100	Rich O Cal pf ww.	24⅛	24⅛	24⅛
800	Salt Ck Prod....	28¼	28⅞	28¼
10900	Texon Oil & Land	4¼	4 1/16	4 1/16
500	Tidal Osage O...	19½	19½	19½
100	Tidal Os O non-vt	19	19	19
200	Venezuelan Pet..	6	5⅞	5⅞
200	"Y" Oil n.......	7	7	7

STANDARD OIL ISSUES AND FORMER SUBSIDIARIES

Sales.		High.	Low.	2.30
400	Anglo Am Oil....	18	17¾	18
3300	A A O non vtc...	17⅞	17	17½
100	Atl Lobos........	3¼	3¼	3¼
100	Buckeye P L....	66½	66½	66½
800	Contl Oil........	17¾	17⅝	17⅝
10	Gal S O pfd old..	45	45	45
1500	Humble O & R...	82¾	81½	82
100	Imp O Can......	67	67	67
100	Ind P L.........	84	84	84
900	Inter Pet Ltd....	41⅜	41¼	41⅜
300	Nat Transit.....	23½	23	23
250	Northern P L....	120	118½	118½
200	Ohio Oil........	64	63⅜	63⅜
600	Prairie O & G....	51	50¾	50¾
250	Prairie P L......	215¼	214¼	215¼
50	Sou W Penn P L.	100¾	100¾	100¾
12300	S O Ind.........	78½	77⅝	78
300	S O Neb........	42	42	42
200	S O Ohio........	76	75½	76
100	S O Ohio pfd....	120	119¾	119¾
1000	Vacuum Oil.....	81⅝	81	81

BONDS

Sales.		High.	Low.	2.30
19	Ala Pow 4½s....	97	96¾	96¾
28	Alum Co Am 5s..	102⅛	101¾	101¾
5	Am Aggre Cor 6s.	104¼	104¼	104¼
63	Am Gas & El 5s..	98	97¼	97⅜
3	Am Nat Gas 6½s	101⅝	101½	101⅝
2	Am Pow & Lt 6s.	107¾	107½	107½
88	Am Roll Mill 5s..	96¾	96¾	96¾
2	Am Sol 6½s.....	113	112	113
10	Anaconda 6s A...	100¾	100¾	100¾
10	Appal El Pow 5s.	100¼	100	100⅛
2	Ark P & L 5s....	99½	99½	99½
13	Asso Gas&El 5½s	104⅜	104¼	104¼
205	Asso Gas&El 4½s	108½	107¼	107⅞
1	Asso D&Ptg 6s wi	100	100	100
5	Asso Elec 5½s....	104⅞	104⅞	104⅞
19	Atlac Plyw 5½s wi	113	112½	112½
7	Beaverboard 8s..	102⅛	102	102
27	Bos & Me 5s AC.	99	99	99
1	Caro Geo Ser 6s A	96¾	96¾	96¾
1	Cent Sta P&L 5½s	97⅜	97⅜	97⅜
15	C M & St P 4½s E	102½	102½	102½
2	Chi Pneu Tool 5½s	100½	100½	100½
10	Childs 5s........	93¾	93¼	93¼
136	Cinn G & E 4s A.	90¾	90⅜	90⅜
7	Cin St Ry 5½s A.	100½	100½	100½
16	Cit Serv 5s......	97¾	97½	97½
1	Cit Serv 6s......	104	104	104
23	Cit Serv Gas 5½s.	95	94½	94¾
13	Cit Ser Gas Pip 6s	100⅛	100	100
81	Cit Serv Pow 5½s.	100⅛	100	100
10	Commerce Invt 6s	98½	98½	98½
16	Cons G Balt 6s A.	107⅜	107	107
1	Cons Tex 8s.....	95	95	95
30	Contl G & E 5s A.	93¾	93½	93½
7	Cont'l Oil 5½s....	96½	96½	96½
3	Cudahy 5s......	100⅞	100⅞	100⅞
2	Cudahy 5½s.....	99¾	99¾	99¾
42	D&R G&W 5s B.	93⅝	93⅜	93⅝
5	Det Cty G 6s A..	107⅜	107	107⅜
16	Det Intl 6½s.....	99½	99¼	99½
41	Det Intl 7s......	94¼	92½	92½
18	Empire O & R 5½s	94	93⅞	94
2	Fed Sug 6s......	82½	82½	82½
8	Fed Wat Serv 5½s.	104¾	104¼	104¾
3	Firest Cot Mil 5s.	94⅝	94½	94½
1	Firest T & R 5s..	96	96	96
2	Fisk Tire 5½s....	96¾	96¾	96¾
26	Fla P & L 5s.....	97½	97	97⅛
12	Gatineau Pow 5s.	98⅞	98½	98½
23	Gen Laun Ma 6½s	116¾	113	116¾
24	Gen Vend 6s....	95½	95½	95½
2	Georgia Pow 5s..	99⅞	99⅞	99⅞
4	Goody T&R 5s 28	99¾	99¾	99¾
4	Grand Trunk 6½s.	109¾	109¾	109¾
2	Gulf Oil Pen 5s 37	101⅜	101⅜	101⅜
5	Gulf Oil Pen 5s 47	102	102	102
2	Hood Rub 7s....	102½	102½	102½
10	HoustonGulfG6½s	99	99	99
4	Houst Gulf G 6s A	99½	99½	99½
5	Ill Pow & L 5½s 57	98	98	98
2	Ill Pow & L 5½s 54	102½	102⅛	102⅛
13	Ind Oil & Gas 6s.	102	102	102
2	IndianapP&L5sA.	100¼	100	100
37	Inland Steel 4½s A	92½	91⅝	92½
8	Int'l Pow Sec 7s E	99⅞	99¾	99¾
6	Int'l Sec Amer 5s.	94¾	94¾	94¾
2	Intst Nat G 6s ww	104	104	104
12	Intersta Pow 5s..	97	96¾	97
3	Interstate Pow 6s.	100⅝	100⅜	100⅜
16	Inv't Cor Am 5s A	106	105	105⅜
5	Ia Neb L&P 5s A	96¾	96	96¾
5	Jeddo H'd Coal 6s	104½	104	104
13	Kelvin Corp 6s...	83⅜	83	83
4	Lehigh Pow 6s A.	107	106¾	107
10	Libby McN&L 5s	95	95	95
1	Lone Star Gas 5s.	99⅝	99⅝	99⅝
2	Long Isl Lt 6s...	105	105	105
1	Louis Pow & Lt 5s	97	97	97
4	Mani Pow 5½s A.	102⅛	102⅛	102⅛
1	Mass Gas 5½s....	104	104	104
1	BeCord Rad 6s...	99½	99½	99½
4	MetEdCoPa4½sD	99¾	99⅝	99¾
1	Midwest Gas 7s A	103½	103½	103½
3	Milwauk Gas 4½s.	101¾	101¾	101¾
16	Narrag Co 5s A..	100½	100½	100½
16	Nat Pub Serv 5s.	91	90½	90½
4	Nichols & Shep 6s	196	193	194
2	Nich & Sh 6s ww.	99¾	99¾	99¾
1	Nor Sts P M 6½s.	103	103	103
2	Ohio Pow 5s 52B.	101¾	101¾	101¾
10	Pac G & E 4½s E.	98½	98½	98½
7	Pac Invest 5s....	101¼	101⅛	101⅛
1	Pen O Ed 6s A ww	103¾	103¾	103¾
2	Phila E 5½s 47..	107¼	107⅛	107⅛
86	Phila E 5½s 72...	105¾	105⅝	105⅝
1	Pitts Scr & B 5½s.	100½	100½	100½
1	Pitts Steel 6s....	102½	102½	102½
16	Potomac Ed 5s E.	99¾	99¾	99¾
5	Proctor&Gam4½s.	99½	99½	99½
3	PubSerE&G4½s..	99⅞	99⅞	99⅞

Sales.		High.	Low.	2.30
132	Pub Serv N J 4½s.	131½	129½	129½
11	Purity Bak 5s...	95⅞	95¾	95¾
12	Rem Arms 5½s...	98½	98	98½
105	Richfld Oil 6s A..	155	147¼	149⅛
3	RochesG&E4½sD.	102⅛	102⅛	102⅛
3	San Ant P S 5s B.	98	98	98
3	Schulte R Est 6s.	105½	105½	105½
10	SchulteR Est 6sX	93⅝	93½	93⅝
19	Scripps E W 5½s..	98½	98½	98½
2	Servel Co Del 5s.	72½	72	72
3	Sharon St H 5½s A	99	99	99
1	ShawinW&P4½sA	95⅞	95⅞	95⅞
219	Shell P L 5s.....	96	95⅝	95¾
51	Snider Pack 6s...	129½	127½	127½
20	S E P & L 6s....	107⅜	107	107⅛
3	Sou Cal Ed 5s '51	102⅛	102⅛	102⅛
5	Sou Cal Ed 5s '52	102⅛	102⅛	102⅛
19	Sou Cal G 5s '37.	94¾	94¾	94¾
20	Sou Asbestos 6s..	129	124	129
9	Southw P&L 6s A	109¼	109¾	110¼
4	Stand P & L 6s...	101	101	101
3	Stutz Mot 7½s...	96	96	96
25	SunMaid Rais6½s.	85	84¾	84¾
1	Sun Oil 5½s......	101	101	101
17	Swift & Co 5s....	100¼	100⅛	100⅛
35	Transcont Oil 7s.	105	105	105
1	Ulen & Co 6½s...	99	99	99
12	Union Pac R R 4s	92¾	92¾	92¾
2	Uni Lt & Rail 5½s	97	97	97
8	U S Rub 6½s 29..	100	99⅞	100
7	U S Rub 6½s '34..	99⅞	99½	99⅞
1	U S Rub 6½s '37..	99⅝	99⅝	99⅝
13	U S Sm & Ref 5½s	102½	101½	102½
12	Util & P L 5½s...	97	97	97
2	West Pow 5½s A..	102	101¾	101¾
20	Wheel Stl 4½s B..	91¼	91¼	91¼

FOREIGN BONDS

Sales.		High.	Low.	2.30
2	Adriatic Elec 7s..	98	98	98
1	Agri Mor Ba 7s'46	105¼	105¼	105¼
3	Agri Mor Ba 7s'47	100	100	100
1	Baden 7s........	97½	97½	97½
1	Berlin 6s wi......	95⅝	95⅝	95⅝
4	BuenosAires 7s'52	102	101½	102
2	Buenos Aires 7½s.	103	102	102
48	Com&Priv Bk 5½s	91	91	91
10	Denmark 5½s...	100¾	100½	100½
36	Denmark 4½s...	95	95	95
23	Estonia 7s.......	94¼	94	94
7	Free St Prus 6½s.	97½	97½	97½
8	Gelsen Min 6s...	97	97	97
15	Ger Cons Mun 7s	100	99⅞	99⅞
5	Ger Cons Mun 7s	94⅞	94⅞	94⅞
120	Guant&WRR 6sA	93	92½	92½
3	Indt M Bk F'ld 7s	101	101	101
14	Isotta Fraschini7s	103¾	103½	103¾
1	Is'ta Frasch7s ww	91	91	91
11	Jugo Sta M Bk 7s	87	87	87
1	Leon Tietz C 7½s.	87	87	87
1	L'nTietzC7½s ww	103½	103½	103½
15	Lom Elec 7s A...	105⅞	105⅜	105⅜
7	Lom El 7s A ww.	97	96¼	96¾
7	Mendoza 7½s....	100	100	100
6	Montevideo 6s A.	98	98	98
2	MorBkBogota7sn	93½	93½	93½
12	MorBkChile 6s'61	96	96	96
2	Muni Medellin 8s	104⅝	104⅝	104⅝
1	Muni Redellin 7s.	98	98	98
8	Nippon Elec 6½s.	94¼	94¼	94¼
15	N Ger Lloyd 6s..	94	93⅞	93⅞
2	Norway 5s '67..	94⅞	94⅞	94⅞
8	Oslo Gas&Elec 5s	94¾	94½	94¾
z12	Parana 7s.......	98	98	98
1	Saarbruecken 7s.	101	101	101
5	Santa Fe City 7s.	97	96¾	96¾
2	Santiago 7s......	100	99⅞	99⅞
1	Sax S Mor In 6½s.	97½	97½	97½
3	Serbs 7s B.......	88½	88½	88½
1	Uni Ind 6½s.....	94½	94½	94½
5	Uni St. Wks 6½s A	91¼	91	91
20	Vienna 6s.......	90⅜	90	90
31	Warsaw 7s......	89⅝	89	89⅝
15	Westp'l U El 6s A	91⅞	91¾	91¾

Ex-dividend today: Carreras A 15%, Carreras B 15%, Nat Sug Ref of N J 1¾, Western Canada Flour Mills 35c, Western Canada Flour Mills par 1⅝, Honolulu Cons. Oil ¾, Home Fire & Marine Ins 40c.

COMMERCIAL MARKETS

PHILADELPHIA, June 4.—BREADSTUFFS—Flour quiet but steady. Quotations, per 196 lbs., in sacks: Soft winter straights, Western, \$8.25a8.75; nearby, \$8a8.50; hard winter, straight, \$8a8.50; short patent, \$8.25a8.75; spring, first, clear, \$7.10a7.40; patent, \$8a8.25; short patent, \$8.30 a8.75; family brands, \$9a9.75. Rye flour, \$7.75a8.

WHEAT—Market nominal.

CORN—Market nominal.

OATS—Market 1c. higher; No. 2, white, 80½a83½c.

BALED HAY AND STRAW—Sold slowly at unchanged prices, We quote; Timothy hay, No. 2, \$15.50a16.50; No.

3, $13.50a14.50.   Straw, straight rye, $23; wheat straw, $15a16; oat straw, $15a16.

PROVISIONS—Steadily held. Quotations: Beef, in sets, smoked and air-dried, 44c.   Beef, knuckles and tenders, smoked and air-dried, 45c.   Hams, S. P. cured, loose, 24c.; skinned, loose, 24c.; smoked, 26c.; boiled, boneless, 40c. Picnic shoulders, S. P. cured, loose, 17c.; smoked, 18c.   Bellies, in pickle, loose, 21c.   Breakfast bacon, 35c.   Lard, 13½c.

BUTTER (Close)—½c. lower.   Top grades, 45½a 48½c.; 92 score, 44½c.; 91 score, 44c.; 90 score, 43½c.; 89 score, 42½c.; 88 score, 41½c.; 87 score, 41c.; 86 score, 40c.

EGGS (Close)—Firmer, extra firsts, 31c.; firsts, in new cases, 29½c.; firsts, in old cases, 28½c.; seconds, 27c.

CHEESE—In moderate demand and firm.   Quotations: N. Y. flats, 25a25¾c.; Single Daises, fresh, 25½c.

POTATOES—White potatoes, new, Fla., bbl., No. 1, $3.25a 3.50; No. 2, $1.75a2; S. C., No. 1, $2.50a3.35; No. 2, $1.50a 1.75.   Sweet potatoes, N. J., basket, $1.50a2; Del. and Md., hampers, No. 1, $2.50a3.50; No. 2, $1a1.65.

LIVE POULTRY—Fowls, not leghorns, 28a29c.; leghorn fowls, 24a25c.; broilers, P. R., as to size, 40a47c.; R. I. Reds, as to size, 35a40c.; leghorn broilers, 1¾a2 lbs. or over, 32a 33c.; 1½ lbs., 28a30c.; 1¼ lbs., 26a28c.; 1 lb., 25c.   Old roosters, 18c.   Ducks, White Pekin, 22a25c.; mixed colors, 18a20c.   Turkeys, 25a30c.   Rabbits, lb., 18a20c.   Pigeons, pair, 45c.; young, 30c.

DRESSED POULTRY—Fowls, fresh-killed, in boxes, 4a5½ lbs., 32a33c.; 6 lbs. or over, 30a32c.; 3a3½ lbs., 28a29c.; 8½ lbs., 26a27c.; 2 lbs. or under, 23a25c.; in bbls., 5a5½ lbs., 29a30c.; 8 lbs. or over, 27a28c.; 4a4½ lbs., 26a 28c.; 3a3½ lbs., 21a23c.   Old roosters, dry-picked, 5 lbs. or over, 21a22c.; under 5 lbs., 18a20c.

LANCASTER, June 4 (Pennsylvania Bureau of Markets). —Hog receipts 425, cattle 425, calves 325.   Market active. Beef steers steady; top, $14; average weight, 1,470 lbs.; bulk of sales $12.25 to $13.25; bulls, she stock and cutters firm; calves steady; top, $17.50; slaughter cattle, calves and vealers; steers, 1,300-1,500 lbs., good, $12.50a14; steers, 1,100-1,300

lbs., good, $12.75a14; steers, 950-1,100 lbs., good, $12.50a
13.75; steers, 950 lbs. up, medium, $12a12.75; common, $8.75a
12; heifers, 850 lbs. up, choice, $10a11.25; good, $8.25a10;
medium, $8.25a9.25; cows, choice, $8.25a9.50; good, $7.25a
8.25; common and medium, $5.75a7.25; low cutter and cutter,
$4a5.75; bulls, yearlings excluded, good and choice, beef,
$8.75a10.75; cutter, common and medium, $6.50a8.75; vealers, milk fed, good and choice, $15.50a17.50; medium, $13.25a
13.50; cull and common, $6.50a13.75.

NEW YORK, June 4.—Cotton futures opened firm. July,
$20.82; Oct., $21; Dec., $20.85; Jan., $20.76; March, $20.76.
Flour firm; spring patents, $7.75a8.25; soft winter
straights, $7.90a8.25; hard winter straights, $7.50a7.90. Rye
flour steady; fancy patents, $7.75a7.90. Rye firm, No. 2
Western, $1.43¼ f. o. b. New York and $141½ c. i. f. export.
Barley firm; No. 2, $1.09¼ c. i. f. New York. Pork steady;
mess, $31.50; family, $34.50a36.50. Lard steady; Middle
West, $12.20a12.30. Tallow steady; special loose, $8; extra,
$8⅜. Hay steady; No. 1, $25; No. 2, $23a24; No. 3, $20a
21; sample, $16a18. Straw steady; No. 1 rye, $30. Beans
steady; marrow, $10.25; pea, $10.25a10.50; red kidney, $8.70
a9; white kidney, $10.25a10.50. Hops steady; State, 1927
and 1926, nominal; Pacific Coast, 1927, $26a30; 1926,
$22a24.
Eggs, receipts, 22,610 cases; market irregular. Extras,
31a31½c.; extra firsts, 29½a30½c.; firsts, 28¼a29c.; seconds, 27½a28c.; dirties, No. 1, 27a27½c.; dirties, No. 2,
26a26½c.; checks, 26a26½c.; mediums, extra firsts, 31a32c.;
brown firsts, 29½a30½c.; storage packed, special marks, 32a
32½c.; storage packed extra firsts, 31a31½c.; storage packed
firsts, 29½a30½c.; storage packed mediums, 27a27½c.;
storage packed dirties, No. 1, 27½a28c. Jersey and other
nearby western hennery whites, closely selected extras, 35a
36c.; nearby and nearby western hennery whites, average extras, 33a34c.; nearby and nearby western hennery whites, extra firsts, 32a32½c.
Butter steady; receipts, 5,652; creamery, higher than extras, 44a44½c.; extras (92 score), 13½c.; firsts (88 to 91
18

score), 41a43¼c.; packing stock, current make, No. 1, 32½c.; No. 2, 31a31½c.

Eggs irregular; receipts, 22,610; fresh gathered, extra firsts, 29½a30½c.; firsts, 28¼a29c.; seconds, 27½a28c.; storage, extra firsts, 31a31½c.; firsts, 29½a30½c.

Cheese firm; receipts, 55,946; State, whole milk, flats, fresh, fancy to fancy specials, 24a25½c.; State, whole milk, held, fancy to fancy specials, 30a32c.; average run, 29a30c.

Dressed poultry steady; chickens, fresh, 30a45c.; frozen, 26a43c.; fowls, fresh, 21a31c.; frozen, 22a31c.; old roosters, 15a21c.; turkeys, fresh, 25a34c.; frozen, 30a47c.

Live poultry firm; broilers, by express, 15a50c.; roosters, by freight, 16c.; no other prices quoted.

NEW YORK PROVISIONS

Sat. Clos.	Opening.	Closing.
Mess Pork—		
Cash $31.50	$31.50	$31.50
Lard—		
Cash $12.20a12.30	$12.10a12.20	$12.20a12.30
Short Ribs—Nominal.		

CHICAGO, June 4 (U. S. Department of Agriculture).—Hogs—Receipts 58,000; market fairly active; steady to 10c. lower than Friday's average; most weakness on choice pigs; top, $9.95 paid for choice 200-250 lb. weights; butchers, medium to choice, 250-350 lbs., $9.25a9.95; 200-250 lbs., $9.30a9.95; 160-200 lbs., $8.60a9.95; 130-160 lbs., 7.60a9.70; packing saws, $8.40a9; pigs, medium to choice, 90-130 lbs., $7.25a8.50.

Cattle—Receipts 21,000. Calves—Receipts 5,000; too many weighty steers here; better grades scaling 1,200 lbs. upward 15c. to 25c. lower; lower grade steers and all grades of yearlings in demand at steady prices. Stockers very scarce. Slaughter classes, steers, good and choice, 1,300-1,500 lbs., $13.25a14.50; 1,100-1,300 lbs., $13.25a14.75; 950-1,100 lbs., $13.25a14.75; common and medium, 850 lbs. up, $10a13.25. Fed yearlings, good and choice, 750a950 lbs., $13.25a14.75. Heifers, good and choice, 850 lbs. down, $13a14.25; common and medium, $8.75a13. Cows, good and choice, $9a11.75; common and medium, $7.75a9; low cutter and cutter, $6a7.75. Bulls, good and choice (beef), $9a10.50; cutter to medium, $7.75a9.25. Vealers (milk-fed), good and choice, $12a15.50; medium, $11a12; cull and common, $8a11. Stocker and feeder steers, good and choice (all weights), $11.75a13; common and medium, $9.50a11.75.

Sheep—Receipts 14,000; fat new crop of lambs uneven. Old crop of clipped yearlings, 25c. down; sheep weak; feeders scarce; lambs, good and choice (92 lbs. down), $17.50a19.25; medium, $16.25a17.50; cull and common, $13.75a16.25. Ewes, medium to choice (150 lbs. down), $5a8.65; cull and common, $2a6.50.

Potatoes, receipts 20 cars; on track, 321. Total U. S. shipments, Saturday 808, Sunday 71 cars; new stock trading good, market stronger; Alabama, Texas, Louisiana sacked, Bliss Triumphs, $2.15a2.35; occasional fancy, $2.50; ordinary, $1.90a2.10; sacked Irish Cobblers, mostly $2.25; Florida barrel, Spalding Rose, $4; South Carolina barrel Irish Cobblers, $4a4.25; old stock trading slow, market steady; Wisconsin sacked round whites, $1.10a1.25. Minnesota sacked round whites, 90c.a$1.05; Idaho sacked russets, $1.50a1.65.

Poultry, alive, steady; receipts, 9 cars; fowls, general run, 23½c.; Leghorn springs, 30c.; broilers, 27a30c.; spring broilers, 38c.; turkeys, 20c.; roosters, 16½c.; ducks, 20c.; spring ducks, 28c.; geese, 14c.

Butter unchanged; receipts 22,828 tubs; creamery extras, 42¾c.; standards, 42¾c.; extra firsts, 41½a42c.; firsts, 40½a41c.; seconds, 38a40c. Eggs unchanged; receipts 35,275 cases; firsts, 26½a27c.; ordinary, 25a26c.; storage packed extras, 29½c.; firsts, 29c.

CHICAGO MARKET

	Sat. Close	Open.	High.	Low.	Close.
Wheat, No. 2—					
July	147½	146¾	149⅞	146⅝	147¾
Sept.	148⅞	148	151¼	147⅞	159¾
Dec.	151¼	150¼	153⅝	150⅛	152
Rye—					
July	129¼	128	131½	128	129½

Sept. .....$121\frac{5}{8}$	$120\frac{1}{2}$	$124\frac{3}{4}$	$120\frac{1}{2}$	$122\frac{1}{2}$
Dec. 122	$120\frac{1}{2}$	$124\frac{3}{4}$	$120\frac{1}{2}$	$123\frac{1}{4}$

Corn, No. 2—

July .....$105\frac{3}{8}$	$105\frac{1}{2}$	$105\frac{5}{8}$	$104\frac{3}{4}$	105
Sept. .....$105\frac{1}{8}$	$104\frac{3}{4}$	$105\frac{3}{8}$	$104\frac{1}{2}$	$104\frac{1}{2}$
Dec. ...... $90\frac{1}{4}$	90	$90\frac{1}{8}$	$89\frac{3}{8}$	$89\frac{3}{8}$

Oats, No. 2—

July—

Old .... $55\frac{3}{8}$	$55\frac{1}{4}$	57	$55\frac{1}{4}$	$56\frac{3}{8}$a
New .... $56\frac{1}{4}$	56	$57\frac{7}{8}$	56	57
Sept. ..... $47\frac{1}{8}$	$46\frac{3}{4}$	$47\frac{1}{2}$	$46\frac{3}{4}$	$46\frac{3}{4}$
Dec. ...... $48\frac{7}{8}$	$48\frac{5}{8}$	$49\frac{1}{8}$	$48\frac{3}{8}$	$48\frac{3}{8}$

Lard—

July 11.97	11.90	12.00	11.90	12.00
Sept. 12.25	12.30	12.35	12.27	12.32
Oct. 12.40a	12.42	12.42	12.37	12.42b
Dec. 12.40a	12.47b	....	....	12.47

Short Ribs—

July 12.30b	12.30	....	....	12.30
Sept. 12.55a	12.55	....	....	12.55

NEW YORK COTTON FUTURES

	Sat. Clos.	Open.	High.	Low.	2.30
January 20.53	20.79	20.95	20.74	20.93
February 20.50	....	....	....	....
March 20.47	20.76	20.88	20.75	20.88
April 20.46	....	....	....	....
May 20.46	20.77	20.85	20.75	20.83
June 20.57	....	....	....	....
July 20.62	20.82	21.00	20.82	20.97
August 20.62	....	....	....	....
September 20.79	....	....	....	....
October 20.76	20.98	21.21	20.98	21.14
November 20.68	....	....	....	....
December 20.60	20.85	21.03	20.85	20.96

	Sat. Clos.	Today's.
SPOT COTTON.		
Middling Uplands 21.15		....

HIDE PRICES WEAKER

CHICAGO, June 4.—Hide prices were again weaker in the American market, brought about by continued easiness in South America and dull leather business among domestic tanners. A practical clearance was effected in the world market at price recessions as indicated by the hide price index of the Shoe and Leather Reporter, which stands at 129.9 for the week ending June 2, 1928. This compares with 132.3 for the preceding week and with 105.3 for the same week a year earlier.

———

—G. V. MacKinnon, president of the John B. Stetson Co., was today elected a member of the Board of Directors of the Fidelity-Philadelphia Trust Co., succeeding J. Howell Cummings, who died recently.

———

METAL MARKETS

LONDON, June 4.—Copper, standard spot, £64; futures, £64; electrolytic, spot, £68, 15s.; futures, £69, 5s. Tin, spot, £224, 10s.; futures, £224. Lead, spot, £21, 10s.; futures, £21, 15s. Zinc, spot, £25, 17s. 6d.; futures, £25, 12s. 6d.

NOTES OF THE STREET

———

—A banking syndicate has sold 44,000 shares of California Dairies, Inc., preference stock, Series A, carrying $6 cumulative dividends.

—Directors of the Oxford Bank and Trust Company declared a special dividend of 2 per cent., marking the tenth anniversary of the institution.

—Bonds called for payment this month now stands at $88,544,500, as compared with $225,666,000 for a similar period in May and $100,641,165 in June, 1927.

—State and municipal borrowing during May totaled $133,882,737, compared with $210,050,710 in the same month a year ago, according to the Daily Bond Buyer.

—Domestic sales of copper in May are estimated at 105,000 net tons and export sales are figured at 90,000 gross tons. These totals are believed to be a new high record.

—Rumors of revaluation of the franc were current said a Paris cable today. These reports had it Poincare decided not to stablize at present rate but would bring it up to 22 to the dollar.

—Franklin Trust Company opened its new branch office today at 52d and Market sts. This is in addition to three other branches, one at Front and Market sts., another at 5708 Germantown av., and the fourth at Frankford av. and Paul st.

—Steel operations in the Mahoning Valley are averaging 70 to 75 per cent., with 108 of 127 Sheet Mills active. Tin Plate operations of independent companies are at 70 per cent. Mills of American Sheet & Tin Plate Company are at 80 per cent.

—Net profit of First National Stores, Inc., for the year ended March 31 was $1,551,919, excluding profit on sale of capital assets. This was equal after preferred dividends, to $2.02 a share on the common. Profit of $1,973,268, exclusive of sale of capital assets, was reported for the preceding 15 months ended April 2, 1927, equal to $2.72 a share on the common.

—One statistical agency has compiled reports of earnings of 700 stocks and extent to which earnings have been discounted in market prices of these stocks. It showed average yield of 4.9 per cent. for 583 industrial concerns, excluding U. S. Steel and General Motors; 4.3 per cent. for 70 utility corporations and 4.6 per cent. for 46 railroads.

—Offering of stocks today included 115,000 shares of common stock of the Industrial Printing Ink Corporation, at $43; 100,000 shares of Oilstocks, Ltd., class A stock at $12; 40,000 shares of class A participating preference stock of the Union Financial Corporation of American at $25, and $1,000,000 of 6 per cent. cumulative preferred stock of the Western Power, Light and Telephone Company.

—New financing today exceeded $45,000,000. The largest was that of $26,000,000 Federal Land Bank 4s, due in 1958 at a price to yield 3.98 per cent. Other new offerings were $5,000,000 Brandenburg, Germany, Electric Power Company first mortgage 6s; $4,500,000 Rockland Light and Power first mortgage 4½s; $750,000 Greenwich Water and Gas Company collateral trust 5s; $1,000,000 City of New Orleans, La., 4½s and $135,000 City of Troy, N. Y., 4¼s.

BANK CLEARINGS UP 1.7%
Philadelphia Reported Decrease of 8.6 for Past Week

Showing the smallest gain in many weeks, bank clearings of leading cities increased 1.7 per cent. last week. Reversing its recent trend, Philadelphia recorded a decrease of 8.6 per cent. The table, compiled by the Commercial and Financial Chronicle, follows:

	1928	1927		P.C.
New York	$5,687,000,000	$5,245,000,000	+	2.4
Chicago	610,861,127	632,017,066	−	3.3
Phila.	383,000,000	419,000,000	−	8.6
Boston	389,000,000	378,000,000	+	2.9
Kan. City	88,248,347	101,496,592	−	13.0
St. Louis	115,800,000	117,500,000	−	1.4
San Fran.	161,276,000	133,854,000	+	20.5
L. Angeles ...	135,233,000	122,950,000	+	10.0
Pittsburgh ...	127,498,320	132,326,546	−	3.6
Detroit	139,000,000	122,129,532	+	13.8
Cleveland	*85,000,000	90,101,750	−	5.7
Baltimore	69,677,523	73,313,058	−	5.0
N. Orleans ...	62,630,564	46,195,216	+	13.9
13 cities 5 days	$7,994,224,881	$7,613,883,760	+	5.0
Other cities, 5 days	972,614,035	1,003,709,060	−	3.1
Totals for all cities for 5 days	$8,966,838,916	$8,517,592,820	+	5.3
All cities, 1 day	1,793,367,733	1,963,991.571	−	8.7
Total for all cities for week	$10,760,206,699	$10,581,584,391	+	1.7

*Estimated.

HOLIDAY AT WINNIPEG

Winnipeg, June 4.—The Grain Exchange was closed today —King's Birthday.

$2,000,000 GOLD TO ITALY

Shipment Made by New York Bank

New York, June 4.—Guaranty Trust Company announces shipment of $2,000,000 gold to Italy on steamship Duilio.

NEW YORK BONDS

(In U. S. Gov. bond prices, fraction in 32ds.)

Sales in $1,000.		High.	Low.	3.00
19	Lib Loan 3½s....	100-13	100-9	100-12
1	Lib Loan 3½s reg	100-4	100-4	100-4
1	Lib Loan 1st 4¼s	101-23	101-23	101-23
70	Lib Loan 3d 4¼s.	100-2	100-1	100-2
27	Lib Loan 4th 4¼s	102	101-31	101-31
1	Lib L 1st 4¼s reg	101-16	101-16	101-16
161	U S Treas 3⅜s...	101-23	101-14	101-14
110	U S Treas 3¾s...	106-2	105-30	105-30
107	U S Treas 4s....	109-29	108-24	108-24
127	U S Treas 4¼s...	113-31	113-16	113-26

Sales in $1,000.		High.	Low.	3.00
9	Antioquia 7s 1945 A	97½	97½	97½
4	Antioquia 7s 1945 B	97	96⅞	97
1	Antioquia 1st 1957.	97⅛	97⅛	97⅛
8	Argentine 5½s 1962	96½	96½	96½
3	Argentine 6s 1957.	100⅜	100¼	100⅜
17	Argentine 6s 1958.	100½	100⅛	100½
19	Argentine 6s 1959.	100⅜	100	100¼
57	Argentine 6s 1960.	100½	99¾	99¾
11	Argentine 6s 1961.	100⅛	99⅞	100⅛
5	Argentine 6½s 1962	96½	96½	96½
233	Australian 4½s '56.	90⅝	90⅛	90½
30	Australian 5s 1955	98	97½	98
7	Australian 5s 1957.	97⅝	97¼	97¼
2	Australian 7s 1943.	104	104	104
10	Bank of Chile 6½s	98	97½	97½
2	Bank of Chile 6¾s	99½	99½	99½
15	Batav'n Pet 4½s '42	92⅝	92	92
4	Bavaria 6½s 1945..	98⅛	98⅛	98⅛
6	Berlin Elec 6½s '51.	96⅜	96	96
6	Berlin Elev 6½s '56	96⅜	96⅜	96⅜
10	Bremen 7s.......	102⅝	102⅝	102⅝
37	Buenos Air P 6s '55	95¾	95½	95¾
10	Caldas 7½s.......	100¾	100¾	100¾
1	Cauca Val 7½s '46.	102	102	102
33	Chinese Gov Ry 5s	28¾	28	28¾
18	City of Berlin 6½s.	98⅞	98¾	98¾
11	City of Bud't 6s'62	87⅝	87⅜	87⅜
5	City of Bord'x 6s..	100⅜	99⅞	99⅞
1	City of Bogota 8s..	105½	105½	105½
2	City of Copen 5½s.	99⅞	99⅞	99⅞
7	City of Copen 5s'52	97¼	97⅛	97⅛
6	City Cord 7s '37 ct	98½	98½	98½
6	City of Lyons 6s...	100¼	100¼	100¼

(In U. S. Gov. bond prices, fraction in 32ds.

Sales in $1,000.		High.	Low.	3.00
4	City of Mars'l's 6s.	100	99¾	99¾
20	City Milan 6½s '52	93⅞	93½	93⅞
1	City of Oslo 6s 1955	101	101	101
2	City P Alegre 7½s.	103¼	103¼	103¼
7	City of Prague 7½s.	105¼	105¼	105¼
7	City Rio Jan 6½s'53	96¾	96½	96¾
1	City Rio Jan 6½s'52	96½	96½	96½
1	City Rio Jan 8s '46	108½	108½	108½
18	City Rome 6½s '52	94¾	94½	94½
2	City Rotterdam 6s	105¾	105¾	105¾
1	City S Paulo 6½s'57	99⅞	99⅞	99⅞
2	City of Tokio 5s...	81⅞	81⅞	81⅞
20	City of Tokio 5½s..	92⅛	91¾	91¾
1	Cologne 6½s '50...	97½	97½	97½
7	ColAgrMB 6s'47ct.	92¼	92	92¼
3	Col Mtg Bk 7s 1946	95	95	95
1	Col Mtg Bk 7s 1947	94¾	94¾	94¾
9	Costa Rico 7s 1951	97½	97⅜	97½
1	Danish M 8s A....	111½	111½	111½
9	Dept of Seine 7s...	106½	106	106½
10	Dpt of Tolima 7s'47	96½	96	96
10	Deuts Bk 6s'32 ct.	98⅜	98¼	98⅜
1	Dom of Can 4½s...	99¾	99¾	99¾
1	Dom of Can 5s 1931	100⅞	100⅞	100⅞
20	Dom of Can 5s 1952	104⅝	104⅜	104⅝
17	Dom Rep 5½s 1942	99½	99½	99½
2	Dom of San 5½s'29	100⅝	100⅝	100⅝
1	Dutch E I 6s 1947.	103	103	103
9	Dutch E I 6s '62..	103	103	103
5	Est R R Com 7s '54	103½	103⅜	103⅜
41	Fiat 7s 1946 war..	117½	117½	117½
8	Fiat 7s 1946 ex-war	94½	94½	94½
2	Finnish Ct 6½s A..	99	99	99
1	Framerica 7½s '42.	108¼	108¼	108¼
2	French Nat S S 7s.	102⅜	102	102¼
1	GerCnAgB6s'60ct.	90½	90½	90½
9	Ger Gen L 6s'48 ct wi	95¼	95¼	95¼
6	Ger CAB 6s '60 Jul	92	91½	91¾
8	GerCAB 6s'60 Oct.	90¾	90½	90¾
2	German Bank 7s..	99¾	99¾	99¾
20	German 7s '49....	107	107	107
1	Graz 8s 1954......	103¼	103¼	103¼
34	Greek 6s 1968 rcts.	88	88	88
9	Holland Am 6s '47.	101½	100⅞	101½
1	Hung Con Mun 7½s	100	100	100

(In U. S. Gov. bond prices, fraction in 32ds.)

Sales in $1,000.		High.	Low.	3.00
7	Hung 7s 1946.....	96⅛	95¾	96⅛
8	Ilseder Steel 7s1946	101½	101½	101½
17	Imp Jap 6½s......	102	101⅞	101⅞
18	Irish Fre S 5s '60 .	97	97	97
29	Italy Pb Ut 7s '52.	98	97⅞	97⅞
5	Ital Cr Cons '47 A	97¾	97¾	97¾
6	Ital Cr Con 7s'47 B	97¾	97¾	97¾
13	JapConPow6½s'50.	96¾	96½	96½
4	JapConPow 7s1944	99¾	99½	99¾
8	King of Bel 6s 1955	100¾	100¼	100½
3	King of Bel 6½s...	105⅞	105¾	105¾
7	King of Bel 7s 1955	108	107¾	108
2	King of Bel 7s 1956	106	105¾	106
3	King of Bel 7½s....	115½	115	115½
2	King of Bel 8s.....	110⅛	110⅛	110⅛
17	King of Denmk 6s.	104⅝	104½	104½
48	King of Italy 7s...	99½	99⅜	99½
9	K of Nether 6s '72.	107	107	107
4	K of Nether 6s '54.	102	101⅞	102
11	King of Nor 5s '63.	97½	97¼	97¼
39	King of Nor 5½s...	100⅝	100⅜	100⅜
3	King of Nor 6s '43.	102½	102½	102½
11	King of Nor 6s '44.	102½	102½	102½
3	K of Serbs Cz Sl 8s	100⅝	100½	100½
1	King of Sweden 5½s	104	104	104
2	King of Sweden 6s.	102½	102½	102½
1	Leipzig 7s 1947....	101	101	101
7	Montec 7s '37 war.	115	114¼	115
3	Montec 7s '37 ex-w	96½	96½	96½
12	New S Wales 5s '57	95½	95⅜	95½
4	New S Wales 5s '58	95¼	95	95
2	Nor H E 5½s '57 ct	92½	92¼	92¼
8	Paris Lyons Med6s	99⅜	99	99
5	Paris Lyons 7s....	104¾	104¾	104¾
4	Par Or 5½s '68 rcts	95⅝	95⅝	95⅝
1	Paris Orleans 7s...	103¼	103¼	103¼
7	Rep of Bolivia 7s..	97½	97⅛	97¼
2	Rep of Bolivia 8s..	106½	106	106½
19	Rep of Chile 6s '60.	96	95⅜	95⅜
8	Rep of Chile 6s '61.	95½	95¼	95¼
87	Rep of Chile6s'61ct	96	95¾	95¾
1	Rep of Chile 7s....	103⅜	103⅜	103⅜
5	Rep of Chile 8s '41.	110½	110⅛	110⅛
23	Rep of Col 6s '61..	94¼	93⅝	93⅝
13	Rep Col 6s'61rcts.	93¾	93½	93½
16	Rep of Cuba 5s '04	101	101	101
1	Rep of Cuba 5½s..	103⅜	103⅜	103⅜
4	Rep of Fin 5½s'58ct	93½	93	93¼
4	Rep of Finland 6½s	99½	99¼	99½
9	Rep of France 7s..	107⅝	107	107⅝
25	Rep of France 7½s.	117⅝	117½	117½
2	Rep of Pan 6½s '61.	104	104	104
31	Rep of France 7½s.	117⅝	117½	117½
5	Rep of Pan 6½s '61.	104	103¾	103¾
31	Rep of Peru 6s '60.	92	91⅝	92
4	Rep of Peru 7s '59.	104	103⅞	104
25	Rep of Peru 7½s '56	106¼	106¼	106¼
1	Rep of Poland 6s..	85½	85½	85½
49	Rep of Pol 7s '47..	90½	90¼	90½
7	Rep of Poland 8s..	101⅛	100¾	100¾
10	Rep of Urug 6s '60	98½	98⅛	98⅛
2	Rhine Un 7s ex-war	99½	99½	99½
2	Rhine Westph7s'50	101⅛	101⅛	101⅛
26	RhineWestph6s'52	93½	93¼	93½
15	Saxon P W 7s.....	102	101½	102
19	Shin'su E 6½s'52 ct	94¼	94	94¼
42	Siem & H 6½s '51 ct	106	105⅞	106
1	St of Pernam 7s '47	97½	97½	97½
6	S of Rio G D S 7s '66	100¼	100¼	100¼
2	St of S Paulo 8s '36	106½	106¼	106½
6	St of S Paulo 8s '50	107½	107¼	107½
1	St of Queensland 7s	113⅞	113⅞	113⅞
1	Styria 7s 1946.....	94⅝	94⅝	94⅝

(In U. S. Gov. bond prices, fraction in 32ds.)

Sales in $1,000.		High.	Low.	3.00
5	Switzerland 5½s ..	103⅛	102⅞	103⅛
1	Switzerland 8s....	111⅝	111⅝	111⅝
5	Tokio Elec 6s.....	100	100	100
4	Toho Elec 6s rcts..	99	98¾	98¾
34	Toho El Pow 7s...	100	99⅝	99⅝
1	Tyrol Hyd Elec 7½s	101	101	101
2	Toho Elec 6s rcts..	99	99	99
16	Ujigawa 7s 1946...	100	99¾	100
1	Up Aus 6½s '57 rcts	90⅛	90⅛	90⅛
3	U K G B & I 5½s '29	118⅝	118⅜	118⅝
7	U K G B & I 5½s '37	105½	105⅜	105⅜
43	U S Brazil 6½s '26.	98½	98	98¼
17	U S Brazil 6½s '27.	98¼	98	98¼
4	U S Brazil 7s 1952.	101	100¾	100¾
9	U S Brazil 8s 1941.	112	111	111
2	U S Stm of Cop 6s.	99⅜	99⅜	99⅜
10	U Stl W 6½s A war	94¾	94½	94¾
10	Uni Stl W Bur 7s..	104	104	104
1	Wuerttemb'g7s '56	99½	99½	99½
23	Yokohama 6s 1961	97⅛	97	97

4	Ajax Rubber 8s...	107	107	107
1	Allis Chalmers 5s..	99½	99½	99½
5	Alpin Mon Steel 7s	96	96	96
6	Am Cyan 5s......	94	94	94
3	Am Agr Chem 7½s.	105¼	105	105
1	Amer Smelt 5s....	101¾	101¾	101¾
1	Amer Smelt 6s....	108⅛	108⅛	108⅛
17	Amer Sug 6s......	104¾	104½	104¾
43	Am Tel & T clt 4s	99½	99⅜	99½
4	Am T & T 5s......	105¼	105⅛	105¼
22	Am T & T s f 5s..	106⅝	106¼	106¼
3	Am T & T 5½s....	108⅝	108⅜	108⅝
1	Am Wr Paper 6s..	88	88	88
9	Amer W W & E 5s.	100	100	100
1	AmWaterWorks 6s	105	105	105
21	Anaconda 6s......	105½	105	105
272	Anaconda 7s......	132½	130	130
74	Andes Copper 7s..	136½	135½	135½
76	Ang Ch con mt co 7s	105⅛	103¼	105¼
26	Armour of Del 5½s.	93½	93⅛	93½
32	Armour & Co 4½s.	93½	93¼	93¼
1	Atchison adj 4s sta	91¾	91¾	91¾
6	Atch adj 4s sta reg	88½	88½	88½
6	Atch gen mtg 4s..	95½	95⅛	95⅛
13	Atch adj 4s sta reg	88⅝	88½	88⅝
2	Atch conv 4s 1905.	92	92	92
2	Atlantic Coast L 4s	95⅛	95⅛	95⅛
1	Atl & Dan 1st 4s..	79	79	79
1	Atl G & W I 5s....	81⅜	81⅜	81⅜
3	Atl C L Clt L&N4s	92	92	92
10	Baldwin Loco 5s..	107¼	107⅛	107⅛
1	Balto & Ohio 4s...	94¾	94¾	94¾
3	Balto & Ohio 4½s..	99¾	99½	99¾
1	Balto & O 5s D....	102½	102½	102½
9	Balto & O ref 5s...	102¾	102⅝	102¾
7	Balto & O ref 6s...	109½	109	109½
6	Barnsdall 6s......	103¼	103⅛	103¼
2	Bell Tel 5s 1948 B.	106	106	106
5	Bell Tel 5s 60 C...	109	109	109
1	Beth Steel 5½s....	103	103	103
27	Beth Steel 6s.....	105⅛	105	105
1	Bing & Bing 6½s...	97	97	97
1	Botany 6½s......	79½	79½	79½
32	BklynManTran 6s.	98⅝	98⅛	98¼
2	Brook City 1st....	93¾	93¾	93¾
8	Bdy&7thAvCon 5s	75½	75	75⅜
6	Brook Edison 5s..	105	105	105
2	Brook Un Gas 5½s.	272½	272½	272½
5	Bklyn Un El 1st 5s	97⅜	97¼	97¼
1	Bklyn Un El 6s...	98½	98½	98½
20	Buff Roch & P 4½s.	94	94	94
6	Bush Term 5s.....	100	99¾	100

(In U. S. Gov. bond prices, fraction in 32ds.)

Sales in $1,000.		High.	Low.	3.00
2	Cal Petrol 5s.....	100¼	100¼	100¼
4	Cal Petrol 5½s....	102½	102½	102½
4	Can Natl 4½s 57...	99	98¾	98¾
1	Can Nor 6½s......	118½	118½	118½
3	Can Nor Dy 7s....	114	114	114
2	Can Pacific 4s....	89	89	89
4	Can Pacific 4½s...	99⅝	99¼	99¼
1	Car Clinch & O 6s.	108⅞	108⅞	108⅞
3	C C C & St L G M 4s	94½	94½	94½
2	C C C & S L 4½s E.	99¼	99¼	99¼
1	Cent Pacific 3½s...	99	99	99
8	Cent Pacific 1st 4s.	93⅝	93¼	93⅝
1	Cent Pacific 5s....	101¾	101¾	101¾
1	Central Steel 3s...	122½	122½	122½
24	Certainteed 5½s...	96	95½	95½
7	Ches Corp 5s.....	100	99½	99½
4	Chesap & O 4½s 30	100	100	100
10	Chi & Alton 3s....	72	71¾	71¾
2	Chi & Alton 3s ct..	71¾	71¾	71¾
21	Chi & East Ill 5s'51	89½	88¾	88¾
14	Chi Gt West 4s...	69⅜	69	69
15	Chi & West Ind 4s.	89¼	89	89
12	Chi & West Ind 5½s	105	104⅝	104⅝
2	Chi B & Q deb g m 4s	94½	94½	94½
3	Chi Ind & L's 5s 47	105¾	105¾	105¾
4	Chi M & St P 4s 89	89½	89½	89½
2	Chi M & St P 6s '34	102⅝	102⅝	102⅝
15	C M St P & Pac 5s A	96	95½	96
1030	C M St P & P aj 5s	77¼	76⅜	76⅞
3	Chi N W 4½s......	100¼	100¼	100¼
13	Chi R I & P 4s....	92¾	92¾	92¾
8	Chi R I & P ref 4s.	95	94	95
3	Chi R I & P 4½s...	94¼	94	94¼
6	Chi Ry 5s........	84	84	84
1	Chi St L Pgh 5s reg	101⅝	101⅝	101⅝
17	Chi Terr S E 5s Inc	95½	95⅜	95⅜
2	Chi Un Sta 5s B....	105⅞	105⅞	105⅞
2	Chi Un Sta 5s '44..	103½	103½	103½
4	Chile Copper 5s...	96½	96⅛	96¼
4	Colo & So ref 4½s..	99⅛	99	99⅛
19	Colum G&E 1st 5s	100¾	100½	100¾
1	Columbus Pow 4½s	95	95	95
2	Con'l Cred 6s.....	99½	99½	99½
3	Computing Tab 6s	105	105	105
1	Consol Gas 5½s....	105⅞	105⅞	105⅞
6	Cons Coal of Md 5s	82	81½	81½
2	Container Corp 6s.	102¼	102¼	102¼
9	Crown Paper 6s...	102½	102	102½
10	Cub Am Sug Co 8s	106	106	106
11	Cuba Cane Sug 8s.	91½	91	91
6	Cuba Nor 5½s....	96½	96½	96½
22	Cuba R R 5s......	99¾	99½	99¾
1	Cuyamel Fruit 6s.	100¼	100¼	100¼
2	Del & Hud 4s ref..	94⅛	94⅛	94⅛
2	Den Rio G & W 5s.	93	93	93
1	Det Edison 5s 1940	104¾	104¾	104¾
7	Detroit Edison 6s.	108	107¾	108
11	Detroit Tun 4½s...	101⅝	101⅝	101⅝
5	Detroit Un Rys 4½s	95⅛	95⅛	95⅛
290	Dodge Bros 6s....	95	94⅝	94¾
7	Duquesne 4½s.....	100½	100	100½
2	Ea T V&G Cons 5s	108	108	108
2	El Coal 6½s.......	95	95	95
2	Erie Prior Lien 4s.	86¾	86¾	86¾
1	Erie cvt 4s ser A..	103	103	103
63	Erie 5s...........	95⅞	95⅝	95⅝
1	Erie & Jersey 6s...	114¼	114¼	114¼
2	Fed Lt 6s 1st......	105	105	105
8	Florida Ea C'st 5s.	89	88½	88½
1	St Smith Lt 5s....	98½	98½	98½
6	Gen Mot Accept 6s	103⅛	103	103
1	Goodrich B F 6½s..	107⅞	107⅞	107⅞
8	Goodyear 5s......	92	91½	91½

(In U. S. Gov. bond prices, fraction in 32ds.

Sales in $1,000		High.	Low.	3.00
1	Gotham Silk Ho 6s	101¼	101¼	101¼
7	Gt North Rwy 7s..	113½	113	113⅛
1	Grand Trunk 6s...	107⅛	107⅛	107⅛
10	Gulf State Stl 5½s.	100	99	100
4	Hack Water 4s....	91½	91½	91½
1	Hoe & Co 6½s.....	92	92	92
3	Hudson Coal 5s...	91¾	91½	91½
6	Hud&Man R ref 5s	100	99¾	100
4	Hud & Man R inc.	92	91¾	91¾
2	Humble Oil 5½s...	101¾	101¾	101¾
2	Ill Bell Tel 5s.....	104¾	104¾	104¾
12	Ill Central 4s 53...	91⅛	91	91
15	Illinois Cent 4¾s...	100½	100⅜	100⅜
3	Ill C Chi St L&N 4½s	99	99	99
1	Ill C C St L&N 5s A	105	105	105
5	Ind Lime 6s......	97¼	97¼	97¼
14	Inter Cement 5s...	99	98¾	98¾
10	Inter Match 5s....	98½	98⅛	98⅜
8	Inter Match 5s....	98½	98¼	98¼
5	Inter Gt Nor 6s...	106¾	106¾	106¾
26	Inter Ber Marine 6s	105⅛	105	105
1	Int Rap Transit 5s	80¼	80¼	80¼
4	Inter R T 5s sta...	80¾	80⅜	80⅜
10	Inter Rap Trans 6s	81	80½	80½
11	Inter Rap Trans 7s	100½	100	100
6	Inter T & T 4½s...	95½	95⅜	95½
2	Inter Paper 5s....	100⅛	100⅛	100⅛
6	Inter Paper 6s....	102½	102⅜	102½
4	Inter Rwy C A 5s.	86⅛	86	86
2	Int Ry Co A 6½s...	98½	98½	98½
6	Kansas Gas 6s.....	106⅛	106	106
2	Kan City Term 4s.	91¾	91¾	91¾
13	Kan City So 1st 5s	100½	100½	100½
7	Kan City Term 4s.	92	91¾	92
8	Lackawan Steel 5s.	102¼	102¼	102¼
4	Laclede Gas Ref 5s	102¼	102¼	102¼
4	Laclede Gas 5½s...	105	104¾	104¾
10	Lake Shore 3½s....	84¾	84¾	84¾
3	Lake Shore 4s 1928	99¾	99¾	99¾
1	Leh Val 4s.......	90½	90½	90½
2	Leh Valley 5s 1933	101¼	101¼	101¼
2	Leh Val Coal 5s '64	97¼	97¼	97¼
1	Liggett & Myers 7s	125¼	125¼	125¼
1	Liquid Carbonic 6s	125¾	125¾	125¾
2	Loews Inc 6s......	109¾	109½	109¾
8	Loews Inc 6s ex-war	100⅛	100	100
11	Lorillard Co 5s....	91⅝	91⅝	91⅝
4	L I N Shore......	100½	100½	100½
2	Manati Sug 7½s...	107½	107½	107½
8	McCrory Sts 5½s..	100⅝	99⅞	100
1	Miag Mill 7s ex-war	93	93	93
2	Midvale Steel 5s..	99⅞	99⅞	99⅞
3	Mil Elec 5s 1961..	101½	101½	101½
1	Minn & St L cn 5s.	50⅞	50⅞	50⅞
1	M St P&S S M 5½s	97½	97½	97½
5	M St P&S S M 6½s	101	101	101
3	Mo Kans & T 4s B	87½	87½	87½
1	Mo Kans & T 4½s.	96¾	96¾	96¾
8	Mo Kan&Tex 5s A	102	101¾	102
21	MoKan&TexAdj5s	104¼	104⅛	104⅛
22	Mo Pacific 4s.....	79¾	79½	79½
17	Mo Pacific 5s A...	102½	102¼	102¼
15	Mo Pacific 5s F...	100¼	100	100¼
32	Morris & Co 4½s...	87½	87	87
45	Murray Body 6½s.	99	98¾	98¾
3	Nassau Elec Ry 4s	60½	60½	60½
14	Nat Dairy 5¼s...	98⅜	98	98¼
8	Natl Radiator 6½s.	89⅞	89½	89½
6	N Eng T & T 4½s..	101¼	101¼	101¼
19	New Orls Term 4s.	92½	92½	92½
5	N Eng T & Tel 5s.	108⅛	108⅛	108⅛
5	N Orl Tx&Mx 4½s.	97⅜	97⅜	97⅜
1	N Or T&M Fy 5s B	100	100	100

(In U. S. Gov. bond prices, fraction in 32ds.)

Sales in $1,000.		High	Low.	3.00
20	N Y Cen cons 4s..	94¾	94½	94¾
5	N Y Central 5s....	108¼	108	108⅛
1	N Y Central 6s....	107½	107½	107½
1	N Y C&St L 5½s B	106½	106¼	106½
4	N Y Chi & St L 6s.	102⅝	102½	102⅝
1	N Y Conn R R 4½s	100	100	100
10	N Y Edison 6½s...	114⅝	114⅝	114⅝
9	N Y G&E H&P 4s	95⅝	95½	95½
4	N Y N H H't 3½s '54	77¼	77¼	77¼
1	N Y N H H't 4s '47	85½	85½	85½
5	N Y N H&H't 4½s	91	91	91
11	N Y N H H't 6s clt	105¾	105¾	105¾
2	N Y N H&H 6s cv	116½	116½	116½
21	N Y State Ry 4½s	55¾	54½	54½
5	N Y Tel 4½s......	101⅛	101⅛	101⅛
9	N Y Tel 6s 1941...	107½	107⅛	107¼
7	N Y Westch&B 4½s	86¼	86	86
2	N A Cement 6½s..	88	88	88
8	Niag F Pow Co 5s.	104½	104¼	104¼
2	North Am Ed 5s..	101¾	101⅝	101⅝
1	Northern Pacific 3s	69¼	69¼	69¼
3	Northern Pacific 4s	93¾	93¾	93¾
2	Ohio Pub Ser 7½s..	116¼	116¼	116¼
3	Ohio River Ed 6s.	105	104⅝	104⅝
5	Old Ben Coal 6s...	95½	95½	95½
20	Ore WRR&NCo 4s	90½	90¼	90½
1	Oriental Dev 6s...	100⅜	100⅜	100⅜
4	Otis Steel 6s......	99⅞	99⅞	99⅞
21	Pac Gas&Elec 5s..	101¼	101¼	101¼
5	Pac Tel & Tel 5s..	103½	103½	103½
8	Pan A Pet 6s 1934s	103	103	103
17	ParFamPlayLas6s.	100⅞	100½	100½
15	Park Lex 6½s.....	101¼	101¼	101¼
35	Pathe Exchange 7s	70⅛	70	70
9	Penn Dixie Cem 6s	100¾	100¼	100½
18	Penna Gm 4½s....	101¼	101¼	101¼
2	Penna 5s 1964....	104	103½	104
1	Penna Gm 5s.....	109⅛	109⅛	109⅛
7	Penna 6½s........	111	110⅝	111
10	Penna 7s.........	103⅝	103½	103⅝
1	Pere Mar 4s......	94½	94½	94½
50	Phila Electric 4½s.	100½	100½	100½
29	Phila Co 5s.......	99⅜	99⅛	99¼
4	Phila Co 6s.......	103½	103¼	103¼
2	Philippine Ry 4s..	42	42	42
22	Phillips Pet 5½s...	93	92⅞	92⅞
1	PCC & SL 4½s serA	100½	100½	100½
1	PCC & SL4½s ser B	100½	100½	100½
1	PCC & StL 5s A..	109⅛	109⅛	109⅛
5	PCC & StL 5s B..	109½	109½	109½
1	Pierce Arrow 8s...	95¾	95¾	95¾
1	Pillsbury 6s......	105⅜	105⅜	105⅜
8	Porto Rican Tob 6s	100½	100½	100½
24	Pub Ser E&G 5s..	104	104	104
5	Punta A Sugar 7s.	105⅞	105⅞	105⅞
6	Pure Oil 5½s......	99¾	99½	99¾
4	Reading 4½s.....	101	100⅝	101
25	Rem Arms 6s.....	100¾	100¾	100¾
12	Rem Rand 5½s war	96	95⅝	95⅝
5	Republic I & S 40.	104¼	104¼	104¼
2	Roch Gas 5½s.....	107¼	107¼	107¼
3	St Joe Lt 5s......	98⅛	98⅛	98⅛
13	StL Iron M&S 5s.	100⅜	100⅜	100⅜
13	StLIM&SR&GD4s	95¼	95	95
9	StL SW con 4s....	97½	97¼	97¼
23	StL&SF Ser A 4s..	89½	88⅝	88⅝
144	StL&SF 4½s rcts..	92¼	91⅝	91⅝
1	StL & SanF Inc 6s	101¼	101¼	101¼
3	StL&SanF ser B 5s	102	101¾	101¾
9	St L & S F 5½s....	102⅜	102⅜	102⅜

(In U. S. Gov. bond prices, fraction in 32ds.)

Sales in $1,000.		High.	Low.	3.00
42	StL & SanF adj 6s	101¼	101¼	101¼
10	StP & KCShL 4½s	97½	97½	97½
1	Schulco Co 6½s B.	103¼	103¼	103¼
5	Seabd A Line ref..	62¾	62¾	62¾
10	Seabd A Line 4s sta	79¼	79¼	79¼
7	Sbd A Line 5s adj	54¼	53⅞	54¼
6	Seabd A Line 6s...	86¼	86	86
6	Shell Union Oil 5s	98	98	98
5	Silesia 6½s........	94¾	94¾	94¾
10	Silesian Am 7s....	100	100	100
1	Sinclair 6s........	98½	98½	98½
8	Sinclair 6½s.......	100⅛	100⅛	100⅛
4	Sinclair 7s........	102¼	101¾	101⅞
4	Sin Crude Oil 5½s.	98½	98¼	98¼
1	Sin Pipe Line 5s...	95	95	95
1	Skelly Oil 5½s.....	94	94	94
2	So Bell Tele 5s....	104½	104½	104½
35	South Pac 4s 1929.	99½	99	99
5	South Pac 4s ref..	95	95	95
1	South Pac clt 4s...	91¼	91¼	91¼
18	South Pac 4½s rcts	98⅜	98	98
12	Southern Rwy 4s..	90½	90½	90½
3	South Railway 5s.	112½	112½	112½
1	Southern Ry 6s....	117½	117½	117½
1	South Rwy 6½s...	124½	124½	124½
15	Southw B Tele 5s.	104½	104¼	104¼
5	S O of N J 5s.....	103⅛	103⅛	103⅛
10	St Oil of N Y 4½s.	97⅜	97⅛	97⅜
1	Stevens Hotel 6s..	100	100	100
2	Tenn Copper 6s...	112	112	112
3	Tenn Pow 6s.....	107	107	107
7	Tex&FtSmith 5½s.	106½	106	106
13	Tex & Pac 5s B...	101¾	101⅜	101⅜
4	Third Av ref 4s...	71⅜	71⅜	71⅜
95	Third Ave adj 5s..	66⅞	66¼	66¾
2	Trumbull Steel 6s.	101⅞	101⅞	101⅞
1	Union Pac 4s ref..	93⅛	93⅛	93⅛
8	Union Pacific 4s..	95½	95½	95½
28	Union Pacific 4½s..	99⅝	99½	99½
16	Union Pac 4½s rcts	99⅝	99½	99⅝
3	United Biscuit 6s..	101½	101½	101½
19	U Drug Del 5s rcts	97⅞	97½	97¾
31	U S Rubber 5s....	91	90½	91
10	U S Rubber 7½s...	102¼	102⅛	102⅛
12	U S Steel s f 5s...	108¼	108¼	108¼
1	Utah Lt 5s........	97½	97½	97½
3	Utah P & L 5s....	100½	100¼	100¼
1	Vert Sugar 7s.....	100¼	100¼	100¼
1	Virginian Ry 5s...	106⅜	106⅜	106⅜
2	Warner Sug R 7s..	92⅛	92⅛	92⅛
44	Wabash 4½s rcts...	92	91⅞	92
10	Wabash 5s B.....	101⅜	101⅜	101⅜
4	Wabash 5½s......	104	104	104
4	Warner S Ref 7s..	92⅜	92⅛	92⅜
1	Western Elec 5s...	104⅛	104⅛	104⅛
13	West Maryland 4s.	82¾	82¾	82¾
2	W Maryland 5½s..	99¾	99¾	99¾
10	Westingh E&M 5s.	103⅞	103¾	103¾
11	Western Pac 5s...	99½	99½	99½
1	W Penn Pow 5s A.	103¼	103¼	103¼
2	West Shore 4s....	91¼	91¼	91¼
10	W Union Tel 6½s..	110⅝	110½	110½
4	West Va C C 6s...	50	50	50
2	Wheeling Stl 5½s..	101¾	101¾	101¾
1	W Eagle O 5½s war	97	97	97
20	Wickw-Sp Stl 7s cv	30½	30⅛	30⅛
10	Wilkes-B & E 5s..	73½	73⅛	73⅛
49	Wilson Co 1st 6s..	103⅛	102¾	103⅛
1	Win Arms 7½s...	107	107	107
74	Young S&T 5s....	100¾	100¼	100¼

CUTTEN GETS ARMOUR STOCK

Transaction Involved 312,500 Shares of Class A Stock

(By Associated Press)

Chicago, June 4.—The final block in the Armour and Company held by the estate of the late J. Ogden Armour, son of the founder, was sold today to Arthur Cutten, of Chicago.

Announcement of the sale was made by F. Edson White, president, and the purchase confirmed by Mr. Cutten. It involved 312,500 shares of "A" common stock.

CRUDE RUBBER MARKET

New York, June 4.—Rubber futures were steady; July, 19.10; September, 19.30; December, 19.30.

BAR SILVER

New York, June 4.—Bar silver 60¼; Mexican dollars 46⅜.

BANK CLEARINGS

Bank clearings today compared with corresponding day last two years:

	1928	1927	1926
Phila.	$94,000,000	$82,000,000	$83,000,000
Boston	66,000,000	65,000,000	67,000,000

Pittsburgh balance $15,100,903.37

NEW YORK

Bank clearings $666,000,000
Bank balances 129,000,000
Federal Reserve balances 126,000,000

STOCKS UP $359,652,045

Increase for 216 Issues Contrasted With $1,213,291,533 in April

The different groups of stocks listed on the New York stock exchange ran at variance during May. Six groups were lower, although the 216 issues listed as a whole increased $359,652,045 since the end of April. This compares with a gain of $1,213,291,533 in April and $1,053,766,756 in May a year ago.

Groups showing losses were leather, railroads, railroad equipment, rubber and tobacco shares. The two latter groups both scored losses during April and May, due to the drop in the price of crude rubber. Tobacco shares reflected the price cutting by leading cigarette makers in this country.

FOREIGN EXCHANGE

New York, June 4.—Pesetas gained 1 and guilders ½ today. Rates were: Sterling cables, $4.88⅜, checks, $4.88; Francs cables, 3.93⅞, checks, 3.93⅝; Lire cables, 5.27, checks, 5.26½; Swiss cables, 19.27½, checks, 19.26½; Pesetas cables, 16.73, checks, 16.72; Norway cables, 26.80, checks, 26.79; Sweden cables, 26.84½, checks, 26.83½; Guilder cables, 40.39, checks, 40.37; Marks, cables, 23.94, checks, 23.93¾.

In the afternoon British sterling and French francs declined. Prices were: Sterling cables, $4.88 5-16; francs cables, 3.93¼; Belgian cables, 13.96; Lire cables, 5.27; Pesetas cables, 16.71.

FIND HOOVER RIGID TARIFF EXPONENT

Manufacturers' Club Head Reveals Correspondence with Secretary Over Crowther Publication

NO 'FREE TRADE' LEANINGS

Herbert Hoover, Secretary of Commerce and outstanding candidate for the Republican Presidential nomination, is revealed as a staunch exponent of a protective tariff, in correspondence between Thomas F. Armstrong, president of the Manufacturers' Club, and George Akerson, assistant to Mr. Hoover.

On May 20, Mr. Armstrong wrote to Mr. Hoover regarding a supposedly authoritative publication, "The Presidency and Hoover," by Samuel Crowther, which gave the impression that Mr. Hoover would not view the tariff question as a major issue.

Crowther took the ground that there no longer is any division between Democrats and Republicans on the tariff question, and that voters in the forthcoming Presidential election, so far as that issue was concerned, could vote for a Democrat as well as for a Republican.

Mr. Armstrong took exception to that statement, pointing out that there was a vast difference between the Underwood-Simmons Democratic tariff and the Payne-Aldrich Republican tariff, which preceded it or the Fordney-McCumber Republican tariff now in effect.

"We believe that in placing you by inference, if not in terms, on an exact level with a Democratic candidate, the Crowther article is doing you a great disservice," wrote Mr. Armstrong. "Hence we believe that you will not find it difficult to state with explicit candor your own position on tariff and protection."

Mr. Hoover's assistant, replying to Mr. Armstrong, wrote: "Mr. Hoover is not responsible for Mr. Crowther's views. Nor is he at all in agreement with the matter you quote from one of Mr. Crowther's articles, even if it bears the interpretation which you put upon it.

"Mr. Hoover is an ardent supporter of the protective tariff. It is obvious that the Democratic party takes pride in its opposition to the tariff.

"I enclose an extract from one of Mr. Hoover's many addresses in support of the tariff, which scarcely bears out the assumption that he views the Democratic party as an advocate of protection."

In a subsequent letter to Warren F. Doane, editor of the Manufacturer, Mr. Akerson said: "You have my permission, and Secretary Hoover's as well, to publish the correspondence which I sent you."

The extract enclosed by Mr. Akerson was from an address Mr. Hoover delivered in California during the campaign of 1924. Mr. Hoover vigorously upheld the Fordney-McCumber tariff and asserted that the Democratic and the LaFollette third party proposed to reduce its protective features. Such a reduction, he said, would bring economic reverses to California.

THE CROSSWORD PUZZLE

Across

1 Encampment without shelter
7 Gem
13 Horse color
14 Game played with numbered balls and cards
16 Pitcher
17 Canadian province (abbreviation)
18 Draw to
20 Meadow
21 Canadian province (abbreviation)
22 Bustle
23 Relatives
25 Football position (abbreviation)
26 Aim
27 Month (abbreviation)
29 Card game

31 Posterior
33 Indian magician
35 Face of pedestal
37 Extra
38 Cleverness
39 Energy
41 Skedaddle
42 Rose red dyestuff
43 Frolic
44 Conflict
45 Light hearted
47 Solution
48 Encountered
50 Otherwise
52 Pry
54 Great quantity

Across

55 Fairy
57 Dress
58 Amusement
59 Long meter (abbreviation)
61 Cut
63 Excavate
64 In the year of the reign (abbreviation)

65 Not at home
67 Praise bestowed
70 Numerical prefix
71 Sudden loud noise
73 Off the center of a vessel
74 Press
75 Woolen cloth (plural)
76 Sicilian city

Down

1 Western horse
2 Electrified particles
3 Large tub
4 Forward
5 Singing voice
6 Bed
7 Greek letter
8 Imitation
9 Again (prefix)
10 Pointed tool
11 Sinister look
12 Browbeat
15 Delude
18 Attach
19 Until
22 Also
24 Doze
26 Give approval
27 Cereal grain
28 Hint
30 Rower
32 Perfect
33 Last

34 Assign
36 Noblemen
38 False hair
40 Investigate
44 Marriage
46 Still
47 Small cask
49 Russian Queen
51 Measure of length
53 Mode
54 Drinking vessel
56 Dude
58 Suitable
60 Draft animal
62 Activity
63 Coin
64 Presently
66 Sailor
68 Abstract (abbreviation)
69 Animal mother
70 Swiss canton
72 Afterthought (abbreviation)
74 Exists

Solution of Saturday's Puzzle

THE CHEERFUL CHERUB

They say we are really
not civilized yet;
Perfection is still
very far —
Considering what we were
started with though
I'm surprised we're as
good as
we are!
R·T·Carn

THE RAGGED PRINCESS

By Edgar Wallace

The Story Thus Far

AUDREY BEDFORD, on her way to London to find work, meets

DICK SHANNON, of Scotland Yard, who is greatly surprised when she tells him her sister is

MRS. MARTIN ELTON, a crook he has been trying to catch.

LACY MARSHALT, soldier of fortune, is in some peculiar way interested in Audrey and hires detectives to watch her.   Next door to Lacy lives the mysterious

MALPAS, apparently a master criminal who is engaged in some plot against Lacy.   Dick is at present trying to find the diamonds of the Queen of Finland, stolen during a holdup.

SLICK SMITH, a crook, had been present shortly before the gems were taken.   Dora Elton is displeased at seeing her ragged sister and is about to turn her away, when it occurs to her to make use of the unsuspecting Audrey in disposing of the Queen's jewels.

BIG BILL STANFORD is an accomplice of the Eltons.

CHAPTER 4

THE ARREST

BIG BILL was no sentimentalist, but in the thing that passed for a soul there was a certain elementary code, the rudiments of which had once been a sense of honor and decent judgment.

"Your sister! Suffering snakes! You couldn't allow a kid like that to take such a risk!"

Dora's smile was her answer.   Her husband was biting his nails nervously.

"There may be no risk," he said, "and if there is, isn't it ours, too?"

19

Stanford stirred uneasily.

"That's so. But we're in this for the profit and the risk. Suppose they caught her and she squealed?"

"That is the only real risk," said Dora, "and it isn't a big one."

The big man looked thoughtfully at the carpet.

"That stuff has to get out of this house and out of the country—quick!" he said. "It is too big to hold and break up here, and I never pass a newspaper boy but I don't hear the squeal that the papers are putting up. Lock the door, girl."

She obeyed. On the mantelpiece was a beautiful gilt and enameled clock, surmounted by a statuette of a faun.

Gripping the statuette firmly, he lifted out the greater portion of the clock's interior, without in any way affecting the functions of the timepiece, which ticked on. Pressing a spring, one side of the bronze box opened and showed a tightly fitting package of silver paper. This he laid on the baize cloth and unrolled. Instantly there came from the table such a flicker of leaping fires, blue and green and purest white, that Dora's mouth opened in wonder and awe.

"There's 70,000 pounds there," said Stanford, and thrust out his lower lip thoughtfully. "And there's also ten years for somebody—seven years for the theft and three years for outraged majesty. You cannot rob a visiting queen without putting something on to the sentence."

The dapper man shivered.

"Don't talk about sentences, my dear fellow," he said petulantly. "If Pierre does his part—"

"Pierre will do his part. He'll be waiting at Charing Cross station at 9.15. The question is, who's going to take the stuff?"

There was a silence.

"Audrey will take it," said Dora at last. "I was a fool not to think of it when I saw her. Nobody knows her, and nobody will suspect her. Pierre is easy to recognize. And then, Bunny, out of this business for good." She nodded emphatically. "There's a little old story about a pitcher and a well."

"Perhaps Mr. Lacy Marshalt will give Martin a directorship," sneered the big man. "When you people get next to what looks like good, easy, honest money, it's surprising how quickly you reform."

"I scarcely know the man," said Dora sharply. "I told you about him, Bunny. He's the man I met at the Denshores' dance. He's a South African and rich, but you couldn't pry loose a nickel without dynamite."

Martin Elton looked at her suspiciously.

"I didn't know you knew him," he began.

"Get back to this stuff," snapped Stanford. "There's one thing I want to know—suppose she's caught?"

Another long and painful silence.

"Why not keep it here till the squeal dies down?" asked Elton. "There's no ghost of a suspicion that they connect us with the job."

Stanford looked him straight in the eye.

"Twelve months ago," he said slowly, "when Leyland hall was cleaned up, you got most of the stuff out of the country through a receiver at Bognor. He gave you a little trouble, didn't he?"

"Yes," said the other shortly, "that is why I hadn't thought of him in connection with this job."

"And you're wise," said Stanford, nodding. "Dick Shannon has been spending the greater part of the day with your friend at Bognor!"

Martin Elton's pale face went a shade paler.

"He wouldn't squeal," he said unsteadily.

"I don't know. If a man would squeal to anybody, he'd squeal to Shannon. The English detective service has gone to blue blazes since they introduced gentlemen. I like police whom you can reason with." He jiggled the loose coins in his pocket suggestively.

"That's why I say that you can't keep the stuff at this house. Bennett may not have squealed. On the other hand, he may have emitted squeak-like noises. What do you say, Dora?"

She nodded.

"The stuff ought to go. I've recognized that all along," she said. "Make a parcel of it, Martin."

They watched the man as, wrapping the necklace again in cotton wool, he packed it in an old cigarette box and tied it about with brown paper, and then Shannon asked:

"If it comes to squealing, what about your sister?"

Dora considered before she replied.

"I am sure of her," she said.

"Let us see her," said Stanford when the parcel had been firmly tied and hidden under a sofa cushion and the top of the clock replaced.

Audrey was sitting in a deep, low chair before the gas fire, pondering her strange welcome, when she heard Dora's footstep on the stairs.

"You can come down now."

She looked at her sister and made a little face and, for all her subtlety, could not hide the disparagement in the glance.

"You're a human scarecrow, Audrey. I shall have to buy you some clothes straight away."

Audrey followed her down to the floor below and into the big drawing room that ran the width of the house. A tall, broad-shouldered man stood with his back to the fire and on him Audrey's eyes first rested. He was a man of fifty, whose hair was cropped so close that at first she thought he was bald. His deep, forbidding eyes fixed and held her as she entered.

"This is Mr. Stanford," introduced Dora. "And this is my little sister."

He held out a huge hand and took hers in a grip that made her wince.

The second man in the room was slight and dapper and his unusual pallor was emphasized by the small black mustache and the jet-black eyebrows. Good-looking, she thought, almost pretty. So this was the great Martin, about whom she had heard so many rhapsodies.

"Glad to meet you, Audrey," he said, his admiring eyes never leaving her face. "She's a peach, Dora."

"She's prettier than she was," said Dora, indifferently, "but her clothes are terrible."

It was not like Audrey to feel uncomfortable. She was so superior to the trials of poverty that, ordinarily, she would have laughed good-naturedly at the crude comment. But now, for some reason, she felt embarrassed. It was the unwavering stare of the big man by the fireplace, the cold appraisement of his gaze.

Stanford looked at his watch.

"I'll be going," he said. "I'm glad to have met you, miss. Perhaps I'll be seeing you again."

She hoped sincerely that he would not.

Dora signaled to Martin to retire with their guest and it was when they were left alone that Dora had her story to tell.

It was the story of an injured wife, who had been obliged to fly from the country because of her husband's brutality, leaving behind her the miniature of her child.

"I don't mind confessing to you that we have secured the miniature, Audrey," said Dora in an outburst of frankness. "I don't think we were strictly legal in our actions—in fact, Martin bribed the servant in Sir John's house to bring it to us. He guessed we have it and has had us watched day and night, and any attempt we make, either through the post— we are sure he has notified the postal officials—or by messenger is likely to lead to failure.

"A friend of this poor dear Lady Nilligan is coming to London tonight, and we have arranged to meet him at the station and hand him the miniature. Now the question is, Audrey, will you be a darling and take it to him? Nobody knows you; the sleuth hounds will not molest you; and you can render this poor woman a great service. Personally I think there's a little too much sentimentality about it, for I don't see why one miniature should be more valuable than another. But evidently this demented lady thinks it is."

"But what an extraordinary story!" said Audrey, frowning. "Couldn't you send one of your servants? Or couldn't he come here?"

"I tell you the house it watched," said Dora, never the most patient of individuals. "If you don't want to do it—"

"Of course, I'll do it," laughed Audrey.

"There is only one point I want to make," her sister interposed, "and it is this: If by any chance this comes out, I want you to promise me that our name shall not come into it. I want you to swear by our dead mother—"

"That is unnecessary," said Audrey, a little coldly. "I will promise—that is enough."

Dora took her in her arms and kissed her.

"You are really a darling," she said, "and you've grown so awfully pretty. I must find a nice man for you."

It was on the tip of Audrey's tongue to suggest that her sister might very well try some other ground of search than that which produced the pallid Martin Elton, for whom she felt an instinctive dislike.

"Of course, I'll take it, my dear," she said. "It seems such a little thing to do. And if I meet the grumpy husband, why, I'll just talk to him firmly."

Apparently Dora's feasts were of a movable kind, for although Audrey had her dinner in her room, the party of which her sister had spoken did not materialize. At half-past 8 Dora came up for her, carrying in her hand a small oblong package, tied and heavily sealed.

"Now remember, you do not know me, you have never been to 508 Curzon st. in your life." She repeated the admonition and described in detail the mysterious Pierre. "When you see him, you will go up to him and say, 'This is for madam'— that and nothing more."

She repeated the instructions and made the girl recite them after her. Audrey was at first amused, then a little bored.

"It seems an awful lot of bother to make about so small a thing, but you have succeeded in arousing that conspirator feeling!"

With the package secure in an inside pocket of her coat, she went out into the direction of Park lane. She had hardly disappeared before Martin Elton came out. Keeping her in sight, he watched her board a bus and, hailing a taxicab, followed.

To Audrey the adventure was mildly exciting. She knew neither of the parties of this family quarrel, and found it difficult even to speculate upon their identity. They were probably two very plain, uninteresting people. Family quarrelers usually were. But she was glad of the opportunity of earning her board and keep, and it relieved her of a sense of obligation, for which she was grateful.

The bus put her down opposite Charing Cross station, and, crossing the congested road, she hurried through the courtyard into the station building. There were hundreds of people in the big approach; the night mail was beginning to fill, and passengers and their friends stood in groups before the barriers. She looked for a considerable time before she saw

Pierre, a short, stocky man with a square, flaxen beard, who seemed to be wholly absorbed in the animated spectacle. Moving to the other side of him to make absolutely sure, she saw the little mole on his cheek by which she was to identify him. Without further ado, she took the package from her pocket and went up to him.

"This for madam," she said.

He started, looked at her searchingly, then slipped the package into his pocket so quickly that she could hardly follow his movements.

"Bien!" he said. "Will you thank monsieur? And—"

He spun around quickly, but the man who had caught his wrist possessed a grip which was not lightly to be shaken. At the same moment somebody slipped an arm in Audrey's.

"I want you, my young friend," said a pleasant voice. "I am Captain Shannon, of Scotland Yard."

He stopped, staring down at the frightened face turned up to his.

"My ragged princess!" he gasped.

"Please let me go." She attempted to free herself. She was horribly frightened, and for a second felt physically sick. "I've got to go to—" she checked herself in time.

"To see Mrs. Elton, of course," said Shannon, scrutinizing her.

"No, I haven't to see Mrs. Elton. I really don't know Mrs. Elton," she said breathlessly.

He shook his head.

"I'm afraid we'll have to talk about that. I don't want to hold your arm. Will you come with me?"

"Are you arresting me?" she gasped.

He nodded gravely.

"I'm detaining you—until a little matter is cleared up. I'm perfectly sure you're an innocent agent in this, just as I am equally sure that your sister isn't."

Dora? Was he talking about Dora? she asked herself with a sinking heart. His tone, the hard judgment in the voice, told the girl something she did not want to know. Something that shocked her beyond expression. Then, forcing every word, she said:

"I'll talk the matter over with pleasure, and I won't make

any attempt to get away. But I have not come from Mrs. Elton's, and she is not my sister. The story I told you this afternoon was untrue."

"But why?" he asked, as they walked together through the store corridor to the courtyard.

"Because—" she hesitated, "I knew you were a detective."

He signaled a cab, gave directions and helped her inside.

"You're lying to shield your sister and Bunny Elton," he said. "I hate using the word 'lie' to you, but that's what you're doing, my child."

Her mind was in a turmoil, from which one clear fact emerged. It was not a miniature that she was carrying from Dora to the mythical wife; it was something more important. Something horribly serious.

"What was in the parcel?" she asked huskily.

"The Queen of Finland's diamond necklace, unless I'm greatly mistaken. Her carriage was held up in the Mall four nights ago and the jewels were stolen from her neck."

Audrey sat up with a grimace of pain. It was as though he had struck her. Dora? She had read something of the affair in the newspaper which he had bought for her at Barnham Junction. Mrs. Graffitt had spoken of the crime. For a time she sat paralyzed with horror.

"Of course, you didn't know what it was," he said, and he was speaking to himself. "It's a hateful thing to ask you to do, but you must tell me the truth, even if it brings your sister to the place that has been waiting for her these many years."

The cab seemed to go round and round; the stream of lights and traffic through the window became a confused blur.

"Do what you can for Dora." Her mother's insistent lesson, almost forgotten, was ringing in her ears. She was trembling violently; her brain had gone numb and would give her no guidance. All that she knew was that she was under arrest—she, Audrey Bedford of Beak farm! She licked her dry lips.

"I have no sister," she said, her breath laboring. "I stole the necklace!"

She heard his soft laughter and could have murdered him.

"You poor, dear baby!" he said. "It was a job carried out

by three expert holdup men.   Now let me tell you"— he patted her hand gently—"I'm not going to allow you to do this mad, quixotic thing.   Didn't you know that Dora Elton and her husband are two of the most dangerous crooks in London?"

She was weeping, her face to her hands.

"No, no," she sobbed.   "I don't know anything.   She is not my sister."

Dick Shannon sighed and shrugged his shoulders.   There was nothing to do but to charge her.

Pierre had arrived at the station before them, and she watched, with fascinated horror the process of his searching, saw the package opened on the sergeant's desk, and the flash and glitter of its contents.   Presently Shannon took her gently by the arm and led her into the steel pen.

"The name is Audrey Bedford," he said.   "The address is Fontwell, West Sussex.   The charge"—he hesitated—"is being in possession of stolen property, knowing the same to be stolen.   Now tell the truth," he whispered under his breath.

She shook her head.

TOMORROW—THE TRUTH

THE PROPHET

When I was less than three feet tall there came a prophet to our town; his voice was great, his learning small, he wore a long and rusty gown. He preached wherever men would stand and listen to him for a while; the end of all things was at hand, he told us with his ghastly smile. Upon a certain day the skies would roll together as a scroll; the hills would fall, the dead would rise, and all the bells of doom would toll. He named the date, he named the hour when these disasters would befall; and so with somewhat vulgar power he tirelessly sent forth his call. At first men laughed and called him crazed, but still he made his ardent spiels; and then, like people charmed or dazed, they followed at the prophet's heels. And as the day of doom drew nigh they gave away their worldly gear; no more they'd sell or trade or buy, their duty in this world was clear. I well recall the fateful day when all things earthly were to end; the prophet and his pilgrims gray were robed, all ready to ascend. Upon a hill they took their stand and waited as the hours dragged by, and naught occurred on sea or land, and nothing happened to the sky. And I recall my wild relief when the appointed time was past; the prophet, with his dream of grief, had made my spirit stand aghast. The lessons learned while we were young are not forgotten while we live; and now no prophecy that's sprung can to me fear or pleasure give. Wise men at intervals uprear and say that this or that will come; and I recall that old time seer and say all prophecies are bum. Not e'en the weather man can hold my rapt attention when he cries tomorrow will be hot or cold, with dazzling blue or murky skies. Not e'en the candidate can chill my ardent soul or quench my grins, when he predicts all sorts of ill for this fair land unless he wins.

WALT MASON.

CAN YOU BEAT IT?

SHUT UP FOR THE NIGHT

ALL TUCKED UP FOR THE NIGHT

HEARS MOTHER TELL FAMILY THAT NOBODY'S TO GO INTO THE NURSERY, BABY'S ASLEEP

BUT OF COURSE HE CAN'T GO TO SLEEP UNTIL DADDY HAS COME HOME FROM WORK

AND HAS TIP-TOED IN TO SEE HIM UNDER THE PRETEXT THAT HE LEFT A BOOK IN THE NURSERY

AND WHEN DADDY'S GONE HE'S GOT TO WAIT FOR GRANDMA TO COME IN

AND PUT ANOTHER BLANKET OVER HIM, SHE'S SURE NO-BODY COVERS HIM WARM ENOUGH

AND AUNT MAY ALWAYS HAS TO TAKE A PEEK AT HIM AND PRETEND TO FUSS WITH THE WINDOW

THEN MOTHER, TO MAKE SURE HE'S ALLRIGHT AND DROP ONE LAST KISS ON HIS CHEEK

AND NOW IT'S SAFE TO GO TO SLEEP

GLUYAS WILLIAMS

"When he stole a kiss from you what did you do?"
"I made him give it back."

"How do you manage to keep your bills down, Jones?" "Easy—by keeping 'em paid up, Brown."

SUCH IS LIFE!

"Er-r—I want some sort of a present for a young lady."

"Sweetheart or sister?"

"Er-r—why, she hasn't said yet which she'll be."

Here's a baseball problem that a big leaguer never has to face, but that is very vexing to the sandlot experts. Unless something is done quickly, the game is ended for the day.

He—"What would happen if you and I ever agreed on anything?"

She—"Why, you'd be wrong, of course."

THE TOONERVILLE TROLLEY   —By Fontaine Fox

THE SKIPPER HAS A PRETTY NEAT WAY OF GETTING HIS TIP WHEN HE HAS CARRIED BAGGAGE UP TO SOMEONE'S FRONT DOOR AND IT LOOKS AS IF THEY WERE NOT GOING TO COME ACROSS

"UNLESS I AM MISTAKEN I FAILED TO ASK YOU FOR YOUR FARE WHILE YOU WUZ ON THE CAR?"

MOM'S HOME!

He—"My motto is 'Every man for himself.'"

She—"Similar to mine. Mine is 'Every man for myself.'"

AUNT HET

"Lettie brags about havin' more sense than her husband, but any woman that's got more sense than her husband has got too much sense to let him find it out."

REG'LAR FELLERS

WINNIE WINKLE, THE BREADWINNER —*The Bathing Girl*

MINUTE MOVIES

TRACKED TO THE **TROPICS**

FILMED BY
ED WHEELAN
~
EPISODE —
TWELVE —

DESMOND STONE RESENTS SAM BYERS' FRIEND-LY ADVICE CONCERNING JUNE. AND TELLS THE OLD TRADER TO MIND HIS OWN BUSINESS —

—By Ed Wheelan

(M)EANWHILE THE FLIRTATIOUS NAKU, WALKING BACK FROM THE POINT, IS SUDDENLY SEIZED BY THE JEALOUS VAHI AND VIGOROUSLY UPBRAIDED FOR HER FICKLENESS

STOP MAKING LOVE EYES AT BAD WHITE MAN OR VAHI KILL YOU — MEBBE VAHI KILL BAD WHITE MAN ANYWAY !!

(A)ND IN HER NATIVE HUT, UNHAPPY JUNE STONE THINKS OF TOM WRIGHT AND THE GRIM TRICK WHICH FATE HAS PLAYED ON THEM BOTH

OH, TOM DEAR, WHY ARE MY THOUGHTS CONSTANTLY OF YOU? IS IT BECAUSE WE ARE BOTH IN PRISON? SURELY MY PRISON IS MORE TERRIBLE THAN YOURS OF IRON BARS !"

(W)HILE NEARING TAHITI PROUDLY SAILS THE SEA SIREN

(L)ITTLE DOES JUNE DREAM THAT TOM HAS BEEN PARDONED AND IS IN THE SOUTH SEAS SEEKING HER !

BEN WEBSTER'S CAREER—*At the Hospital*

—*By Edwin Alger*

BRINGING UP FATHER (© 1925)

—*By George McManus*

TAILSPIN TOMMY—Tommy's Got the Goods

THE NEBBS—Reflections

ELLA CINDERS—Situation Wanted—Female

—By Sol Hess

ROR
OF AN
K OF
LOOKS
AT
VERY-
S OFF
SO
CTION

SAY, IF YOU LOOKED LIKE THAT BIRD, ALL YOUR WALL PAPER WOULD BE MIRRORS = RIGHT NOW YOU GET A LOT OF COMFORT FROM YOUR APPEARANCE = I'VE SEEN YOU PLAY FACE TAG WITH THE MIRROR FOR HOURS, YOU UNDER-SIZED FLOCK OF JEALOUSY.

VOTE FOR JUDGE SABATH

W. A. Carlson.

—By Bill Conselman and Charlie Plumb

U WORK
REST, AND
NG IS HARD
SITION, I'LL
'M TAKING
EONE WHO
IF I DON'T
G ME TO
LL!

AH! LIKE A FLY IN A FURNISHED ROOM, AN IDEA BUZZES INTO MY BRAIN! MAYBE THAT NICE MR. CUMMINGS, WHO RUNS THE COMMUNITY CENTER, COULD FIND A JOB OF WORK FOR A WILLING WOMAN! SOMETHING WHERE I COULD BE OF SERVICE TO POOR PEOPLE WHO NEED IT!

MUTT AND JEFF—*The Lion Tamers Make Ready*

for the G. O. P. Convention.—By Bud Fisher